MW01532228

Stand up America!
Stand now!

Jug Kell

The Final Branch

REFLECTING ON THE HEART OF AMERICA

Jeffrey J. DiQuattro

CROSSBOOKS
PUBLISHING

CrossBooks™
A Division of LifeWay
1663 Liberty Drive
Bloomington, IN 47403
www.crossbooks.com
Phone: 1-866-879-0502

Scripture taken from the Holy Bible, New International Version®. *Copyright* © *1973, 1978,
1984 by International Bible Society. Used by permission of Zondervan. All rights reserved.*

©*2011 Jeffrey J. DiQuattro. All rights reserved.*

*No part of this book may be reproduced, stored in a retrieval system, or
transmitted by any means without the written permission of the author.*

First published by CrossBooks 08/19/2011

ISBN: 978-1-6150-7572-0 (sc)
ISBN: 978-1-6150-7573-7 (hc)

Library of Congress Control Number: 2010940904

Printed in the United States of America

This book is printed on acid-free paper.

*Because of the dynamic nature of the Internet, any Web addresses or links contained in
this book may have changed since publication and may no longer be valid. The views
expressed in this work are solely those of the author and do not necessarily reflect the
views of the publisher, and the publisher hereby disclaims any responsibility for them.*

To God, who endowed the citizens of The United States of America with so much; to our forefathers, who possessed such foresight; to my wife Kimberly, who encouraged me over the years to aspire to a book of this magnitude; to my son Benjamin, who deserves the right to live under the guardianship of liberty; and to patriots of all generations who have heard liberty's call!

COVER DESIGN

The design for the cover of this book finds inspiration from two sources—one personal and one historical. During the 1990's, I had the opportunity to live and work in Washington, D.C. for seven years. To a small town boy, navigating Washington, D.C. was daunting until I found the location of the Washington Monument, a memorial, dedicated to our first president—President George Washington. It became my reference point whenever I was lost or needed help in finding my way home. Little did I know some sixteen years later it would remain a reference point for this book and for America to find her way home.

The second source comes from President William Howard Taft who captured the majesty of the Washington Monument in an article titled *Washington: Its Beginning, Its Growth, and Its Future* featured in a March, 1915 edition of *The National Geographic Magazine*. Listen to the words of the twenty-seventh President of the United States.

With a new character for each new hour, a different aspect for every change of light and shade, the Washington Monument seems to link heaven and earth in the darkness, to pierce the sky in the light, and to stand an immovable mountain peak as the mists of every storm go driving by. With a height of 555 feet, a base of 55 feet square, and walls tapering from 15 feet at the base to 18 inches at the top; with its interior lined with memorial stones from several States, from many famous organizations, and from a number of foreign countries; with its stately simplicity and high qualities of manhood it honors, it is fitting that the aluminum tip that caps it should bear the phrase "Laus Deo."

Laus Deo, a Latin term, means *Praise be to God!*

Contents

PROLOGUE

― ∼⦿∼ ―

When I set out on this journey, my quest was quite simple: to discover the heart and soul of America. As the journey began, I had no idea the depth and breadth of America's roots, for my heart was just drawn to begin digging. I was awestruck at how our Christian heritage was so intertwined with the American call to liberty and the birth of the greatest nation ever known to mankind—The United States of America. I hope this book blesses anyone who desires to look through the pages. As a nation we are reaching a tipping point where Americans must choose to either return to our roots or to sever our ties with the past. America's heritage, history, and faith in God are the wellsprings of our American life and the source of direction when we wander. For the last half of a century, we have tested the boundaries our forefathers handed down to us, like an adolescent who desires to strike out on his own. There are few, if any, boundaries we have not crossed, but when a boy grows up into a man, he too must choose the way he will go. The political theatre in America is a mere reflection of a soul in turmoil. With each passing political cycle, we place our hope in one political movement after another, only to discover that peace cannot be found in the works of man; rather, the peace which transcends life is found when we declare one nation under God.

How long will we struggle with one another? Can a house divided against itself stand?[1] There is no adversary or ideology we cannot defeat, except our Achilles heel, known as the enemy within. Will we succumb to the fate of those great empires that stood so tall and accomplished

---

1   President Abraham Lincoln speech given on June 16, 1858, in Springfield, Illinois, after accepting the Republican Party's nomination for United States Senator. The words "A house divided against itself cannot stand" were taken from Matthew 12:25.

so much? They fell not from the enemies abroad, but from divisiveness amongst their ranks. It would be much easier to write about an America which was one election away from a panacea. Unfortunately, the dilemma facing our nation is not contained on the surface; it is a matter of the heart. If we are to rediscover the greatness of America, we must return to our nation's roots: the Constitution, the Bill of Rights, and the Declaration of Independence. I hope that through the pages of this book your heart will be captivated by the majesty of America!

Section I—The American Crossroads

INTRODUCTION

⋰⊙⊙⋰

"This is what the Lord says:
Stand at the crossroads and look; ask for the ancient paths,
Ask where the good way is, and walk in it, and you will find
Rest for your souls. But you said, "We will not walk in it.""

Jeremiah 6:16 (NIV)[2]

Never in the history of this nation has the urgent beckoning of liberty been so apparent. As the twenty-first century unfolds, the world groans for freedom. The *land of the free* and the *home of the brave* must again muster the fortitude to unearth and recapture our shared destiny: *life, liberty, and the pursuit of happiness.* This nation is no stranger to service or the demands of sacrifice, as our proud heritage has consistently stood the tests of each generation. From the Revolutionary War, to the War of 1812, to the Mexican-American War, to the Spanish-American War, to the Civil War, to World War I, to World War II, to the Korean War, to Vietnam, to the Cold War, to Desert Storm, and presently, the ongoing wars in Iraq and Afghanistan; America knows the gift of freedom, and unlike any other nation on Earth, America has been willing to shed our blood to usher in the gift of freedom across the globe. After all, freedom was birthed with the founding of this nation, refined with the development and dominance of the United States of America, and has been defended by

---

2   Scripture taken from the Holy Bible, New International Version®. Copyright © 1973, 1978, 1984 by International Bible Society. Used by permission of Zondervan. All rights reserved.

us throughout the globe. Americans should be captivated by our heritage and energized with our high calling.

Urgency is defined as the calling for immediate attention[3], that is, America's attention is being called as socialism, fascism, communism, totalitarianism, terrorism, and all out tyranny are progressing in almost every sphere of the globe. From Hugo Chavez in Venezuela, to old Europe, to Vladimir Putin and the reemergence of Russia, Iranian President Ahmadinejad and the Iranian regime, and, most shockingly, America herself. Yes, within the borders of the United States of America, our Coca-Cola, Chevrolet, and apple pie culture is under an assault from within. Is America falling prey to the same forces the founding fathers fought so hard to rid themselves of? "Let Freedom Ring." It's so simple, yet so difficult to maintain, especially in an era of instant information and constant activity.

This is neither a book of fear, nor a book to be feared. It is a book which calls for a revolution, neither a violent movement, nor a military engagement. Rather, a revolution to fight for the heart and soul of America and to invigorate each American to uncover our individual purposes and realize our common destiny heralded from heaven herself—*"Liberty for All!"* Our story, our call, as it was in the beginning has not changed. What's different is that America has changed.

The business community promotes the agent of change. Politicians promise it, people are told to embrace it, the speed of technological development demands it, so it is only natural for people to bend America into the convenient image of the moment. It isn't our image to mold or our right to change the responsibility entrusted to the United States of America some two hundred years ago. Americans can attempt to change and re-direct our destiny, but when the television is turned off, the computer closed, children put to bed, and America is still, Americans will hear the still-silent voice of freedom beckoning each of us to an unashamed and shared set of values which promote and preserve our common faith, family, and community.

What happened to America that we find ourselves virtually divided between red states and blue states? When did America enter the era where there are no limits? How did our political institutions become so polarized? How is it that a country with the heritage, the resources, and the abundance endowed to America finds itself with the largest financial deficits ever

---

3   *The New Oxford American Dictionary, Second Edition*, Erin McKean (editor), 2051 pages, May 2005, Oxford University Press, ISBN 0-19-517077-6.

known in the history of the world? Why is a nation whose character has sent our young to die for the freedom of others been so willing to embrace a culture of death? Why has a nation who has written on its currency "In God We Trust" begun the slippery slope of removing God from the public square? Why are we so embarrassed to acknowledge our Judeo-Christian roots when those roots have produced a harvest one hundred fold? How has political correctness become more acceptable than the truth? Where is Superman, an icon representative of *truth, justice, and the American way?* Our academic institutions have become plagued with anti-Americanism. Our media has become biased, our government encumbered with bureaucracy and labeled with incompetency. When did Americans develop this entitlement mentality where life owes us something? When did we erase the memories of immigrants flocking to Ellis Island with the one promise that their individual efforts and gifts could offer a better life for them and their families? When did the lawyer replace a man's word? How did we get here? Has America lost her fight, or is America at a crossroads? Has our Creator offered us a choice to return to our roots, or the alternative—to follow that of Europe as its churches shrink and its culture resorts back to the bondage of old?

Our responsibility, even more acutely, our duty to our Creator and our fellow man is to rediscover what invigorated the men and women of those great historic moments to risk life and limb to preserve freedom. It is our call and each American's choice to accept the demands of destiny. The call of this book is to *let freedom ring,* from the family dinner table, to our churches, to the schoolhouses, and ultimately, to the halls of Congress.

Stand up, America. Stand now, and set loose those rugged cowboys who roamed so free!

A Search for Our Soul

――――――― ⨍⨶⨎ ―――――――

"Come to me, all you who are weary and burdened, and I will
give you rest. Take my yoke upon you and learn from me, for
I am gentle and humble in heart, and you will find rest for
your soul. For my yoke is easy and my burden light."
Matthew 11:28–30 (NIV)[4]

The mission in this book and the ensuing analysis is to discover the heart of America and its foundation without the aid of scholars, historians, and lawyers. We are on a quest to find the pulse of America, not unlike the Protestant Reformation, which decidedly took Christianity back to its roots after centuries of societal structures placed man and institutions between the followers of Christianity and the inerrant Word of God. Our goal is to remove the institutions, remove man, and remove two hundred years of barriers that are standing between *"We the People"* and the next great awakening in America. Our hope is to allow you to sit on your grandfathers' laps and listen to their voices, the convictions of their souls, and the warmth of their hearts. We desire to allow America to hear the unencumbered words of Thomas Jefferson, George Washington, Benjamin Franklin, John Hancock and the like without the noise and the distractions of twenty-first-century America. America has lost her way, but America has not lost her hope. Now is the time to grab a cup of hot

―――――――――――――

4   Scripture taken from the Holy Bible, New International Version®. Copyright © 1973, 1978, 1984 by International Bible Society. Used by permission of Zondervan. All rights reserved.

chocolate, cozy up next to the fire, and bask in the radiance as we reconnect with the heart and soul of America. *The Declaration of Independence*[5], *The Constitution of the United States*[6], and *The Bill of Rights*[7] were given as gifts from above as cornerstones whenever America drifts with every doctrine of the wind. They were given to us for when we were cold, lost, depressed, and hungry, and we need to hear directly from the heart that birthed America to restore comfort and security to our soul. We have lost our way, America, but not all is lost!

The journey you are about to enter into is going to be filled with truth, comfort, excitement, and moments of great depression. America has found herself with a great chasm between the voice of our soul and the reality of twenty-first-century America. There is so much noise and so many distractions in modern America that we are unable to pause and look across the gorge. If we did, it would bring certain heartbreak. There are those moments in history, those watershed events, which for a brief instant illuminate our eyes to some of the stark realities facing America, but there is something in the American psyche these days, which opens for but a moment to reality and returns to the cover of denial. In our denial, in some strange way, America finds comfort, finds solace in pretending as if all is well in the world, and if we merely hide our heads in the sand, the bad will go away and the good will return. Oh, if life was that easy. We see a problem, ignore it, and all of a sudden the problem is cured. Well, Land of Liberty, we have collectively been running from our problems for too long, depending upon the next great scientific discovery or the latest technological gadget to be the salve we have been looking for. The irony of life is that we can run from our problems by changing churches, moving to a new city, changing careers, or exchanging one spouse for the next, yet the more we change the heavier our load becomes. America, we have become so encumbered with our problems that we are about to come to a screeching halt where we will have but one hope to finally confront our problems, lighten our load, and to bring ultimate relief to our soul. Our goal of this book is to begin the confrontation process so by the end of this book, we can begin the intervention, which will bring America lasting relief from our ailments.

For those of you who like only good news, the first several sections of this book are a presentation of the stark realities confronting America. It is downright ugly, nasty, and dirty. Our light is growing dim, and when you

---

5   See Appendix A – The Declaration of Independence.
6   See Appendix B – The Constitution of the United States.
7   See Appendix C – The Bill of Rights.

look across many segments of our society, some believe it is a sign of the times, and the end of America is right over the horizon. You don't have to overhear many conversations before you hear the comparisons to Rome and its fall from glory. Culturally, morally, economically, and spiritually, America is bankrupt. It pains my soul to listen to the voices of depression, despair, and defeat from those cultural warriors who have fought so valiantly to reverse the degradation of our American culture. Many a man and woman have given their life's work and physical lives to see America turn the corner, to no avail. For the faithful in America, it would appear the harder you fight for your morality, values, and the right to raise your children in the ways of the ancient path, the more hostile the culture becomes. America, we are depressed. There is a sense of hopelessness, and we are beginning to shut down emotionally as a nation. We are withdrawing into ourselves and cannot see clear of the walls of depression. America, we need help!

As with problems in life, we as a nation need to walk down this ugly path together and allow ourselves to accept the reality of our nation and our bankruptcy. Like an alcoholic or drug addict, they do not change until they hit rock bottom. America, we are at rock bottom. We just need to open our eyes for a few moments and keep them open to a nation who has drifted astray. It is in the pain of this reality where we can begin to pull back the layers of American culture and come to terms with rock bottom. For many, you are there, and you have been there. For others, you have been skipping through life one decision after the other, pretending there were no wolves out there. For others, you may be somewhere in between. In the spirit of unity, honesty, and love, we Americans need to walk side-by-side to collectively confront one another. We will draw strength during the hard spots, and we will provide strength to others, but to restore America back to preeminence, it will only be done as *one nation, under God*.

The Cowboy

The fascination with the cowboy is so deeply engrained into the American character. To some the cowboy and America are virtually synonymous. Truthfully, the fascination isn't unique to America. People from all over the world visit the United States of America with the purpose of going out west to a dude ranch to watch a rodeo, or plan a getaway to discover what it is like to be a real cowboy. Why is it girls and boys alike still pretend to be cowboys? The cowboy, the American emblem of freedom, strength, and ruggedness, still pervades the American psyche. This rugged cowboy went places where others feared to venture. He dealt with the roughest of living conditions, and most all, he just desired to roam free. The cowboy—one man, his horse, his God, and the open range—is a portrait of the pure American dream. Today, many have exchanged their horses for Harleys and their open range for outer space, but the heart of America, born to be free, still "... lives to ride and rides to live." The cowboy is uniquely American, and it defines us around the globe. The cowboy within has been corralled for far too long and longs to be set free. A popular children's movie, *Toy Story*[8], depicts the change that occurs between the cowboy character, Woody, and Buzz Lightyear, the new high-tech toy. Woody ultimately becomes second fiddle to Buzz Lightyear as the favorite toy. As a result, Woody becomes jealous and he attempts to find a place in the heart of the boy, Andy. The story line advances with the competition between Woody and Buzz Lightyear. When both characters are ultimately thrust out of a second floor window, they go on a journey to return home. The journey is really more about reconciling the modern technological toy, Buzz Lightyear, with the old, rugged, traditional toy, Woody the cowboy. Where Buzz works off of batteries and laser beams, Woody operates off of a pull string, cowboy hat, and a rope. What's amazing about this movie is it speaks so clearly about the modern cultural battle being fought in our midst: the battle for modern society to reconcile itself with its origins and the simplicity of design implanted into the hearts of America and recorded in *The Declaration of Independence* and *The Constitution of the United States of America*. America, our hope, strength, and security will not be found in looking forward. Rather, it lies behind.

Will you journey with me, America, as we look at our past, as we walk down this road through the layers of despair? Will you sojourn, America, as we make our way past the ailments of today and unpack those precious gifts known as the Constitution of the United States, the Bill of Rights, and the Declaration of Independence? Can we walk together toward the light of our past as we by-pass centuries of layers and leap from the year 2010 to eighteenth century America? I'm excited! America, let's dive in. Let's sit with the voices of old as we pick up on their cadence, their convictions, and the spirit of the greatest nation on earth! Let's go, America. Let the quest begin!

Stand up, America. Stand now, and set loose those rugged cowboys who roamed so free!

---

8   *Toy Story*. CD. Directed by John Lasseter. United States: Pixar Animation Studios, Walt Disney Pictures 1995.

Section II—
The Fall of An Empire

Is the End Near?

❦

*"Then you will know the truth, and
the truth will set you free."*

John 8:32(NIV)[9]

When we look across the scene of the American culture, it would be easy to conclude Armageddon is about to take center stage. Our culture, once described as a shining city on a hill, has darkened for sure. We have witnessed the emergence of a liberal worldview, which stands in stark contrast to those values of yesteryears. This transformation of our culture did not occur at the hands of one man. Rather, this decline in American potency occurred gradually, over decades, perhaps centuries. For some it appears America's future is full of despair. Those not-too-distant memories of an America that stood for what was right, true, and good in a very harsh world have become just that—memories. As we read our history books, we sat at the edge of our seats when we learned about young America bursting onto the world scene in 1776. Yet in the year 2010, our enthusiasm for this nation appears to be dwindling. It isn't just the older generations of the land, so the excuse that the times have changed does not apply. It cuts across the entire spectrum of our society—the young, the old, and all those generations in between. America, the light of liberty given to the world appears to be growing

---

9   Scripture taken from the Holy Bible, New International Version®. Copyright © 1973, 1978, 1984 by International Bible Society. Used by permission of Zondervan. All rights reserved.

dim, and the inspiration of hope seems so far from our grasp. The truth is America is depressed. We are confused, and we are searching for meaning in a culture which erupts with hostility at every turn. Those traditions that were once thought of as sacred are being torn to shreds. Those values we held near and dear are being thrown out for those that are less enduring. What is right has become wrong, and what is wrong has become right. We value comfort over reality and emotions over truth. There are some in our land who frankly desire our demise, for in some demented way their view of history has been skewed to see this nation as a force for evil, not for good. This is not the image of America we have in our hearts. This is not the same nation as that of George Washington, Thomas Jefferson, John Adams, and Benjamin Franklin. What happened, America? Is the end near?

No authority on earth can answer that question with any degree of certainty. Some may think our empire is about to meet the same fate as that of Rome, others believe this is just what happens when a nation moves out of the days of its youth. No matter your perspective or your point of view, one thing is for certain. We cannot begin to answer any of these questions without an honest dialogue on the ailments of our land, where for but a moment we can let down the veil of pretend, get real with ourselves and our neighbors, and take a look at the truth of the condition plaguing this land.

Personally, this journey has been sobering for sure. If you are like me, depression and despair walked close as I faced the reality of the American dream. There is no doubt our culture has drifted. Well, truthfully, we have made a wholesale change of course. Our land is tugging and pulling, not against the restraint of the world, but amongst ourselves. It has been said a house divided will not stand, and in this moment we are anything but united. I beg you, the reader of this book, to hang onto hope. Let's begin this open dialogue, where truth meets America's reality. It will sting, it will bruise, and it will hurt. Our goal isn't to depress or cast your spirit with despair, for at the core of this book is the belief that all things are possible.

So all is not lost, but the first part of any recovery is allowing the light to shine, bringing truth to bear, and admitting where we have failed. As our journey toward recovery begins, we must face up to our time and admit to ourselves the cultural plagues which are depressing our land. With the explosion of information, we have become obsessed with intellect at the expense of common sense. We cater to the few of society and avoid the truth, for to acknowledge the truth would mean someone's feelings might get hurt and life wouldn't be fair. From there, perhaps we need to unpack a culture that has become so hostile to life, while it embraces death. As if death wasn't enough, somewhere we must face the fact that Americans have forgotten their independence, as they seek greater dependency from Washington. Our homes are a wreck, our finances are a disaster, our morals have collapsed, and oh, the maniacs we have running the media!

Hang with me, America, as we have some straight talk. It will be painful and ugly for sure. By the conclusion of this section, you may be convinced the fate of this great nation is that of the great Roman Empire. Perhaps that is correct, or the Provider from above is asking us to return to our roots.

THE INFECTION OF INTELLECTUALISM

⸎⧫⸎

"For my thoughts are not your thoughts, neither are your ways my ways declares the Lord. As the heavens are higher than the earth, so are my ways higher than your ways and my thoughts than your thoughts."

Isaiah 55:8–9 (NIV)[10]

In the last two decades the world has witnessed an explosion of information. A person from one continent can reach information on a different continent in a matter of seconds. The information technology explosion has revolutionized our world. People are armed with information and access to knowledge now more than any other time in history. The Internet has accelerated business and research projects, and provides virtually instantaneous communications at a fraction of the cost of more traditional methods. We have shifted from an economy that produces goods to a service economy driven by knowledge. Terms like "knowledge management," the "chief knowledge officer," and "intellectual property rights" are commonplace in our corporations. The hard sciences are making breathtaking discoveries at breakneck speed. Things only dreamed possible some fifteen years ago are now becoming a reality. America has arrived into the intellectual era. For all of our accomplishments, all of the scientific discoveries, the advancements in medicine, operating our businesses at the speed of change, are we the wiser for it? It depends.

---

10   Scripture taken from the Holy Bible, New International Version®. Copyright © 1973, 1978, 1984 by International Bible Society. Used by permission of Zondervan. All rights reserved.

Our knowledge through virtually any measurement has most certainly increased, but somewhere in this information explosion America lost her common sense. We can send men to the moon, drop a missile from 25,000 feet into a window of a home, and cure some of the most impossible diseases, but when it comes to making commonsense decisions, we are lost. What happened, America, to our common sense? When did life become so complicated that you need a Ph.D. to decide whether to eat white bread, wheat bread, or organic bread? How come we are so smart, but so fearful to drive our automobiles because we assume we will destroy the planet? What happened to the KISS principle (keep it simple, stupid)? Have we lost our way, America?

There are limits to our knowledge, and there are limits to man's intellectual abilities. To admit this is to recognize something greater and grander exists and is in control of the universe. To deny this places man and our capabilities as the central source for the quest for answers. America is off balance. I recall speaking to a Christian man a few months ago. We began to discuss world events, politics, and other issues. The man clearly knew more about world history than me, and had a firm grasp of the various theories behind his thought processes. When the topic of abortion came up, I simply stated it was wrong, period. My friend went into a diatribe on the tenets of the Constitution, on how he would never want an abortion, but didn't want to take the right away from women. After an approximately two-hour discussion on the topic, it became clear to me that I was arguing from a perspective of convictions (common sense) and he was arguing from a perspective of intellectual superiority. Even though this well-meaning gentleman was a walking, believing, church-attending Christian, he placed more emphasis on intellect and his capabilities than in his faith.

Global warming: the end is near. The planet will be destroyed, and it is all because you soccer moms are driving your children to practice in sport utility vehicles. Beside the fact that the statement just simply sounds ridiculous, inherent in the global warming theory is the idea that man is in control of the most sophisticated aspects of our planet, and man has within his grasp the ability to control our planet, including the climate. Common sense would say take a trip to the Petrified Forest out west, now surrounded by trees that have turned into stones over the centuries. This almost desert-like area of the world was at one time a lush forest that supported some impressive foliage. So how can a forest turn into rocks and barely support any kind of vegetation? Simple. Our earth is a changing, dynamic planet that has changed climates throughout the ages and will continue to change in ways we may or may not understand. To overplay the impact and/or man's ability to control those forces is to place our intellect over acknowledgement of our limitations. Think about the billions of dollars consumed in the global warming debate of governments across the globe when the entire thing could be resolved through common sense and a few principles:

- Conserve as it makes sense;
- Acknowledge man can't control the natural forces of the universe;
- Admit our environment has always changed and will always change. The change doesn't necessarily mean destruction. Perhaps the earth will be an even better place to live;
- Refuse to be governed by fear.

The other day, I had the opportunity to spend some time with what I would call two typical teenage boys. Between their computers, cell phones, iPods, Wiis, X-Box 360s, and their ever-growing virtual lives, I began to notice something was very peculiar about them. These children possessed an immense vocabulary, had knowledge about things I'm not sure I will ever know, being three times their age, but they plainly lacked good old common sense. I recall the days of my upbringing when I spent hours with my grandfather, my uncles, and my cousins working at a family owned junkyard. We worked together, we talked together, we dealt with customers, we dealt with conflict (sometimes scuffles between brothers), we tore vehicles apart, and we put vehicles together. We learned to drive and we learned to work. We learned about running a business, and we learned much about working with family. At the time I didn't think a thing of it, but the commonsense skills we learned during this period of life have paid perpetual dividends. I share this because I'm beginning to recognize the children of America no longer have those experiences. Those experiences have been traded in for video games, online gaming, interactive Internet studies, and texting. The things we grew up with—both hard skills and relational skills—many children in America are frankly missing. They can tell you how to defeat the most sophisticated video game, but lack the ability to carry a normal, meaningful conversation. It occurred to me that these teenagers are stuck inside of their heads and have lost touch with the relational aspect to life. Am I getting old? Perhaps, or just maybe some of the commonsense lessons of growing up within the context of mentors, a business, and good old hard work are inscribed in my character in a way our youth cannot obtain through the virtual lives they lead. I believe there will be some unintended consequences to the American culture of which I wouldn't even begin to attempt to predict. Wake up, parents! Wake up, America, and let's restore some good old common sense back into our homes!

Look at the financial debacle of 2008, 2009, and now into 2010. At the root of the financial mess were people borrowing money they could not afford, lenders lending money the people would never be able to repay, and a government that established the market conditions to support such dysfunction. We saw a housing market with 15% to 20% gains year after year. The irony of the whole affair is we were actually shocked when the market changed course. Was it greed? Probably, to a degree, but it was plainly just a lack of common sense. I recall living next to an eighty-eight-year-old neighbor and a seventy-six-year-old neighbor in Montgomery, Alabama. I had the unique opportunity to get to know these two gentlemen and learn from the wisdom they gained over the years. They had gray hair for a reason, and it was no surprise they understood a few things about money that we've somehow forgotten. They were not super smart or overly educated, but they lived their lives by a few simple financial principles. They never bought anything they could not afford to pay for in cash. If they couldn't pay for it, they waited and saved their money. They never took out a loan on a vehicle, a piece of furniture, or a television. They bought what they could afford. Yes, they were from a different generation, but some life principles are enduring. As a matter of fact, they never took out a loan on a home for longer than five to seven years. One doesn't have to look long to find stories of young couples with an adjustable rate mortgage on a fifty-year loan. So if you are thirty years old, you might have the home paid off if you make it to eighty! It is true. You can't make this stuff up. A few short generations ago, men and women understood that if you couldn't pay for something, you didn't buy it. We have created a generation in which we actually believe a fifty-year adjustable rate mortgage is a deal too good to pass up!

As a nation, we have some very difficult choices ahead of us. Our economy implodes due to overextended credit, and what do we do? We overextend our government. I believe it was Senator John McCain who said we are committing generational theft. Yet, we have a cadre of politicians and a strong number of Americans who actually believe you can restore fiscal responsibility by utilizing the same methods which created the problem to begin with. Where are my eighty-eight-year-old and seventy-six-year-old friends? They weren't the most intellectual of persons, but boy they understand if you do not have the cash to pay for something, don't buy it. The infection of intellectualism and the destruction of common sense have blinded America, and sooner or later, as a nation, we are going to have a reckoning with the ignorance of our intelligence.

At the root of this dependence upon intellect is fear. Fear that we are not in control of our environment, fear we cannot completely depend upon ourselves, and fear of a God who continues to govern the affairs of man. Without a degree of faith, man lives in a state of fear. Over the past fifty years we have witnessed the removal of faith from the public square and the adoption of intellect as our god. America, no matter how smart we become, no matter how explosive the Internet is, we will never have perfect information, and we will always have limitations. Always. There is no way around it, end of story!

It is time. It is overdue, America. We can no longer afford (literally) to witness the removal of common sense through the replacement of intellect. Both have their proper place in balance and in check, but we have shifted to favor our smarts and we are on the path toward adopting an intellectual worldview. We have decidedly removed our confidence in the wisdom from above, ignored the wisdom of generations before us, and markedly changed American culture. Restore America's common sense to the public square, restore common sense to our homes, our churches, and our schools.

Stand up, America. Stand now for common sense, and set loose those rugged cowboys who roamed so free!

DON'T HURT MY FEELINGS

⟨⟩

*"They exchanged the truth of God for a lie, and worshiped and served
created things rather than the Creator - who is forever praised."*

Romans 1:25 (NIV)[11]

What is political correctness and who defines it, anyway? Americans can no longer call white people white, black people black, an Islamic extremist a terrorist, people who lead a generational existence on welfare as irresponsible, a marriage as between one man and one woman, and a spade a spade. America has been hijacked by fear of the truth. Today's culture places more emphasis on making people feel good rather than seeking, speaking, and embracing the truth. Look at our federal governmental institutions. They are plagued with political correctness, which paralyzes action and effectiveness. Most of the federal agencies have ethnic committees, sexual-orientation committees, race committees, and then somewhere in there, performance actually becomes a factor. Look at the debate raging in America regarding building an Islamic mosque within close proximity of the World Trade Center. Proponents believe it is acceptable to build a mosque within feet of perhaps the gravest tragedy in American history. In reality, it is an obvious stab at a historically fresh and tender wound to most Americans. The building of this mosque represents a symbolic statement to the world about the impairment

---

11 Scripture taken from the Holy Bible, New International Version®. Copyright © 1973, 1978, 1984 by International Bible Society. Used by permission of Zondervan. All rights reserved.

of political correctness upon this nation. Unbelievably, Americans must relive the agony of September 11, 2001 as political correctness supersedes truth and common sense.

Children are now confused every Christmas season. Is it "Merry Christmas," or "Happy Holidays"? No wonder our children are morally confused. We can't even call Christmas by its true name because we must accommodate and typically dumb it down to the most minority voice. During a recent news broadcast, a story ran about the city of Seattle banning any religious expressions during the Christmas season in the state capitol. They were allowing a Christmas tree, but the tree couldn't be called a Christmas tree. It had to be called a "holiday tree." We are dying, America, and it has been occurring for fifty years. One or two more blinks and we will be gone. The cancer of political correctness is killing America, and it must be treated and treated seriously. The most recent attack in Fort Hood, Texas, is thankfully bringing the discussion of political correctness to the forefront. Our hope is that it remains there. Our fear is that it will be fleeting. We can't even call an Islamic fundamentalist who has had multiple contacts with Al Qaeda and made formal presentations likening a suicide bomber to a US soldier who falls on a grenade to save his platoon a terrorist. He is a terrorist, period; accept it. If it offends Muslims, then Muslims can clean it up. If it offends the politicians, then too bad, because we want the truth more than we want to feel better.

Why does America fear the truth? Stated another way, why is the truth so fearful? Truth is a blessing, but when truth confronts us, it hurts. It hurts because we know we must change. It hurts because we know we've done something wrong. It hurts because we must admit we aren't in control, and it hurts because we are reckoned with judgment from a divine being, and it forces us to accept the fact that each of us sooner or later must answer to a God who believes in accountability. In America we actually think if we deny the truth, run from it, the truth will go away. Perhaps if we pretend it isn't there, somehow we don't have to change. Eventually, if we ignore it long enough, we can become immune to its effect. The net result is an America who has entered the feel-good era. Life is all about comfort and not about consequences. When the financial firms mess up, we bail them out with money we don't have. When the automotive industry runs itself into bankruptcy, our government purchases a controlling interest in private companies. When people take out loans they could never afford, we reward them not with consequences, but with mortgage relief programs. This isn't a statement where we should run from our societal responsibilities, but natural consequences are God's corrective mechanism. When we feel consequences, we typically turn away from the direction causing those consequences and move toward a healthier place. Look at drug, alcohol, and sex addicts. They never change until the consequences are severe enough to force them out of their addiction. Then and only then do people change. America, we are addicted to feeling good and we are afraid of feeling consequences. Unfortunately, we have pursued this comfort society for over half a century, beginning with the love and drug revolution in the 1960s all the way to the present, where the truth is something to be feared, not something to be embraced. We cannot run from consequences forever. Each time we run or hide from a consequence it multiplies until there is no more running from that consequence. I heard a quote recently from a Hollywood tough guy who said we are raising a generation of teenagers. That's right, teenagers. When you compare today's men to the men who went off to World War II, we are raising a feel good, don't offend culture that does everything and anything to avoid consequences. Was this star correct? I'll let you make the judgment. Just look at the push for parental healthcare coverage to be extended until children are well into their twenties. I can appreciate the need to help our children out, but if they never have to provide medical care for themselves, then they never have to be responsible, and then they will never have to truly grow up. Perhaps, just maybe, this lone voice in Hollywood was onto something.

You don't have to watch the news long to hear a story about some military person who did something wrong in Iraq or Afghanistan. Recently, there was a story about a captured terrorist bringing soldiers up on abuse charges for giving him a bloody lip. Look around at the constant barrage of cell phone videos depicting our law enforcement members as beasts. Here's a truth for you: war sucks. It is violent. Bad things happen and people die. War isn't supposed to be a gentleman's sport. It brings out the worst and the best in people, and to expect us to ever conduct a war with the fullness of civilized manners is unrealistic and plainly naïve. The brave men and women who place their lives on the lines to protect the streets and the neighborhoods in America everyday, who face constant scrutiny, should be given some grace. These unsung heroes transport people on a daily basis who may urinate in their backseat, who attempt to stab them and/or pose serious medical risks (e.g., HIV), and at the very least, never fully knowing whether they have said their last goodbyes to their families when they walk out the door to do society's dirty work. I'm not justifying behavior which clearly violates the honor given to an officer or soldier, but what I am saying, America, is our search for political correctness and the "never offend" culture denies the dirty, rotten realities of war and our officer's daily lives. Every citizen should go through a week of training at a law enforcement academy doing mock drills apprehending suspects, or going into a dark, desolate house while making split second decisions for your life, the safety of your fellow officers, and the lives of those in the home. Having worked in law enforcement, one of my greatest fears is taking the life of an innocent person. Believe me, police officers are faced with decisions like these in fractions of a second. Try their shoes on for size!

Look at our politicians today. This goes to both parties. We are promised one thing and then they vote another way. We have the public voice and the news story, and miss the private vote or private action. I used to blame the politicians, but I've begun to think Americans like feeling good about themselves. We don't want to confront the dark realities of truth seeking. In recent years, we witnessed an era of Republicans who promised fiscal conservatism and provided the exact opposite, followed by a Democratic party who promised "pay as you go" and passed the largest deficit spending bill, labeled as a stimulus bill, which didn't breed freedom but created bondage to foreign governments. We blame the credit card companies for outrageous interest rates, and then our government outrageously borrows from China. All because America is afraid to accept the cold, hard reality that we can't borrow our way out of pain. The truth is we have gotten fat, dumb, and happy, and it isn't politically palatable to let the cards fall where they may and try to pick up the pieces. We have punted the pain to another generation for another time, but we can deny the existence only for so long. Eventually, we will be called to account. Suffice to say, our politically correct, put-off-pain, do-not-offend, and run-from-consequences culture seeks to demonize the truth, and for it we are comforted for a time, but it acts to atrophy our American strength.

Return, return, America, to the search for truth. Return to Superman's motto: *"Truth, justice, and the America way."* America, come back from your preoccupation with comfort, your search for pleasure, and your desire to deny reality. We must dare to dream of the day where seeking truth is valued more highly than seeking pleasure.

Stand up, America. Stand now for truth, and set loose those rugged cowboys who roamed so free!

THE CULTURE OF DEATH

❧☙

"Lo, children are a heritage of the Lord;
and the fruit of the womb is his reward."

Psalm 127:3 (NIV)[12]

Americans should be stricken with grief over the growing contempt for life. Our culture, including many Christian denominations, has grown increasingly hostile toward what can be called "inconvenient life." Inconvenient lives are those lives who are chosen to end before they begin, those lives of our elders who were too difficult to care for or too time consuming, or those children who were born with some type of handicap or were just plain "different." Just a few evenings past there was a news report on parents who utilized human growth hormones to ensure their children would be tall enough. Was there ever anything wrong with a so-called short person? Look at all the genetic testing that is performed on embryos and infants still in the womb. Granted, some is for legitimate purposes, but truthfully, a large portion of the testing is done to provide the parents with the choice of whether or not they desire the child. Oh, America, how sad a state we have become where we value our own conveniences and selfish agendas over life. We place our careers, our finances, our goals, and what we want out of life over those of the unborn, the elders, or the disadvantaged. My heart is shredded with sadness for our land. We are intentionally and freely allowing innocent blood to be shed

---

12   Scripture taken from the Holy Bible, New International Version®. Copyright © 1973, 1978, 1984 by International Bible Society. Used by permission of Zondervan. All rights reserved.

in our midst. We are creating a culture that almost promotes it. This is perhaps the greatest travesty of the American story.

Stunningly, our society is outraged over supposed torture of the terrorists who possess intelligence relating to saving American lives, yet in the next breath, they believe in health care rationing, abortion for inner-city pregnancy issues, unfettered research on embryonic stem cells, and the like. Somehow, there is greater value placed on terrorists than on the complete innocence of life in the womb or the elderly.

More pointedly, the church should be ashamed of itself, without question. It doesn't take much research on church doctrines to determine that there are a large and growing number of so-called Christian churches that are proponents of this "death culture." Most of those churches have sophisticated reasoning. It's terrible, utterly terrible, for our churches to be debating and struggling with this issue. It should be simple. We believe in life, we support life, and we go to great lengths to protect life. Look at the church of Pergamum in the book of Revelation.

> "*12*To the angel of the church in Pergamum write:
>
> These are the words of him who has the sharp, double-edged sword. *13*I know where you live--where Satan has his throne. Yet you remain true to my name. You did not renounce your faith in me, even in the days of Antipas, my faithful witness, and who was put to death in your city--where Satan lives. *14*Nevertheless, I have a few things against you: You have people there who hold to the teaching of Balaam, who taught Balak to entice the Israelites to sin by eating food sacrificed to idols and by committing sexual immorality. *15*Likewise you also have those who hold to the teaching of the Nicolaitans. *16*Repent therefore! Otherwise, I will soon come to you and will fight against them with the sword of my mouth. *17*He who has an ear, let him hear what the Spirit says to the churches. To him who overcomes, I will give some of the hidden manna. I will also give him a white stone with a new name written on it, known only to him who receives it."
>
> Revelation 2:12-17 (NIV) [13]

---

[13] Scripture taken from the Holy Bible, New International Version®. Copyright © 1973, 1978, 1984 by International Bible Society. Used by permission of Zondervan. All rights reserved.

As I read this passage of Scripture, it gives me a couple of clear insights into God and God's character. First, God is keeping a watchful eye on us, on His church, and on this nation. He is acutely aware of our transgressions. Second, God's truth goes straight to the heart of man's intentions, motives, and sin. After all, "... these are the words of him who has the sharp, double-edged sword." Even though in our relativistic culture it may seem acceptable to embrace aspects of the culture of death, the author of truth will discern this quite differently. There are really two paths in life: God's way or the world's way. In life, there is little middle ground afforded to us, especially as Christians. Third, God desires for us to repent for our sins. He wants us to repent, He desires reconciliation, and He sends warnings in advance of His punishments. Recall the prophets of old who would tell the ancient kings what God would do. Look at Samuel, who told King Saul he had lost God's blessing. America, we have sinned, we are sinning, and we continue to sin in the culture of life. It is undeniable and frankly obvious to anyone remotely paying attention, whether they are Christian or not. Fourth, God will take action to punish the church if it does not repent. God warns the church by saying "... otherwise, I will soon come to you and fight with the sword of my mouth." He will not tolerate disobedience forever. Finally, God has a reward for those who repent and for the church that repents: *hidden manna.* God is telling the church there are blessings in obedience and destruction in disobedience. So, where do you stand? Where does your church stand, and where do you think God stands? Truth, Scripture, and just plain old common sense would point decidedly to a culture of life.

Gifts from God: Abortion

Have you ever visited the site of the 1995 bombing of the Federal Building in Oklahoma City? The memorial conjures up such strong emotions, which move the hardest of hearts to the tragedy and loss of innocent life. The difference separating Oklahoma City from other national tragedies was the field of chairs used to represent the death of each person or child in the Federal Building. The chairs were positioned to symbolize the location where each person was thought to be located in the building. This somber memorial is touching for sure, but that somberness transitions into the realm of gut-wrenching with the awareness that the small chairs represent each child killed during that tragic day. Funny how naturally and instinctually the tears well up when our hearts are tugged by the suffering of our young. If you walk across the street from the memorial, you will see a large statute of Jesus Christ with his back toward the memorial. As you circle the statue and glance into the eyes of Christ, it is readily apparent that Jesus is in tears. What a visual for Christ's sentiments on the death of any child: Jesus weeps.

John 11:35 states "Jesus wept."[14] The shortest verse in the Holy Bible conveys such profound meaning. Contextually, Jesus arrived on the scene of his dear friends Mary, Martha, and other close friends after his dear friend Lazarus had died. Mary and Martha were grief stricken, and even though Jesus knew he was going to raise Lazarus from the dead, Jesus was overwhelmed with the outpouring of sorrow being experienced by his friends. Jesus, for a moment, allows us to see squarely into his character and his emotional makeup. Jesus demonstrates his partial humanity and his unique compassion for those he loves. In view of abortion, if Christ found the death of Lazarus, a grown man, worthy of great sorrow, then what type of reaction does Christ have over the estimated forty-five million children in the United States alone (not too mention the millions of children who experienced a similar fate through United States government indirect aid to groups who do abortions overseas) who have been victims of abortion since Roe vs. Wade came into effect?[15] Jesus wept.

Various Christian denominations have developed varying positions on when abortion is acceptable or when it is not acceptable. We have tried to theologically define it while the constant acceptance grows. "Jesus wept" rings loud and clear each time another innocent life falls prey to abortion. The seared condition of the collective American conscience is a result of decades of moral decline. The community of those who call themselves Christians should be outraged and they need to take a stand in their midst. Pastors and priests need to be direct, firm, and resolute as they preach and minister to their congregations. Politicians need to be held accountable, and community groups who are proponents of abortion need to be boycotted. Make no mistake about it, as we debate it, with each passing of innocent life, Jesus weeps. If this topic does not tear at your heart, then you really should question your heart.

We all have friends or couples we know who want to have children. Couples who would love any child from any family, but for some reason in the providence of God, they aren't able to have a child. In contrast, a society that virtually encourages the taking of innocent life is perplexing,

---

14 Scripture taken from the Holy Bible, New International Version®. Copyright © 1973, 1978, 1984 by International Bible Society. Used by permission of Zondervan. All rights reserved.

15 http://www.guttmacher.org/pubs/fb_induced_abortion.html

to say the least. Our society should be advocating adoption as the first and best means of dealing with an unwanted child. Women, there is something in the wiring between a female and a baby which, upon sight, brings you to utter joy and elation. There is something in your makeup that explains why you walk down a street, see a baby in a stroller, and feel you must take a second look. Infants have the ability to bring out the tenderness in our souls. So to think that a woman can go ahead and end the life of an innocent child in her womb, override the God-given instincts toward children, and have no long-term mental or emotional scars is logically impossible to conclude. Even if the abortion is legal, even if you have the procedure done under proper medical supervision (if this is possible given the Hippocratic Oath), and even if you do it early in the pregnancy to rationalize the guilt away, there is something deep within which tells you it is wrong. I'm no psychologist, but perhaps the rampant bouts of depression for some could be explained by the quick decision to end a pregnancy. This isn't about guilt or condemnation, because the same Jesus who weeps is the same Jesus who forgives. His heart is full of compassion for all. Simply stated, abortion has been touted as a woman's right, and logically it is incompatible with the essence of womanhood. The right to have an abortion does more to diminish women's rights than to aid them. In its best form, it says here's a sure method to create a life of pain, agony, depression, and inner turmoil. Look at a mother who loses a child before that child reaches adulthood. Inevitably, the parent will say, "My child was not supposed to die before I died. This isn't the way it works." The way what works? The way God designed it to work.

You men out there, both Christian and non-Christian alike, listen up! At our core we are designed to be the protectors and providers of society. We are supposed to be the chivalrous ones defending the rights of the innocent, and we are failing and failing miserably. Legalized abortion may have given something to a woman—the right to choose—but it also removed a huge right of a man—the right to make decisions concerning his child. Men, our Supreme Court kicked us right to the curb and told the men of America we no longer have a right to determine what happens with our children. Again, to be a man and not to be outraged should be incompatible. Our place as a father, and at least as an equal member of society, has been shattered as we find our authority marginalized. In the eyes of the laws of America, American men are subservient when it comes to taking the life of the unborn. The old saying "the end does not justify the means" is exactly what abortion represents. Men, stand up and take your place at the table. Wouldn't it be great if we saw a wave of men across this country begin to stand up and demand their rights to their children back? Wow, after fifty years of methodical destruction of men, how would that rock America?

Parents, you too need to heed this warning. Believe it or not, in some states your teenaged daughter can have an abortion without your knowledge or permission. If you are a parent, you should be outraged. The government and some community health groups are providing the funds and the means for your child to end a pregnancy without you ever knowing it. How many homes out there have had teenaged girls have abortions to avoid the shame of an unwanted pregnancy, and now sit with the blood of this child on their hands for the rest of their lives? What makes me so angry is most if not all of these teenagers do not possess the mental or emotional maturity to really understand the consequences of an abortion. As a society and as a nation, we are robbing the rights of our parents and destroying our teenagers' souls.

Abortion is utterly destructive to the virtues of honesty, accountability, and responsibility. Many abortions are performed as convenience abortions, as birth control, or to remove a child who possesses some type of handicap. As they say, " ... you can't make this stuff up." Our teenagers learn to take the quick way out, our society reinforces instant gratification, and the abortion laws support the performance in an almost secretive atmosphere. In the end, there is no accountability for the loss of the child in exercising such a violent right.

Recall how often George W. Bush would be brought to tears over the daily reports on the loss of men and women during the wars in Afghanistan and Iraq and the emotional and mental toll it took on the leader of the free world to knowingly send people to die. Our society grieves each time we lose a soldier. The parents, wives, children, and friends who knew that person are changed forever. War is absolutely devastating. So why do we think ending innocent life for the sake of convenience is any less devastating? Perhaps we cannot see the impacts or the long-term ramifications on the American psyche, but they are there. They are absolutely there. We can rationalize it away, we can manipulate our Constitution, and we can make it culturally acceptable, but in the still of the night there is something in the heart of a person that knows it is wrong. Wake up, America! It is time to end this, and end this now!

Finally, from a purely logical point of view, abortion makes absolutely no sense. There are really two central arguments which are philosophically at odds. First is the core argument that man is capable of determining when life begins, and therefore has the right to end a pregnancy because it isn't life to begin with. This logic then sets up the debate over whether life starts during the first, second, third trimester, or upon birth. The debate rages forward as we attempt to find the precise point after conception where an embryo is considered life. Unfortunately, there will never be and can never be a logical conclusion to the argument, because the logic is based on momentary values, momentary scientific knowledge, and it creates an argument not based in an absolute. The embryo isn't life yet? Wait just a second. If it isn't life, and you believe in the theory of evolution, it would stand to reason that if the earth and man evolved from a random explosion of subatomic matter that ultimately evolved into human life, then, logically, you would have to surely conclude that the moment a sperm and egg create a unified cell it becomes life. Okay, my point here isn't to get into some fifty-page dissertation on "pro-choice" arguments. It gets pretty confusing, quite convoluted, and creates twisted logic, which at best is incongruent with science and can only be based in what the individual thinks, feels, and believes at that moment in time. These things change based on the age, the value system, and life experience of the individual. It is moral relativism at its finest. Where is the end to this debate? There cannot be an end, because truthfully the argument isn't based in an absolute. It is based in momentary feelings and emotions. So, I take you back to the decision of sending our young into war. At the very least, we have gone through lengthy political elections, placed someone in the Office of the President of the United States, and daresay the decision for war has never been entered into lightly, and not without a lengthy vetting process to get there. Why are we so flippantly free on the decision regarding life or death of the unborn? The "pro-life" side advocates it is not our decision to decide where life begins or life ends, because it is God's prerogative. At least the conclusion of the "pro-life" side is based in an absolute, which won't change each moment. Whatever your conviction, when we have a philosophical divide, we as a nation must make a choice. If we will never agree morally, doesn't it at least make better sense to err on the side of life, not death, in those areas where there is such divisiveness?

Abortion is wrong. As a Christian community we need to love those who are victims of abortion, but as a church fellowship we need to firmly root ourselves in protecting life and to unabashedly proclaim to our people the abhorrent nature of abortion and the obvious disconnect with our Christian faith. We should be outraged at politicians, business and civic leaders, and community leaders who proclaim to be Christians, yet support abortion. *We the people* need to hold our leaders accountable, and we the church need to absolutely make a unified stand against every leader who claims to be a Christian and supports abortion. It is not optional.

Our God and Creator looks with great compassion upon children, and even more so orphans. If we could sit down with God, I bet he would shed tears for each orphan who has never known the love, security, and affection of a family. Orphans matter because our God says they do, but they also tell the world something about American culture. They show we care for those who cannot care for themselves. It says America is different. We don't abandon the helpless to the streets, and we don't shut out the feeble to the fringes of society. No, not America; we take in the homeless, we take in the helpless, and we bring to them what life so maliciously took from them. America, let's become a nation where every orphan has a home, where every child has multiple good homes bidding for him or her, where our less fortunate find fortune in good, strong, loving homes. It is through our caring and compassionate character that our united national character trumpets the cause of freedom across the globe and displaces the all too familiar accusation of American self-centeredness. May we see a day where children become our prized possession over careers, possessions, and comforts.

We are a nation where our past, our present, and our future are sources of great strength and stability. Our past defines where we have been. It provides us with our accomplishments, our failures, and gives inspiration and insight into the destiny of our nation. Our future and our young possess the strength and the ambition to climb new heights and to reach new stars. Without the activity of the young, we would cease, progress would halt, and our old would be less invigorated. Our present generations are the transitory generations. They are the people who meld the past into the future. A constant cycle of heritage and hope, acting as a wheel of progress and governor ensuring our society progresses, yet doesn't over-stretch its aim. The beauty and wisdom found in having multiple generations intertwined so delicately into the direction of our nation is that our elders are the source of wisdom and bring with them memories of our heritage. During biblical times it was considered the duty of the elders to mentor the young. There is something calming, something soothing about a voice who has seen a number of cycles of life that interjects to guide, to instruct, and to lead. We are stronger, wiser, and better equipped because of our elders. They have seen more, they have experienced more, and many of them have the literal scars to prove it. We are one nation made up of many ages and races. Our strength lies in our diversity, where each generation has great gifts to offer the other generations.

To the young of America and those who have the drive to move America forward: you are full of ambition, full of the desire to make things different, bigger, better than your parents did. You have the intellectual ability and the technological capability to do things, go places, and achieve things the older generations never dreamt of doing. Your vigor and strength are so necessary to propel our nation forward. After all, when it is time to defend our nation, we call on you. You are the strength of America, but you lack what the elders bring to the table. You lack the wisdom and the fortitude of character developed from a lifetime of trials. This isn't to say the elders possess all the answers, because in them we find resistance to new ideas, but in the very least our old need to have a seat at the table. They need to be welcomed, cherished, and encouraged to participate and made to feel like they matter, because they do.

America has shifted to value youthfulness over wisdom where our elders are looked upon as burdens to care for and a drain on our resources. As the healthcare debate rages on throughout America, even the consideration of not doing everything and anything possible to prolong and/or keep our elders alive means we have moved beyond greatness and are settling for mediocrity at best. America, what defines us as great, what distinguishes us from other nations, is that we do whatever it takes whenever it's required to protect and preserve the lives of our old. They are our heritage. Furthermore, by allowing room in America for those former generations, we are honoring our past, caring for our present, and ensuring our future. They are the anchors which keep our society from overcorrecting on impulse. They are the ones who, through the gravity of their years, ensure that the spontaneity of youth doesn't forego the lessons of the past.

The Christian faithful need to lead by example. Our faith is rooted in love, and love always serves and always protects. The Christian church should be the first to demonstrate respect for their elders, the first to take an aging parent into their home instead of shipping them off to a home of sorts. The Christian church should be the place where the elders are cherished, encouraged, uplifted, and listened to. It amazes me how long the people lived during Old Testament times and the value they placed on the father and the eldest son. No, the number of years on this planet does not equate directly to wisdom, but there is merit in the idea that with age comes experience, and with experience comes wisdom. Not always, but the law of averages kicks in somewhere. The Ten Commandments say to honor your father and your mother, and therefore we must.

The church and America need to honor our fathers and mothers. We need to honor them in our churches by celebrating the old, in our families by wanting to care for them and keeping them around, in our communities and political debates. It simply isn't right that we make our elders feel like a burden when they can no longer work or completely care for themselves. It isn't right we have churches that only cater to the young and intentionally dismiss the old. It isn't right we talk about cost benefit analysis when discussing medical treatment. We are Christians, and we are Americans. We care for them because that is who we are, not because the numbers on the profit/loss statement make sense. We are the nation who never leaves a man behind in times of war. That, even though it risks the lives of other soldiers, sailors, pilots, and marines, is the defining character of our American military. Why can't the care of our elders with every inch of possibility, sacrifice, and effort reach into the American heart and become institutionalized as part of our defining national character?

In Search of Perfection

The Hollywood culture found in America has established a level of human perfection which is virtually unachievable. Our culture desires thin, but curvy women around five-foot-six inches, along with muscular men approximately six feet in height with six-pack abs. Just look at the television commercials for a moment. The majority of the television commercials are centered on the idea of the perfect body. The pornographic industry attempts to sell perfection, and by statistical measurements it is a huge industry. In the year 2010, genetic testing is common to determine abnormalities with unborn children. For some parents this is just a part of being informed, for others this is the step where they choose to end the life of their child because of the imperfections revealed in the test. There was a recent news article that discussed parents giving children human growth hormones to ensure the children would be tall enough to meet the parent's expectations. At some point, the American measurement system has gone astray. For some reason, those who are not born perfect, who possess a physical or mental disability, or who do not meet the artificial standards of our society are considered less valuable. How vain! There isn't a man or woman reading this who hasn't struggled with this dilemma within themselves, their children, or their spouse. We have become a society intensely hostile to imperfection. The roots of this culture are terribly destructive and have far reaching ramifications.

The inconvenient truth in America is if we do not achieve this artificial standard, there is a societal shame that is placed on this person—a guilt and sense of being less valuable. We are designing entire industries with the goal of achieving physical perfection. In the book of Ecclesiastes, King Solomon, who had every possession imaginable and hundreds of concubines, discovered the truth of the fleeting nature of chasing perfection thousands of years ago. *"Vanity of vanities," says the Preacher, "Vanity of vanities! All is vanity" (Ecc 1:2)[16]*. Look at Proverbs 31:30. *"Charm is deceptive, and beauty is fleeting; but a woman who fears the LORD is to be praised[17]."* These Scriptures are completely counter to the societal values that are streamed into our homes through the television, the Internet, magazine racks, radio, and every other billboard on our way to work. The promise is that if we only achieved some level of perfection, we would find happiness. The point of this discussion on perfection is that it is a root that feeds the culture of death in America. It is our fixation with perfection which influences our decisions on ending pregnancies, obtaining divorces, and the pursuit of cosmetic surgeries to enhance our appearances to fit societal norms.

There isn't an American alive who hasn't been impacted by or infected with this need for perfection. If love means perfection, and happiness is a result of perfection, and "perfection" is not attainable, is it any surprise we have a record number of people taking antidepressants? America, wake up and open your eyes to the culture of death, which is so prevalent. It finds its expression in taking the life of the unborn, pushing our elders to the fringes of society and facilitating their smooth exit out of this world. Even more despairing is how the fixation with perfectionism has driven many decisions of ending a pregnancy or requesting a divorce. America, God hurts for us as a nation. He longs for our return to life.

Stand up, America. Stand now for life, and set loose those rugged cowboys who roamed so free!

---

16 Scripture taken from the Holy Bible, New International Version®. Copyright © 1973, 1978, 1984 by International Bible Society. Used by permission of Zondervan. All rights reserved.

17 Ibid.

The Plague of Entitlement

⟨⊙⟩

*"But my **God** shall supply all your need according*
to his riches in glory by Christ Jesus."
Philippians 4:19 (NIV)[18]

As a nation we give billions to the poor both domestically and overseas. Our charitable organizations and not-for-profits are some of the most generous the world has ever known. In recent years, the continent of Africa has received large sums of money from America alone to fight the AIDS epidemic. The American churches and faith communities consistently give and reach out to the poor throughout this land.

Was America intended to have the multitude of entitlement programs provided by the government (funded by tax dollars) where we actually paralyze the individual's ability to provide, force their dependency upon the government, and push people away from God and their God given gifts and talents? Just visit a Wal-Mart when food stamps are about to expire and you will see a cadre of perfectly capable human beings wearing decent clothes, speaking on cell phones, furiously going about their shopping as not to leave a food stamp unspent. There are some in our society who truly need food stamps. They have hit a rough spot in life or have a legitimate disability, and we should help them out. Then there are others who have adopted an entitlement mentality as a way of life. The spirit of

---

18   Scripture taken from the Holy Bible, New International Version®. Copyright © 1973, 1978, 1984 by International Bible Society. Used by permission of Zondervan. All rights reserved.

the entitlement programs means well, but the reality is they end up creating dependency, complacency, and most alarmingly, the entitlement programs undermine the traditional role of the husband to provide for his family. Go on a mission trip, America, into those welfare communities. You will find some who need help, you will find others who expect it, and you will find an even larger group who have been destroyed by it. Please don't misunderstand, Christ wants us to help the needy and give to the poor, but the question remains: How is the best way to "give to the poor," through handouts or through some mechanism which promotes accountability and demands improvement? Fundamentally, over-dependence on entitlements can rob a person of their dignity, and their ability to fulfill their God-sized purpose in life. What a political hot potato! Many of these people need to wake up, because we are on the verge of a government which can no longer afford the handouts.

Put another way, government dependency has roots of jealousy, envy, and covetousness, and as Christians we are commanded to grow beyond these deficiencies of the heart. The unintended consequence of this entitlement culture is America has raised a generation who believe they are entitled to certain benefits, certain rights, and certain wealth regardless of their effort, sacrifice, or investment. We have elected entire political blocs who view their ordained mission as returning resources to the poor through the vehicle of government assistance, and as we study the lessons of history, this approach never works.

Should we help the poor? You bet, but when we help the poor by destroying their ability to realize their God given gifts, the ability to have faith in a God who can provide, and to develop healthy habits that would eliminate their dependency on the government, we create permanent economic dependents who are motivated by envy, held captive to government assistance, and never fulfill the America dream "in pursuit of happiness." The truth is that God calls us to a life filled with faith, dignity, and respect. Yes, we should depend upon our brother, but when entitlement becomes a matter of the heart, it is at that point where we do more harm than good!

From Dependence to Independence

Let's remove our three quarter of a century entitlement mentality and let's dream again. A dream of an America that brings freedom to those held captive by entitlements. Let's carry out the mantra of caring for the poor by creating independent, fully functioning, fully contributing citizens. Let's organize government programs where dependence is not the end state, it is the first step with the end goal of independence.

Look at today's government programs. There are strong political pressures against changing programs to focus on results as opposed to permanency. Politicians are given incentives to keep people on the books instead of providing them the tools to have their own means of support. This is no different than what Christ told Peter. Come with me and I will make you a fisher of men. Jesus could have just done all the work himself, but instead He taught the disciples to fish for men themselves. He taught the apostles that they would have the Great Comforter to guide their personal relationship with God, that they would be guided and provided accountability and responsibility. Perhaps Christ is now calling us to teach our poor, to instruct the disadvantaged in how to become fishers of men. Perhaps God would like each of us to learn to have a personal relationship with Him, not one that is dependent upon some institution or priest or pastor. What would happen if, as a government, we instilled this principle into our legislation and our assistance programs? What if politicians would ask themselves before each vote whether this program creates independence or dependency? What would happen if we established a culture where Americans didn't feel entitled to anything other than the opportunity to grow, achieve, and aspire? What would happen if we unleashed the fifty years of bottled creativity into our economy?

John F. Kennedy's famous words: "Ask not what your country can do for you, ask what you can do for your country,[19]" ring with historical permanence. The class envy and the expectant attitudes that pervade our culture were destructive during Kennedy's days, and they are destructive now. Those addicted to entitlements are victims of a destructive force in America; a force which desires to marginalize people and ensure their God given gifts and talents remain dormant. Recall the stories of immigrants who worked in mills, the steel factories, and production plants six or seven days a week just to provide food. The entitlement culture has cheapened America and weakened our individual and national character. We are losing sight of hard work, persistent savings, patience, endurance, long suffering, respect, and humility. These values are being superseded by instant gratification, instant communication, and an attitude of "the world owes me something." The world owes us nothing. To pretend

---

19   Source: http://www.jfklibrary.org/white%20house%20diary/1961/January/20

otherwise is to rob our children of enduring national attributes which will be needed to sustain this land during times of national testing.

Stand up, America. Stand now for the liberation from entitlements, and set loose those rugged cowboys who roamed so free!

Who's the Boss Around Here?

⎨◉⎬

"Obey your leaders and submit to their authority. They keep watch over you as men who must give an account. Obey them so that their work will be a joy, not a burden, for that would be no advantage to you."

Hebrews 13:17 (NIV)[20]

"For rebellion is like the sin of divination, and arrogance like the evil of idolatry. Because you have rejected the word of the Lord, he has rejected you as king."

1 Samuel 15:23 (NIV)[21]

During the mid 1990s the nation, and especially the metropolitan area in Washington, D.C., experienced an explosion in technological jobs and the salaries for those who possessed such skills. Technology companies and consulting firms were paying first year graduates from college hefty salaries with little to no professional experience. Computer science programmers could make $70,000 to $100,000 right out of college. Computer skills were in demand while the Y2K scare was full steam ahead. A panoramic view of the metropolitan area showed the signs of a housing explosion where bidding wars were common. It was an era where twenty-five year olds had half a million dollar homes

---

20 Scripture taken from the Holy Bible, New International Version®. Copyright © 1973, 1978, 1984 by International Bible Society. Used by permission of Zondervan. All rights reserved.

21 Ibid.

and drove better automobiles than their parents ever dreamed. What wasn't right with this picture was that a college graduate with virtually no experience obtained such a dowry at such an early age. The technology boom was the culmination of a culture that had thrown off authority for the past fifty years by creating a generation of entry level Chief Executive Officers (CEOs), CEOs with virtually no experience, but full authority to be a player and call the shots. Unlike the generations before where employees worked their way through one company step by step over time, this generation's perspective was pay me, promote me, or I will skip on out the door. This generation believed in instant communication, which translated to the expectation that their opinions mattered and what they had to say should be heard at the highest levels. Gone were the days of the chain of command, the respect for authority, or the humility that youth brought with it much folly.

America's rebellion against authority has been occurring for many years. We have fought to remove the divine hand of Providence from having any influence across the public square. We have undermined the husband's role in the household through the extreme feminist movement, we have allowed children to dictate to their parents, we have witnessed increased hostility toward anyone who resembles a person of authority, like a police officer, and we have torn down any cultural norm which held us to account. Take a moment to ask a police officer if they have noticed a change in the public's attitude towards law enforcement in the last twenty to thirty years. It might surprise you how they respond and the stories of disrespect you may hear. The dismal spiral of rebelling from authority is occurring across America and has infected our homes, our schools, our governments, and our communities. No wonder we have a generation of politicians who desire to remove the effectiveness of our *Constitution,* or pretend as if the sentiments in *the Declaration of Independence* need not apply.

Look at Washington, D.C. The politicians no longer respect the authority of the will of the people. We have judges who create laws from the bench, a congress that believes it can spend itself without answering to any authority, and the creation of entitlement programs with no method for paying for them. Our leaders use mental gymnastics to deceive us into believing their way is right, while in their hearts they are pursuing a political agenda rooted in rebellion. Look around at our church leaders who believe they are above the accountability of the Word of God, or those with wealth who buy their way around the law of the land. The roots of rebellion and America's disdain with authority are far and wide. Our forefathers knew this land would be a land of rugged individualism accompanied by freedom and independence. Unbridled independence, free from the demands of faith, which inspires submission to authority, is a friend to rebellion and a foe to authority.

Just say the word "submission" to a group of women and you will get an almost violent reaction. The women's movement of the last forty years has made this word synonymous to something evil, something to be repelled and destroyed. It is almost like we have become a generation of rebellious children who desire no boundaries, will not be told what to do, and believe we answer only to ourselves. The story of the prodigal son who left home with his inheritance in hand. He smugly and confidently left the authority of his father's home. He spent his wealth on women and entertainment until he found himself in servitude to repay his debts. This is a story about a father's love to reconcile with a lost child, but it is also a story about what happens when a child goes out from under the authority of God. Under one position, he found great turmoil and met rock bottom. Under the other, he found comfort, acceptance, and blessings within the authority of his father's house. America, will we learn from this story as we drift out on our own by throwing off the protective arms of authority only for us to meet our bottom?

America, what went wrong? When did we begin to look upon authority as evil, bad, or wrong? When did we consider rebellion as virtuous and boundaries as bad? We were given this gift of authority to provide order, structure, and security. It helps all of us know how things are done and who will make the call. Have you ever tried to play a game of football when everyone wanted to be the quarterback, how about a game of basketball with a team full of point guards, or a game of baseball where everyone had standing as the head coach? It is impossible to achieve with no clear sense of authority. Do we really think it will work, America, to leave authority behind and to place all of us in charge?

Stand up, America. Stand now for authority, and set loose those rugged cowboys who roamed so free!

LAWYERS, LAWYERS, AND MORE LAWYERS

—————————— ∼⊙⊙⊙∽ ——————————

"An honest man's word is as good as his bond."
J Ray's English Proverbs published in 1670[22]

"Simply let your 'Yes' be 'Yes,' and your 'No,' be 'No';
anything beyond this comes from the evil one."
Matthew 5:37[23]

B y the sovereignty of God my job recently relocated us from Buffalo, New York to Lubbock, Texas. Upon learning the news of the transfer, my wife and I were excited to be in a much warmer climate. Then we became anxious when we discovered Lubbock, Texas is six hours west of Dallas, and a virtual impossibility to reach without two to three stops by airplane. It is an island locked by land, not the oasis of beach resorts, but it does have some of the most beautiful sunrises and sunsets. After our initial visit to look for a home, we discovered Lubbock was much greener than we had seen from our initial Internet results. Truthfully, Lubbock is not the prettiest part of America. Lubbock sits on what is known as the high plains in west Texas and is extremely flat, surrounded by fields of cotton, which are irrigated by some of the worst tasting water I have ever experienced. During the spring, there are wind

22 *Everyman Dictionary of Quotations and Proverbs*, Chancellor Press, first published 1951.
23 Scripture taken from the Holy Bible, New International Version*. Copyright © 1973, 1978, 1984 by International Bible Society. Used by permission of Zondervan. All rights reserved.

and dust storms, and it seems everyone we meet has allergies. It may not be pretty, but beating right under the surface of this city is Old America. Old America, a land where "...an honest man's word is as good as his bond."[24]

It almost seemed too good to be true. Do people still stand behind their word? Does someone's integrity still mean more to him or her than making the quick dollar? Recall the movies of old and stories of heroes of the past that described this era of America. For all of my life, I never experienced it. The Lubbock standard hit my wife and I on two occasions, and both involved buying a home. After seven days of looking for a home, we found five acres of land in the exact area of town where we were looking. The land, in our opinion, was God's gift to us as we began the next chapter of our life in Lubbock, Texas. I called the owner of the land and we spoke for approximately forty-five minutes that evening. The gentleman was nice and respectful. We really hit it off. There was one problem with the land, though. The owner had given his word to another interested buyer that he would hold the land until Friday. When I asked if he was open to other offers, the owner simply stated, "I gave him my word, and so I'm obligated to wait." In that moment, I realized this man really meant it, and this transaction was less about money and more about integrity. We ultimately did not get the land, because the owner sold it to the other person, but we did learn this man's word was his bond. On the second occasion, my wife found a home she absolutely fell in love with. It was more expensive than we had desired to spend, but the home, the price, and the remodels done on the home made it an extremely attractive proposition. We contacted the woman selling the home and arranged a showing. The homeowner told us upfront she would show it to us, but there was already someone interested in it. We followed through despite the verbal offer on the home, and you guessed it, we fell more in love with the home (great for all you husbands out there). My wife asked the seller if she was open to other offers, and the woman responded by saying: "I gave the man my word that I would wait for him and meet with him this weekend and get the agreement in writing." Wow! It still exists. Old America still exists where people value their word more than they value the dollar.

The irony of those two experiences is there were no lawyers involved, no contracts between the two parties, and no money exchanged, just simply the seller and buyer's word. That's it, simple, Old America, where a person's handshake was not given quickly or lightly. Many of us would feel quite convicted over the deficiencies in our own character. Unbelievably, there

---

24 *Everyman Dictionary of Quotations and Proverbs*, Chancellor Press, first published 1951.

existed a societal culture where there was shame associated with breaking a person's word. There was no need to legislate morality when the culture itself reinforced a strong, good old-fashioned American character.

Somewhere between the founding of America and the present day, America has become dominated by a culture so paranoid by legal liability we take out insurance policies for virtually every risk, have an attorney involved in the simplest of transactions, and sign more documents to minimize our liability. We have become a cover-your-you-know-what culture where we trust nobody and we sue everybody. When we moved to New York state and attempted to close on our home, we learned there were three attorneys involved in the process and a minimum of forty-five days closing, with the most likely closing on a home around sixty days. This was the standard just to cut through all the red tape involved. This is not about lawyer bashing or negating the value of what the legal profession adds to our society. Rather, it exemplifies how deeply astray the American value system has drifted and how desperately we need to return to the days when a man's word was his bond. Lawyers serve a good purpose, but our political institutions, government institutions, business, homes, and yes, you got it, churches have become absolutely inundated with legal liability paranoia to the point where the paper has more power than the person's word.

Having worked as an employee of the federal government, the vast majority of the institutions are so weighted down by liability and documentation trails that the average employee spends a significant part of his day performing administrative tasks associated with managing away the potential legal liabilities, and an even smaller proportion of his time goes toward delivering and providing services to the general public. Ask the average government employee about their jobs. They will tell you they would love to remove the administrative burden, as it destroys morale, slows them down, and frustrates their customers. A change has occurred in America where we have moved beyond the tipping point of common sense toward a culture of legal paranoia. The root of this paranoia is caused by a breakdown in our moral integrity. As Christians, we are commanded to live differently and to distinguish ourselves from this amoral culture. Hear the words of Christ:

> *You are the salt of the earth. But if the salt loses its saltiness, how can it be made salty again? It is no longer good for anything, except to be thrown out and trampled by men. You are the light of the world. A city on a hill cannot be hidden. Neither do people light a lamp and put it under a bowl. Instead they put it on its stand, and*

gives light to everyone in the house. In the same way, let your light shine before men, that they may see your good deeds and praise your Father in heaven.

Matthew 5:13–16 (NIV)[25]

We are the salt of the earth, all of us who call ourselves Christ-followers. Salt acts as a preservative. It adds flavor, it makes people thirsty, and it purifies. If we become the salt, then we are supposed to be preserving those values which Christ himself taught and died for while here on earth. Wherever the Christian finds his or her sphere of influence, whether in our homes, our businesses, our communities, or our churches, he or she should be defined and known for their integrity. Salt adds flavor, meaning it changes the taste of the original substance to which it is added. As Christians, our integrity should be changing and influencing those around us to such a degree that people see almost no need for legal protection, and no reason to question whether a Christian will take advantage of people or honor the commitments they've made. Look at Joseph in the Old Testament. Potiphar trusted Joseph and placed him in charge of his entire household. Talk about a path to promotion. Salt makes people thirsty. Salt purifies. Therefore, it should change those around us.

America, our value system must turn the corner and we must return to the days where our cultural value system placed preeminence upon our word. May America change our used car sales mentality and call back the days of old when a man's word was valued. Imagine a nation with empty courtrooms, attorneys going out of business in droves, and contracts where the average person could read, understand, and digest the contents in a few moments. It is time to simplify America. It is time to restore our integrity and restore the sacred trust we have lost with one another. It is time for the hearts of each American to change to value character over cash. Could we dream to be men and women who rush to correct our wrongs and stop hiding behind the veil of legal protections? Could America be known as a nation where yes means yes, and no means no? It starts with you, it starts with me, and its starts now. We can do it, America. We can be different than the rest of the globe. We can set the standard and become the envy of the world. Can you envision a day where corporations find our cultural

25 Scripture taken from the Holy Bible, New International Version®. Copyright © 1973, 1978, 1984 by International Bible Society. Used by permission of Zondervan. All rights reserved.

integrity a competitive advantage, where our integrity reduces unnecessary expenses and puts more into the hands of the shareholders, the employees, and to the bottom line? Let's turn the corner, America. Let's restore the bond with our fellow man, and let's live with a clean conscience with our Creator. We've all fallen short, but together we can become a nation of three hundred million strong, pushing hard and strong toward a culture of absolute integrity! Try that on for size, China. Get a glimpse of that, Europe. Perhaps Russia and its hard-knock tactics could learn a trick or two. We can, America. We can set the bar and raise the standard.

Stand up, America. Stand now for integrity, and set loose those rugged cowboys who roamed so free!

Media Mania: Another
Guardian of Liberty

⌘

"That the freedom of the press is one of the great bulwarks of liberty,
and can never be restrained but by a despotic government."
James Madison[26]

There is probably no other source of information so influential in our society as the media. In modern America, we have virtually limitless opportunities to access current events, and we have become a wired culture with instantaneous access to news. Just look at the 24/7 news channels streaming into the average American home. Some of us have become news junkies, achieving an almost drug-like high by being in the know. The media can be a great comforter during uncertain times and can become lethal during moments of personal public disgrace. Without a doubt, the media holds a near and dear place to our democracy. It keeps politicians in check, exposes government waste and abuse, and communicates broadly during national tragedies and celebrations. More than any time in history, the media has more access points to influence the public and to sway the public's perspective while taking a prominent role in water cooler conversations. With this awesome power comes awesome responsibility. The media's influence must be matched with its character, or else it moves from a force for good to a force for evil.

In a democracy such as ours, the media's primary purpose is to seek and present the truth in an impartial manner. There remains a role for

---

26   Source: http://www.archives.gov/exhibits/charters/virginia_declaration_of_rights.html

editorial articles, partisan based talk shows, and opinion columns. We are a democracy that draws strength from diversity of opinion, but the pure media needs to be different. You are the truth seekers of our society. Jefferson and his cohorts understood the value of the media. It acted like another aspect of government, exposing issues and keeping the other branches in check. It governs the undue expansion of the government's power and counters power's ability to corrupt. The media should be impartial—the staunchly independent auditors of society who seek the facts, not flirt with the whims of politics. So, for all of you in the media: if you are affiliated with an organization that embraces the truth and encourages informed, frank reporting, you are a great public asset. For those of you who find yourselves stuck between your journalistic ethics and the tone of the organization, either take a stand or move on to an organization that values you for both your integrity and your profitability. There are many who dismiss the role of the media as a bunch of paparazzi running around just trying to hound out the next great story with their invasive natures, microphones in hand, and camera-in-the-face mentalities. Despite their disdain for your profession, *the Constitution of the United States* recognized the need for the freedom of the press. The press is absolutely critical to a fully functional democracy, and serves a noble purpose in America. However, there is a war being waged over this freedom and the degree to which it is influenced by partisan political whims. With this race for the headlines and the ever-present politically postured news organizations, our media is letting America down and placing dysfunction into our democracy. America needs the media industry to set the standard for integrity, truth, honesty, and honor. As I write this, I'm reminded of the movie *We Were Soldiers*[27], where Mel Gibson plays the main character, Lieutenant Hal Moore. The movie depicts a major battle between the Americans and the North Vietnamese, where both sides faced tremendous loss and the harsh realty of a possible massacre. At one point, Lt. Moore turns to the sole reporter on the ground and requests the reporter tell the story of what occurred there so the American people would know exactly what happened and how their men died. The reporter may never win a military commendation for his story, but his purpose was every bit as noble as Lt. Moore's.

During the second Iraq War, the disconnect between what the men and women of the armed forces were experiencing on the ground and what was being reported was unbelievable. It seemed the news would depict, in

---

27 *We Were Soldiers.* CD. Directed by Randall Wallace and Arne L. Schmidt. United States: Icon Productions, Paramount Pictures (US) 2002.

horrendous detail, the horrors of roadside bombs, suicide bombers, and the deaths of American soldiers. As members of the military, it must have felt like Vietnam all over. The media neglected all the good and minimized the number of lives on the ground that were experiencing freedom for the very first time. Historically, the number of Iraqis receiving freedom was comparable to our own Revolutionary War! Perspective was rarely reported, context neglected, and the courage of our men and women in uniform minimized. Never will you see a story that analyzes the impact of democratization in Iraq and the impact it had several years later on during the Iranian election protests or the opening up of Syria's government. The Iraq War is far from perfect, but the anti-war slant taken by many in the media and their desire for the United States to fail is wrong. It was cruel for those who had loved ones in harms way and for those who had lost loved ones, and it almost seemed like the media itself was hoping for American failure. The media needs a renewal, a return to the roots of its profession, and a cleansing from the inside out.

In today's instantaneous news cycle, where news from a remote corner of the globe is broadcast across the world in seconds, the media has an even more extraordinary responsibility. The information shapes public opinions, governmental policies, and actions and reactions all over the globe. The frequency and the emphasis placed on a particular story will leave the consumer of the media with an out of perspective perception. If the news continues to report on the four thousand lives lost in Iraq, but neglects to mention that historically, for the size, scope, and duration of the war, this is a small number of casualties, it leaves the public with the wrong historical perspective. This isn't to minimize the efforts of those who have paid the ultimate sacrifice, it just helps America keep this war in perspective. The globe is interconnected, and the competition in the media sector has never been greater. Speed to press earns the ratings, but there is a moral imperative to ensure the speed to press is coupled with unbiased accuracy and a balanced perspective, placing the stories of today into historical context.

Passive Americans

On the other side of the coin of responsibility lie the viewers. Today's consumer of media has never been savvier to technology. With the onslaught of media thrust upon Americans and the split second society we live in, Americans face the temptation to become analytically lazy, allowing what we see, hear, and read to be adopted outright as truth. While the media has a responsibility to produce accurate, unbiased, and historically balanced news, the consumer has the responsibility to question, challenge, and critically analyze what they are taking in. If the consumer is remiss in his responsibility, we the citizenry fail our democracy as well. If the media acts as a system of checks and balances on our democracy, the citizenry is the system of checks and balances on the media. The argument could be made that to critically analyze the media is just as dutiful as voting for your political candidate of choice. The media are held in check by ratings and viewer sentiments. There is power in the ratings for any news outlet. In fact, they live and die by those metrics. America, there is much power in your choice of news outlet. Believe me, the news may not agree with your perspective, but they will listen to the ratings. It is just how the business works.

The frightening part of the American culture is we have become very passive in our consumption of information. The Internet brought many breakthroughs by placing more information at the fingertips of the people. Many citizens have become passive users of the media as opposed to active consumers. An active consumer is engaged, thinks about the information, questions it, and doesn't assume the author of any article is infallible. When digesting news, regardless of the source, we must refuse to allow the media to set our mental thought processes and refuse to turn off our own analytical capabilities, no matter how trusted the news source. Think about using a GPS in your automobile to try to get to your destination. While driving, have you noticed that you just kind of trust the GPS? We depend on its next command, and darn if those maps aren't updated, because we put our natural sense of direction into hibernation. When we are led to the wrong location, we cannot even remember which direction is North, South, East, or West! This is like the news. If we shut off our analytical mind and just go into receive mode, when the news leads us to the wrong address, we have no idea how to get home!

The New Standard of News

To hold the media accountable is our civic duty. The media has a critical role in the functioning of our democracy. Accountability of the media cannot be dictated from Washington or forced upon news organizations from above. Accountability occurs when an engaged and informed citizenry challenges and actively participates in the news delivery and consumption process. Speak up, America, when you listen to a news story and it doesn't make sense. Speak up, America, when one day a news organization says the economy is recovering only to deliver worse employment numbers the very next day. Let's demand consistency from our media. Let's demand news in historical context, and let's demand news based in facts, research, and good old street journalism. Media, it is time to restore the trust in the relationship once adorned to your industry from the public. Let's call for integrity boards to be established in news organizations across America. Let's call for fact audits prior to the presentation of stories. Let's call for quality metrics tuned towards integrity, not sensationalism, and let's target audiences who desire truth. Let's call our American newsrooms to a new standard, a standard worthy of protecting the liberty entrusted to America!

Stand up, America. Stand now for truth in our newsrooms, and set loose those rugged cowboys who roamed so free!

Death to Rome: The Moral Demise

⸎

"When there is moral rot within a nation, its government topples easily. But wise and knowledgeable leaders bring stability."

Proverbs 28:2 (NIV)[28]

America, we have a problem. America, you have a problem. America, I have a problem. We can no longer deny the reality of the existence of perversion, violence, and the general demise of morality within America. Explicit violence, sex, and virtual redefinition of our morality are on the rise and have been for over fifty years. This isn't the result of a single generation, nor can it be solved within the confinements of a generation. The damage is deep, the demise is widespread, and now is the time for action. No longer can we afford to hide the lamp any longer. It is high time to bring to light the perverse nature of our society and initiate a national dialogue beginning with the Christian community.

America the Perverted

It is difficult to author a chapter dealing directly with a topic that has affected and infected so many Americans. There are virtually no Americans who have not been affected by the sexualized culture, the violence amongst us, and the collapse of American morality. Young men are taught at an early age that women are to be looked upon as objects. Boys are socialized to tie

---

28   Scripture taken from the Holy Bible, New International Version®. Copyright © 1973, 1978, 1984 by International Bible Society. Used by permission of Zondervan. All rights reserved.

their self-worth to the relative attractiveness of their lady friends. Even the most wholesome boys in America have a difficult time remaining sober from the tentacles of pornography. Just drive down any freeway and the billboards will amaze. Turn on the television, or simply walk through the checkout at the grocery store. Our society bombards us with perversion everywhere we look. As a result, our society develops distorted views of sexuality, self-worth, and the beauty of virtues. The pornographic industry is designed to create the ultimate sexual experience and the sky's the limit. With the explosion of the Internet, we are now able to access sexually perverse material at any time from anywhere. Recent news reports state more people watch pornographic movies than any other genre. Can you believe it? America's appetite for the sexually perverse has grown to insatiable levels. Many have grown up in a culture that normalized pornography, strip clubs, and promiscuous sexual behaviors. Boys at a young age feel the pressure to become sexually active or risk being labeled abnormal. In America, a young man's senses of masculinity are called into question at younger and younger ages based upon their ability to engage in sexual behaviors. The net result of this overdose of sex is distorted views of the opposite sex and distorted views of sexual relationships. The average American wouldn't recognize a healthy, functional sexual relationship if it slapped them in the face. The exposure to sexual material is occurring at younger and younger ages, driving children to have sex at earlier ages, and forcing them to cope with the adult consequences well before they are emotionally ready. Look at the typical bachelor party in America. It involves a group of guys getting together, drinking, and hiring a stripper for the groom or going to a strip club. This ritual has almost become a rite of passage. Even more disturbing, the father of the grooms often times organizes the bachelor party by pre-selling tickets, including drinks, dinner, and oh yes, exotic entertainment. For both the religious and the non-religious, there is something in our wiring which becomes conflicted as we engage in behaviors that are the exact opposite of what marriage represents. There are harsh ramifications of such sexual behavior upon a society. It weakens the institution of marriage, it undermines the security found in the social fabric of America, and it shifts our culture to place greater emphasis on those fleeting pleasures in life. Even more epidemically is the number of Christian men who find themselves addicted to pornography, participating in adulterous relationships, and seeking divorce out of the desire to find greater pleasure.

The depths, destruction, and the costs associated with being addicted to something as lethal as pornography seems like overkill. Boiling beneath the surface of this overdose of sex, is the alteration to how men and women relate to one another, costing families hundreds if not thousands of dollars, victimizing children, destroying marriages, and driving a wedge between America and matters of faith. America is facing a major crossroad in our moral calling. We can either choose the path of sexual perversion, which leads to further destruction, or return to our more puritan roots. This isn't to say sexual perversion was nonexistent during American history. Rather, the culture has widened its acceptance, and behaviors and lifestyles once thought of as shameful have become an acceptable part of American life and entertainment. Our spiritual institutions are often afraid to discuss the delicacies of this subject for fear of offense. Our politicians continue to fall prey to their own indiscretions, and our cadre of sports heroes are tainted by the constant stories of one of their own being brought up on charges of rape. All the while, our culture promotes, accepts, and encourages our children to sow their oats. The moral demise of America is certain for sure, and unless we make a change, we are going to see greater chaos, confusion, and certain demise of our land.

Our boys are particularly susceptible to the enticements of the sexual culture, but to my surprise it doesn't just end with the idea that boys will be boys. The tentacles of sexual perversion have begun to reach deep into the ranks of women. It was always thought of as the male teacher preying on the young female students, but something has changed. Statistically, one of the fastest growing segments in the pornographic market are women. Perhaps as women begin to take on more of the traditional male roles (i.e., breadwinner), they are now becoming plagued with the same sexual issues that have plagued men for years. Our teenagers are under constant assault to participate in sex, our young adults frequent dance clubs that have podiums dedicated to girls dancing explicitly with other girls. Women are taught to use their sexuality to their advantage. Just look at the number of advertisements as you drive to work, walk through the checkout line, or read a magazine. The sexual infection dominates how women dress, how they perceive the need to succeed, and yes, also distorts their views of men and healthy sexual relationships. Sex does sell, but in the process the selling of sex is destroying womanhood and redefining femininity. Yes, women, your sexuality, your perception of yourself, and the heart of womanhood is being undermined, and it is time for it to stop. It must stop, and it must begin with those who call themselves faithful. It must start by the faithful renewing their perceptions of femininity and digging into God's Word to rediscover the unique design and inherent dignity of being a woman. We owe it to our daughters, our granddaughters, and most of all ourselves. What is needed in today's America are women who willingly take a stance and begin extending their influence to touch, teach, and transform American culture and the perception of women. Our young girls are crying for mentorship. We need an uprising of ladies who begin to combat the culture where femininity is under assault.

The number of sexual predators in America is staggering. Federal, state, and local law enforcement agencies across America have units dedicated to targeting persons exploiting children. America has broken a sacred vow with our children as we continue to see the growing exploitation of children. Gone are the days when a child pornographer fit a certain stereotype. Now it cuts across virtually all social and economic strata. It could be the twenty-six-year-old gym teacher, the priest who has served the community, or the sixty-year-old man who lives at home with Mom. They are bankers, lawyers, churchgoers, nurses, doctors, teachers, and firefighters. Recently, there was a story of a firefighter who was being interviewed by law enforcement. When confronted with his conduct of molesting a child, the firefighter asked to use the bathroom and then attempted to commit suicide. How many times in the news do we hear about the polygamy groups out west who target young girls? The extent, the growth, and the gravity of sexual exploitation of children is staggering in America.

It is time to turn the corner on this and take a stance for purity, for chivalry, and for absolute honoring of women, and to restore the ideals of sex given to us from God. The current has flowed for too many years in the wrong direction. Perhaps, if we could just begin to stand together, shoulder-to-shoulder, perhaps we could trigger a revolution; a revolution to restore the virtues of sex between one man and one woman. We might even discover wonderment in true masculinity and femininity.

The Hidden Epidemic: Sexually Transmitted Diseases (STDs)

Occurring within our nation is a hidden epidemic called sexually transmitted diseases (STDs). According to the video titled *Teen Sexually Transmitted Disease: The Rules Have Changed*, produced by MASE (Mothers Against Sexual Exploitation), 25 percent of the United States (US) population has an STD. Two-thirds of the victims who have contracted an STD are estimated to be under the age of twenty-five years old. Despite advancements in the medical profession, the number of STDs has risen from two to three to upward of thirty different STDs in the past fifty years. There are two primary categories of STDs: bacterial and viral STDs. The bacterial STDs, such as chlamydia, gonorrhea, and syphilis, are thought to be STDs that are curable if caught early. However, 85 percent of people who contract an STD do not have any symptoms and are often unaware they have an STD.[29] To further complicate the matter, the strains of bacteria are becoming increasingly resistant to traditional medical treatments, which makes it more complex to combat this epidemic. Regarding STDs contracted from a virus like herpes II, human immunodeficiency virus (HIV), and human papillomavirus (HPV), it is even more concerning since there are no known cures. HPV is thought to lead to cervical cancer, a type of cancer that just a few short decades ago was isolated to middle-aged women but now is rampant among our teenagers. Due to the physiological immaturity of teenage girls, it is estimated that 46 percent of teenage girls will contract HPV after having intercourse once. [30] According to the Centers for Disease Control in 2008, there were more than 65 million people in the United States living with an incurable STD and each year an additional 19 million people become infected with an STD.

Over the past twenty years we have witnessed an increase in the use of condoms as part of the safe-sex ideology taught in our schools, our governments, and our media. The safe-sex ideology has resulted in a substantial increase in the use of condoms and a significant decrease in the number of pregnancies, but along this same twenty-year period there has been a dramatic rise in STDs.[31] Therefore the safe-sex ideology may have been effective in combating teen pregnancy, but it has sorely failed at combating the hidden epidemic of STDs. If only the ramifications of sexually active teenagers ended with the physical impacts of the disease, that would be bad. But we are witnessing staggering emotional impacts. An estimated 33 percent of all sexually active teenagers struggle with depression.[32] Sexually active boys are twice as likely to struggle with depression as boys who are not sexually active, and girls are three times more likely to struggle with depression than girls who are not sexually active. Girls who are sexually active are three times more likely to attempt suicide whereas sexually active boys are eight times more likely to commit suicide. Taken together, these are staggering statistics.[33] Recently, Dr. Armand Nicholi from Harvard Medical School made the following statement:[34]

> Sexual permissiveness has not led to greater pleasure, freedom and openness, more meaningful relationships between the sexes, or exhilarating relief from stifling inhibitions, but has often led to empty relationships, feelings of self-contempt and worthlessness.

---

29 *Teen Sexually Transmitted Disease: The Rules Have Changed.* CD produced by MASE (Mothers Against Sexual Exploitation) in a project with The Constitutional Coalition, 2004.

30 Ibid.

31 Ibid.

32 Ibid.

33 Ibid.

34 Ibid.

The evidence is clear and convincing: we have an epidemic on our hands. The response of the culture has been to promote the safe-sex ideology. This approach at best prevents unwanted pregnancies but at worst has lulled us into a false sense of security. We are at a crisis America and those under the age of twenty-five are in the crosshairs. We must begin to confront our culture and develop a strong set of responses to meet this hidden epidemic or face even greater consequences. To place the blame solely on the back of the safe-sex ideology would not be fair. The safe-sex ideology is the government's and culture's response to a social problem—a problem rooted in the collapse of virtues. Since the 1960s we have witnessed a liberalization of Americans' views and behaviors regarding sex. Along with this liberalization came the weakening of the church as a voice for purity, chastity, and temperance in our culture. We must rediscover, reeducate, and revive the virtues of purity, chastity, and temperance within our culture. Individually and collectively, America, we must begin the transformational process within our own hearts and across our nation to promote a change in attitude toward virtues, which are the only lasting answer to combating the hidden epidemic of STDs.

Violence Within Our Ranks

Beyond the sexualized culture, which has come to define America, we have arrived at a time where violence is commonplace. Turn on the news. There seem to always be stories of shootings, mass killings, a husband killing his wife for another lover, and yes, Americans who desire to kill Americans in the name of some radical ideology. Students throughout schoolhouses must now walk through metal detectors before entering the buildings. Our schoolhouses are like prisons, secured by a staff of paid security professionals. It seems about twice a year our nation experiences mass shootings where our schools, churches, colleges, military, businesses, and homes wake up to the reality of brutality in our midst.

What is at the root of all of this violence? Truthfully, the only explanation of why America is becoming more desperate, depressed, and decidedly angry is the continued breakdown of the family, our internal morals, and our lack of focus on God himself. For some reason, people feel helpless and hopeless, and in an attempt to reconcile themselves with these emotions, they turn toward violence. When these violent episodes occur, the immediate reaction is to blame the lack of gun control, access to violent video games, or other outward expressions. The plague cannot be solved with a pill. It is much deeper than that. We have always had guns, and boys have always wrestled and played war or cowboys and Indians. Somehow, people have lost hope and have begun to place greater value on death over life.

With our culture's violence against biblical values and the breakdown of the home, people lack mechanisms to interpret and place life into proper perspective both within our homes and in the community at large. In times past, when someone's home environment was falling apart, the societal Christian values provided alternatives and hope for a different way and vice versa. When societal values breakdown, the home is supposed to pick up the slack. Sadly, today we are left with a breakdown of both the home and our communities. This cycle of weakened families, weakened communities, and greater hopelessness, in my opinion, expresses itself in the extremely violent acts we witness all across our land. It's like the expression "you don't know where you are going until you look at where you have been." America, whether we like it or not, our nation was birthed from European Christians some two hundred years ago, and it is in this rear view mirror perspective that we will find our way back from the era of violence we have embarked upon. America, it is time to choose. We can either choose to adopt a biblical worldview that defines our culture, or we can choose a worldview that, at the end and at its roots, results in no hope—none at all.

Those Greedy Americans

Capitalism is the best economic model the world has known, and has been used to bring more people out of poverty than any other theory of how a society should function. At the heart of capitalism is the desire to be rewarded for one's hard work, ingenuity, and talents. It is in the heart of this capitalistic mindset where America's rugged individualism has created a synergistic effect upon the economic engine around the globe. However, between the years 2007 and 2010, we have witnessed the most significant economic meltdown of the capitalistic economies for the past seventy-five to one hundred years. Just when we thought it was over, we hear of a nation like Greece on the verge of collapse and wonder when the negative ramifications of a society hampered by deficits and debt will reach America. We are on very shaky ground for sure. The issues surrounding this economic meltdown are complex, multi-faceted, and there is enough blame to go around. There are many economists who still believe there is more economic calamity to come, and investment firms who are warning their clients that the recovery we have experienced in late 2009 until 2010 will be short-lived. To fully explain and articulate reasons for the meltdown could be a book in and of itself. However, what is evident to an outsider is that there were two economic issues driving the collapse. On one side of the table we have the entitlement mentality where we were providing loans and credit to people who could never afford it. In our nation and for those who desire to take the wealth of this land and provide it to others, we established a situation where a critical mass of people found themselves in financial positions which they would never be able to correct. On the other side of the spectrum, there was a ton of excess on Wall Street where profits and payroll were flowing. It appeared to the novice that Wall Street and the financial genies were creating complex investments based upon mere speculation instead of tangible deliverables or products. Who brought more wrong to the mix we will never know, but at the root of both sides of this equation lies greed, the greed to get rich, to have more, and to generate wealth. It became the objective, whether it was to buy a home you couldn't afford or to sell an investment which was shady at best. The collapse of the world economy wasn't the result of capitalism. It was the result of a nation that had reached the tipping point, where more of the motives were impure than pure. America had finally come to terms with the fact that we had lost the governor, which our founders placed upon our nation—our Christian heritage. I can recall during the 2000s when we witnessed Enron, MCI, HealthSouth, and other large corporate brands go belly up because they too had committed fraud on their investors for way too long. The government's response to this crisis was the creation of the Sarbanes-Oxley Act, which was supposed to institute greater governance upon corporate entities. After several years, the results are mixed over the relative success of the legislation, and considering it didn't prevent this latest calamity, it would be hard to argue it was a success. The business profession learned it was impossible to legislate morality through its experience with the Sarbanes-Oxley Act. The government can, for periods of time, put things into place that may help stop the bleeding, but fundamentally, laws do not change hearts. America finds herself with a collapse of her moral character, and we are helpless for answers. Perhaps this is what happened to those empires of old like Rome.

Look at the Roman Empire

How often has America been compared to the great Roman Empire? How many times do pastors, priests, and scholars attempt to place America into the cyclical spiral up and down of the Roman Empire? Are we truly the Roman Empire, a powerful yet brief experiment with history, or will we meet the test of endurance, developing dynasty after dynasty? To fully explore these questions and to comprehensively compare our existence to that of the Roman Empire would be a novel to itself. However, like the Roman Empire, America has witnessed the demise of our morality, and we are raising generations of children who believe morality is relative to the time, place, and situation. We live in a day and age where there are no absolutes, just what is convenient for the moment. You don't need to be a Roman scholar or a historian to know the strength of any civilization is the strength of the collective character of its citizenry. The moral character of the citizenry must be rooted in something, and our past rooted it in the Christian faith. We will either derive our character from faith or from self. Faith, heritage, and in particular, a Christian worldview possess absolutes which are not dependent upon moments in time, a worldview dominated by self and experience which are transitory at best. Many in America would have you believe this is a progressive perspective, and to hold to absolutes is old fashioned and doesn't fit America. Contrary to thought, our relativistic culture is injecting chaos, confusion, and disorder into America.

Fortunately, absolute morality breeds stability, security, and strength, whereas relativism breeds insecurity and weakness. Moral absolutes allow all of us to know what is expected, what will be judged, and what the consequences for our actions are, no matter what is going on around us. The relativistic culture we live in now adopts the view that what is wrong today may change tomorrow, so if you hang in there long enough, you will be on the side of society's so-called virtues. This mentality doesn't promote stability and security, it promotes confusion, chaos, and convenience at the expense of stability, security, and strength. Think about children for a quick second. When children are given clear boundaries for bedtime set by both parents, the children learn they either go to bed or they will be disciplined. When a child tells a lie and both parents put him into timeout for each lie or remove a privilege from the child, the child typically responds by telling the truth, or will at least think about the consequences the next time. Read children's book after children's book, and they will tell you kids like routines and consistency. It provides them a sense of security and stability. So how have we come to believe that once we reach adulthood, we are no longer in need of the boundaries of moral absolutes? You must admit it sounds foolish when put this way.

Our founding fathers believed in moral absolutes, and those principles were instilled into the writing of the Declaration of Independence and the Constitution of the United States. Both documents have stood the test of time and are in no way designed to be changed—at least not without meeting some pretty high thresholds. If our founders possessed a moral relativistic value system, they would have created these documents to allow for almost constant change. They didn't do this, because they knew America must be rooted in something more secure. Our founders knew all too well what happened when morality changed based upon the whims of society. They saw what happened with the establishment of the Church of England and the tyranny of the King of England, where a tyrant could do what he pleased when he pleased. It is simply just inconsistent with history and with the inherent design of these documents to assume relativism. Were the authors who risked life and limb wrong, or have we become so arrogant to believe we somehow possess greater foresight than the men who history called to divinely scribe these documents and create perhaps the greatest nation ever known on the planet?

So here is our choice, America. We can continue to fan the flames of sexual perversion until we have a virtually anything goes culture, or we can rediscover and reeducate our culture on God's sexual standards. We can deny the existence of God and continue to produce and perpetuate violence and hopelessness, or we can attempt to restore civility and hope to America. We can pretend we have some supreme knowledge and cast aside moral absolutes, or we can cultivate a society that embraces the security, stability, and strength which comes when a culture is firmly rooted in moral absolutes. The decisions have arrived at our doorsteps after fifty years of heading wildly in the wrong direction. America can continue onward toward greater moral flexibility, or take a stance and choose the difficult road, the road rarely traveled, of restoring moral absolutes to our land. It's true, America. Some people won't like it. Many self interest groups will be upset. We will offend some, and yes, there will be consequences; there always are, but the costs of not restoring our morality are debilitating for sure. The moral decline has affected virtually all areas of our culture, but probably not more than that of our homes.

Stand up, America. Stand now for virtues, and set loose those rugged cowboys who roamed so free!

THE CRISIS IN OUR HOMES

—————————— ✐⊚⊘∿ ——————————

*"Husbands, love your wives, just as Christ also loved the church and
gave Himself up for her; ²⁶ that He might sanctify her, having cleansed
her by the washing of water with the word, ²⁷ that He might present
to Himself the church in all her glory, having no spot or wrinkle or
any such thing; but that she should be holy and blameless."*

Ephesians 5:25–27[35]

I t has become a very sad day across the United States of America. The
nucleus of our society, the traditional family, is under such violent
attack one must wonder what the average American family will look
like ten, twenty, and or even thirty years from now. Outside of abortion,
there is no greater social issue plaguing our nation. The simple fact that
we are even entertaining the conversation over homosexual marriage is
alarming and heeds warning to the spiritual bankruptcy of America.
God intended marriage to be between one man and one woman. He
commanded Adam and Eve in Genesis 1:28 to be fruitful and multiply.
America has drifted so far from God's intended plan that our public policy
on marriage is on the verge of changing across America. Several states like
Massachusetts have already passed gay marriage rights, and other states
like New York are strongly considering it. Personally, I'm deeply troubled
by the condition of our society, the state of marriage, and the apparent

35   Scripture taken from the Holy Bible, New International Version®. Copyright © 1973,
     1978, 1984 by International Bible Society. Used by permission of Zondervan. All rights
     reserved.

runaway train toward an anything goes culture, especially in the realm of marriage. Many cast blame and blast hateful messages onto the advocates of same-sex marriage. All of us are responsible, and especially the church for this moral failing.

Yes, much of the accountability for the breakdown of the traditional family rests at the footstool of each and every person who shows up to a church and calls Jesus Christ their Lord. We have failed one another, our fellow citizens, and our nation. Our marriages, our divorce rates, and our happiness are statistically no different than the secular community. As Christ says in Matthew 7:5, *"You hypocrite, first take the plank out of your own eye, and then you will see clearly to remove the speck from your brother's eye.*[36]*"* This is akin to marriage counseling 101 you receive from a counselor worth his weight in salt. What a light bulb moment! Our battle with the traditional family in America cannot and will not be won by trying to change our opponents. We need to love them, and remove the logs from our own marriages first. The Christian community is infected with the same failed statistics as the secular world. Why, then, would someone take our word for it?

The American Christian needs radical repentance of our marriages and our homes. For most, we need to spend less time attempting to attack, destroy, and defend against our opponents and more time repenting, reflecting, and renewing our own marriages and families as we allow the grace of God to transform our homes. If we believe God should be the center of our nation, the center of our lives, and the center of our families, then in return we should put some teeth to these beliefs and allow the Holy Spirit to invade those areas of our lives. You see, we keep attempting to change our culture through works and through our own strength, and it is by grace we were saved, not through works. It is time to surrender our marriages and families to an almighty God who can save and can transform. It is through the transformation in our own homes, marriages, and families in which we will begin to touch, change, and transform our culture. Truthfully, the culture is running on empty for answers, but the Christian family is not providing the salve.

What do you mean just lie down and let the proponents for redefining marriage run rough shot over us? How can we just give up on traditional marriage? We aren't, we are just being much more strategic and allowing

---

36   Scripture taken from the Holy Bible, New International Version®. Copyright © 1973, 1978, 1984 by International Bible Society. Used by permission of Zondervan. All rights reserved.

the release of the Holy Spirit by getting self and self works out of God's way. It is called backwards planning. The goal is strong marriages and strong traditional families. This approach advocates for reliance upon God to first change ourselves, and when our pride and our sin is out of the way, then God can unleash his spirit upon the rest of the culture through the faithful. This approach argues for a re-salting of the American family. This idea builds on the old motto "Build it and they will come." If the average American Christian home had a marriage and family firing on all cylinders, if the love of Christ was so prevalent in their homes, and the fabric of their marriage was rooted and secure in Christ, our society would change. People are naturally attracted to God, the work of God, but it must be genuine transformation only accomplished through the great I Am. As the Bible says in Mark 1:3, *"... a voice of one calling in the desert, 'Prepare the way for the Lord, make straight paths for him.'"* That's our responsibility to repent, and through repentance we prepare the way for the Lord. Think on it. I know I will. The years I have wasted blasting the left, blaming others, and feeling like a victim. Our point of control to change this thing called marriage is through repentance, humility, God's grace, and finally, to allow the flowing of the Holy Spirit to touch the lives around us.

Traditional Family

God designed our families to be a marriage between one man and one woman under God. At the most simplistic of terms, our anatomy points to the natural design of marriage and the design of the family. America is either passed or very close to the tipping point where cultural institutions are more against the traditional family than supportive of it. I recall listening to a radio broadcast of Dr. James Dobson's "Focus on the Family" several months ago. During the program, Dr. James Dobson expressed his concern that for the first time he could recall, we were losing on so many fronts in the cultural battle for the heart of America. This was a big wake up call when a man who has devoted his entire life to strengthening and defending marriages and families has a dim outlook for the American family.

The recent healthcare legislation passed through Congress and signed by the President contains provisions that make it economically less feasible to be married than to be living with a partner. This may satisfy a few special interest groups, but the net result is a nation that places less value on marriage and the traditional family. We see it occurring across corporate America and state governments. There are no benefits to building a strong traditional marriage, and in many cases it is even better not to get married. The arguments will come that this is the civil rights issue of the twenty-first century, but what is never discussed is what happens when people have no incentive to raise children in a loving, stable, and secure environment. Sure, there are some same-sex couples who have long lasting partnerships, but our non-commitment based culture will give rise to generations of children who do not know the stability, security, and emotional strength found in a committed-for-life marriage between one man and one woman. Many fear the death of making a distinction for the traditional marriage will end in an anything goes society.

Men and women of America, we must take up the call and rally to support men like James Dobson in defending the traditional family. We are quickly approaching the edge of the cliff, and if you have ever tried to climb up a side of a steep mountain, it is much more painstaking than backing down from the edge. We are here, America. The church is here, America, and if we do not make some serious changes within our own homes, families, churches, and communities, America is going to fall off of that cliff. America, will you join together with men like James Dobson and rally to protect and support the traditional family? When the traditional family goes, so goes America. The stakes are high. It isn't good enough to put the blinders on, put our heads down, and move forward with life assuming it doesn't affect us or that it doesn't matter. It does matter. It matters to God, it matters to your children, and it matters to the future of America. We, the American church, are in the driver's seat, and need to make some tough decisions. We need to be decisive with our beliefs. We need to be unwavering, and we need to have convictions of steel to hold to the truth. It is the truth that will ultimately touch people's lives, not accommodation.

The University of Virginia, the National Marriage Project, and the Institute for American Values produced a report titled *The State of Our Unions: Marriage in America 2009.*[37] Contained within the report is an annual assessment along with key findings regarding the status of marriage in America. Provided below are four of the findings which should cause some concern to advocates for traditional marriage. First, the American divorce rate today is nearly twice that of 1960, but has declined since hitting the highest point in our history in the early 1980's. For the average

---

37 *The State of Our Unions: Marriage in America 2009.* Editor W. Bradford Wilcox. The National Marriage Project at the University of Virginia and the Institute for American Values, 2009.

couple marrying for the first time in recent years, the lifetime probability of divorce or separation remains between 40 and 50 percent.[38] Second, marriage trends in recent decades indicate that Americans have become less likely to marry, and the most recent data show that the marriage rate in the United States continues to decline.[39] Third, the percentage of children who grow up in fragile—typically fatherless—families has grown enormously over the past four decades. This is mainly due to increases in divorce, out-of-wedlock births, and unmarried cohabitation. The trend toward fragile families leveled off in the late 1990s, but the most recent data show a slight increase.[40] Fourth, the presence of children in America has declined significantly since 1960, as measured by fertility rates and the percentage of households with children. Other indicators suggest that this decline has reduced the child centeredness of our nation and has contributed to the weakening of the institution of marriage. Although the divorce rate has remained around 50%, the number of people considering marriage has declined at a time when our society places less value on rearing children and providing a stable environment for children. The truth is traditional marriage in America, once thought of as the bedrock of our society, is also up for grabs. Symptomatically, we are now witnessing the emergence of the anything goes family structure.

Our hearts must be saddened when we hear of someone trapped in the homosexual lifestyle or someone who struggles with being transgendered. These people, like the rest, are attempting to find acceptance through the culture. Our hearts break, for most of us have no idea how deep, difficult, and painful their struggle is. God loves them the same as any other human being, but God is very clear about His perspective on sexual immorality. The Bible is clear about homosexuality, adultery, and all forms of fornication. This is one topic where there isn't much room left for interpretation. Often times, when we stand for traditional marriage, we are accused of being old fashioned, out of touch, and discriminating. What is even more frightening in many western European nations is that churches are being accused of hate crimes when they speak God's truth about sexually immoral lifestyles. America, the fringes of the European culture have begun to reach the shores of this land. Pressure will be brought to restrict what truths will be allowed to be spoken in our churches. This brings flashbacks of Paul, Peter, and the rest of the apostles who, in the Book of Acts, had to speak truth

---

38 Ibid.
39 Ibid.
40 Ibid.

even if it meant imprisonment by the government. Peter and Paul knew they were to be submissive to their authorities, but they possessed an even greater loyalty to Jesus Christ himself.

Men of America and men in the church, we (as I place myself in this category) need to take a stand! Unequivocally, unapologetically, and unashamedly, we need to take a stance for the traditional family and for our own families. We need to put away our childish ways, because there is an epic fight going on and we are in the middle of it. We are acting as if everything is normal, just going along on autopilot. We, men of America, are the warriors of our society. Our rights as men are being subjugated and our families are being undermined at each turn. God placed us at the head of the home, and two of our core responsibilities are provision and protection. It is no longer acceptable to shrug off our responsibilities for our children, our churches, and our communities or toss them onto our wives. What happened to that John Wayne ruggedness? Where did the chivalry go? We are men, and we are Americans. We stand tall, we stand brave, and we stand courageous because we live for God and live in the red, white, and blue. It is clear in Scripture God holds the man responsible for the priesthood of the home. Perhaps, God will hold men much more accountable for the success or destruction of the traditional family in America. It has to work that way. The leader must stand to account. Therefore, men, account for our morality, for our churches, for our marriages, and for our children. Stand up, men. Stand tall because God made you a man, so He knows you have what it takes to start fighting. Start fighting for the heart of your home, the heart of your bride, and the hearts of your children. Few know what this looks like or feels like. It is probably slightly different for each of us, but start fighting for the things that matter. Do not allow the media, the culture, your friends, your past, your wounds to stand in your way. No more excuses, no more shallowness, no more shrinking back from our responsibility, from our honor, and from our dignity.

This is a battle cry which needs to reach beyond the intellect of our American men and into their hearts; a battle cry to tap the enormous will to fight, will to win, and will to persevere which is sewn into the design of every man. Many men have been wounded by their childhood, gotten caught up in addictions, made some blatantly horrendous choices and mistakes, but with God there is redemption. Who cares? Move beyond and move above. We men need to rise to this occasion. We are warriors. We are lovers. We are victors. Therefore, men, get right with God. Get right with your wife and children, and get back into the fight. When you get knocked down, cowboy, dust off your pants and get back in the saddle. That is who you are. You watch. As we become those men who fight for the truth, for our God, for our marriages, our children, churches, and communities, you watch how supportive your wives become. You watch how your dignity and self-respect rise. You watch how your life satisfaction meter blows off the chart. We were designed for the fight, not designed for the little corner office with a twenty-minute commute to work. We are rough, we are wild, and we like a good fight every now and then. Let's fight men as we turn to look at our better halves!

My wife, an educated and accomplished professional, is the consummate advocate for women and their role in the family and our society. I have never met anyone with such an iron-clad compass of convictions. My wife is college educated, and prior to becoming my bride, she had a bursting career. She found herself in leadership positions with high-pressure jobs paying some generous salaries with additional wealth and status to come. She also quickly rose to various charitable boards and boards of other professional organizations. She was an overachiever who excelled past her peers with a wicked amount of professional potential. As much as my wife enjoyed the spotlight, the charisma of her position, the status, the influence, and the potential, she clearly understood this was but a season of her life.

A mother's legacy begins well before the baby is born. Her DNA takes over as she prepares the home for the arrival of the most precious gift God has given to mankind. It transitions into sleepless nights, the reckless havoc it causes on the female body, and the hoops a mother will jump through to feed, care for, and raise her children. You see, my wife could see past the temporary nature of jobs, money, careers, status, fame, and position to the enduring legacy she was building in her child. This isn't to say she doesn't miss the fun business trips and nights to just hang out and order room service. Believe me, the audience is small and the recognition tiny for the numerous nights spent with a sick child.

My wife chose greatness not in the form of professional accomplishments, success, or money. Rather, she chose to stay home with our child despite the fact she had the capabilities to be as successful as her heart desired in the workplace. Over the years, the more women I meet in the workplace who have young children at home, they appear very conflicted. They love their kids, but enjoy the interaction and the professional challenges offered to them at work. The working environment is enhanced and careers may blossom, but our children, our families, and our society are paying the price. Something in a woman's DNA says to her, "God blessed me with this child I cannot imagine a greater gift and responsibility to be entrusted with. I should be home influencing, raising, protecting, teaching, caring for my child because no one else loves them more than I do." Greatness is defined differently for all of us, but strategic windows of those little lives open and then they close quickly. The purpose of this chapter is not to judge or condemn a woman who cannot be at home. There are certainly many circumstances, and the demands of life are hard for sure, but there was something comforting, something soothing, and something calming during the days when a wife was at home managing the affairs of the house, welcoming our children when they got off the bus, helping a neighbor during mid-day, or just plainly embracing and accepting the greatness of being a mom, and especially of being a wife. Go to the average neighborhood during the day. They are ghost towns. How can America rebuild our sense of community when our only interactions occur when we are pulling in and out of the garage? The world will tell us we can have it all, but life forces us to choose where to invest—in the things which are temporal or those which are eternal.

We have a choice, America, as we stand at the canyon's edge. The traditional family is under assault. Our children are confused over what it means to be a man or a woman, as we've entered the era of such gender confusion. Our neighborhoods have become ghost towns as women who take pride in motherhood and the role of a wife are belittled and minimized. Our mothers, who once stayed at home to raise our children, are being forced into the workplace due to the unstable state of our homes. Our men, who once felt the deep need to provide and protect, are becoming the "other child" in our homes. They lack the know-how or the respect to provide paternal leadership. The flurry of our activity has been much, and we must ask: Is America better off? Everyone gets what they want, but was there really anything wrong with a man and woman marrying to raise a family together? Was there anything wrong when generations before, built upon the legacy of enduring marriage, reached down to mentor the young? Oh, America. Return, Land of *Liberty,* to those "Little House on the Prairie" days. Why does it have to be so complex?

Stand up, America. Stand now for the simplicity of the traditional American family, and set loose those rugged cowboys who roamed so free!

THE FINANCIAL ABYSS

─────────── ✥ ───────────

*"If taxes are laid upon us without our having a legal
representation where they are laid, we are reduced from the
character of free subjects to the state of tributary slaves."*

Samuel Adams[41]

*"We must not let our rulers load us with perpetual debt. We must make
our election between economy and liberty or profusion and servitude.
This is the tendency of all human governments. A departure from
principle becomes a precedent for a second: that second for a third;
and so on, till the bulk of society is reduced to mere automations of
misery, to have no sensibilities left but for sinning and suffering ...
And the fore horse of this frightful team is public debt. Taxation
follows that, and in its train wretchedness and oppression."*

Thomas Jefferson[42]

W hat's the point of owning anything? Why should you aspire for the American dream of staking your claim to a piece of land, purchasing your first home, or passing a heritage onto your children? Has America become the land of tax and rent, where the

---

41 *Harper's encyclopedia of United States history from 458 A.D. to 1912,* Benson John Lossing, Woodrow Wilson, Harper Bros., 1912.
42 The Jeffersonian cyclopedia: a comprehensive collection of the views of Thomas Jefferson classified and arranged in alphabetical order under nine thousand titles relating to government, politics, law, education, political economy, finance, science, art, literature, religious freedom, morals, etc., John P. Foley (Editor), Funk & Wagnalls Company, 1900.

ownership society we once proclaimed as a beacon of our liberty has gone by the wayside? Have we forgotten how the world converged upon America to head west for the American dream? Has the American dream become such a figment of our imagination? Can we recapture the excitement possessed by those young settlers who saw a land full of such hope and promise, or has America left the roots of our ownership society and drifted into a tax and rent culture? These are profound questions with lasting effects upon our children and our children's children.

The Constitution of this great land foresaw the need to guard property rights, and its authors understood the pitfalls of a state with the power to tax and the power to own. The premise behind property rights was not just to provide people with some land. It was to cultivate an ownership society where people possessed a personal stake in the successful outcome of their communities, states, and the nation they called their own. Unfortunately, America—unintentionally for some and intentionally for others— has slipped into a tax and rent culture where our citizens see everything as transitory and nothing as their own. There is no sense of ownership, no sense of responsibility, and no sense of accountability. This is most evident with our politicians who vocalize their intent to be fiscally responsible on one side of their mouths, then spend out of the other side of their mouths as if the country's credit card possessed unlimited credit with no minimum payments and no interest to bear. The plague of financial irresponsibility has put America into a position of bondage and has made our nation vulnerable. We may have the greatest military on earth, but our tax and rent culture, combined with our spend more than you have mentality, is about to bring America to her knees. Our politicians measure success in our economy by the level of consumer spending. If consumer spending is up, then America is doing well. If consumer spending is down, then America is doing poorly. This is absolutely ludicrous. We should be encouraging modest spending with emphasis on savings and debt-free living. The recent financial crisis has brought many of our ailments to the surface. We saw people who bought homes who could never afford them, we witnessed banks who would place mortgages on homes for fifty years with adjustable rates, and we saw irresponsibility on Wall Street, Main Street, and probably, most pointedly, within the ranks of the federal government itself. There is no doubt the investment community is motivated by greed, but our tax and rent culture has invaded Washington, D.C. and taken a hold of our fiscal policies. America, the land where people worked a lifetime to afford a home, the nation where people staked their claim to land, worked it with blood, sweat, and tears so their children could have a better life. The American work ethic where hard work, pride in workmanship, and patient success symbolized the American dream. Somewhere in the last thirty to fifty years our beloved heritage was shelved for something more gratifying, something more immediate, and something attainable without the perceived cost. The era of tax and rent has come of age with almost certainty. If you are like most, perhaps you will begin to say, "Well, I own a home. I pay a mortgage, and in fifteen years I will have my mortgage paid off and I will own it free and clear." Well here's a different twist on this American remnant. Six months ago I was having a conversation with an aunt on my mother's side of the family. We were discussing the atrocity of the taxes across the state of New York and the outrageous amount of personal income that goes directly to taxes each paycheck. My aunt happened to make the remark that in America, we are not property owners any longer. We have mortgages, and even after we pay off our mortgages there remains a tax burden on the property indefinitely. In many cases, the property tax is equivalent to or even more than the actual mortgage. So, here you go: I have worked thirty years to pay for this home only to be rewarded with the equivalent payment on the home for the next thirty years in the form of property and school taxes! Oh, yeah! Don't forget about the taxes on your electric, your heating, your gasoline for your automobile, your phone bills, and the good old water you use, otherwise known as surcharges, or fees. Oh, and please don't remind us of the taxes on telecommunication services. Taxes abound in America, and they abound across socialist Europe, which is on the brink of financial disaster. This isn't even taking into consideration the growing interest payments to service our national debt.

Somehow, we have shifted from an ownership based society to tax and rent culture for sure. It would be very interesting if you could get a complete picture of the actual tax burden the average American family pays each year. Think about it. Most people pay federal income taxes, Social Security, Medicare, state income taxes, state property taxes, sales taxes, gasoline taxes, taxes on telecommunication services, taxes on utilities, alcohol taxes (if you smoke, major cigarette taxes), local school taxes, the death tax, the gift taxes, and soon enough, we have some who desire to tax us for our personal carbon footprint in the name of national security. By all means, if you own cattle you better watch out, because they have one heck of a carbon footprint! It would be hard to argue we are anything but a tax and rent society. Truthfully, what percentage of annual incomes go toward taxes? 40%? 50%? 60%? Perhaps higher? The average American citizen has no idea of an accurate picture of the tax burden. Look at some states where you pay personal property taxes on the same automobile year after year, and somehow it doesn't qualify as double taxation. Your ailing parent dies and you pay an extraordinary amount of taxes on the estate, which has already been taxed once. Try to live in large cities like New York and you will see taxation taken to a whole new level. There are some who would estimate taxes in the city of New York around 60% or greater of income, and as the Bush tax cuts expire at the end of 2010, some people could approach 70% of their income being paid as taxes. What is wrong with America that instead of erring on the side of the citizens we err on the side of the government? This movement toward increased taxation isn't what was intended in the Constitution of the United States. In fact, the Constitution makes clear *"We the People"* not *"we the government"* should get more and get bigger. The question Americans must ask themselves is at what point have we passed the point of no return, where our fiscal irresponsibility is irreparable?

Placing the Constitution of the United States into historical context, the authors were attempting to escape the class-based society where land ownership was based upon birthrights rather than on the simple fact of being a citizen of that nation. The spirit behind The Revolutionary War was that *all men are created equal,* not the existence of some exclusive club where the state controlled the rights of land ownership. Our forefathers knew land ownership had to be protected constitutionally, or tyranny would begin to breathe again and socialism would gain strength. It wasn't consistent then and isn't consistent now with our heritage, nor our foundation, to have such a tax and rent culture. Our level of insensitivity towards the tax and rent culture and the "society owes me something" mentality is frightening. It has gotten to the point where we believe it is normal for taxes to increase each year no matter what the economic circumstances. Think through this for a second. Look at the average property taxes on homes. The tax rate is tied to the increased value of the home. Townships, cities, schools, and entire states depend upon increased tax revenues from homes to grow and to survive. Therefore, we have an entire cross section of our economy that reinforces itself to perpetually raise the tax rate, from homeowners, to realtors, to the city, the state, the schools, and any other entity sucking the financial life blood out of your home. Where is the independence in the system, and where are the anchors that restrict part or all of these entities? During the recent housing bubble, it didn't take a genius to determine that at some point housing prices were going to slow down or at least drop. They must when they outpace the people's ability to pay for the land. In this interconnected economic world we live in, the domino theory is alive and well. Everything has become so interconnected, so richly taxed, and self-reinforcing it is catastrophic when something goes awry. Amazingly, we are shocked when we witness the American work ethic, the desire to contribute to our society, and our sense of ownership, deteriorate before our eyes. Recently, there was a statistic that on average almost half of American households will pay no federal income taxes at all for 2009. Either their incomes were too low, or they qualified for enough credits, deductions and exemptions to eliminate their liability.[43] Tell me how that can be healthy for propelling a nation forward. American pride is a dying pastime.

Get to know men and women in their late sixties, seventies, and eighties. There is just a different mentality. Last summer, when my wife and I moved from Buffalo, New York to Lubbock, Texas, we had several pieces of furniture damaged. The moving company contracted the damaged property out to a local company run by a man named Bill. Bill was around seventy years old and believed in sweat equity. What was right was right, and he provided his customers with exceptional service even beyond the profit. Bill came over to our home in a little old pickup truck, he meticulously repaired our furniture, and in some cases restored the furniture to even better condition than we bought it in! Bill did a better job than the assembly line non-ownership tax and rent culture we are producing in America. We were very grateful for Bill, but saddled with the burden of how America had changed. Bill is a true American hero, and there is much we could learn from his generation.

America, the beautiful, we must be vigilant. Our freedoms are under siege from within, and even more concerning, from outside our borders. Our tax and rent culture, where we spend more than we have and pass the responsibility off to the next generation, will come home to roost. Out on the horizon, we can see the tip of the iceberg emerge as we move into the twenty-first century. Our struggles will not be fought with tanks and planes, but with the strength of economies. No doubt we will have military conflicts, but the victor of the twenty-first century will most assuredly be thrust into the winner's circle through the sheer strength and robustness of their economy. Make no mistake; nations like China, Russia, India, the European Union, and Middle Eastern States understand the

---

43 Ohlemacher, Stephen, Associated Press Article titled: *Nearly Half of US Households Escape Fed Income Tax.* April 7, 2010.

fundamental linkage between economic strength and political strength. Suffice to say, each would welcome their turn as the top dog on the world stage and take great pleasure in a diminished America. Be wary, America. There are movements across the globe for the creation of world governance structures, structures which we will be told will produce worldwide stability to financial markets, promote the common good of all, and expand the economic security across the globe. In early 2010, I read an article that indicated the United Nations was attempting to institute a tax on worldwide commerce. Of course, they said it would go to benefit the United Nations health programs across the globe. The net result will be the loss of even greater freedoms for each of us, and a dramatic reduction of the sovereignty of the United States of America. As they say, you can't make this stuff up.

Stand up, America. Stand now for responsible financial stewardship, and set loose those rugged cowboys who roamed so free!

A WORLD GOVERNMENT

⟿⟾

"If anyone does not provide for his relatives, and especially for his immediate family, he has denied the faith and is worse than an unbeliever."

1 Timothy 5:8[44]

The Constitution of the United States, as fitting to its title and true to the desires of its drafters, applies solely to the United States of America. It was intended for the birth and development of the high calling of this great nation, not as a subservient document to the United Nations, the European Union or any other global body. We are America, and we fought hard, we fought strong, and we fought long for the right to be the finest nation on earth. History spoke clearly when we took the stance against the tyrannical rule of the king of England over two hundred years ago that established America as a sovereign nation. These brave men and women who died for freedom did the exact opposite of the global governance movement. They shed their blood for freedom and independence. Shockingly, there is movement afoot where citizens of this nation have partnered with like-minded individuals who desire to place a world ruling body and its dictates over the dictates of the Constitution of the United States. The band of global governance radicals place preeminence on global governance and international law at the expense of the Constitution of the United States. This is unconstitutional

---

44   Scripture taken from the Holy Bible, New International Version®. Copyright © 1973, 1978, 1984 by International Bible Society. Used by permission of Zondervan. All rights reserved.

and disregards over two hundred years of our blood and treasure shed on virtually every continent in this world. America passed the test of time by dying for freedom then, and Americans today should stand on the shoulders of the patriots of our birth to re-defend the right of America to be a free and sovereign nation.

Amazing how quick the memories have faded about American men and women who died all across the continent of Europe, how America stamped out imperialistic Japan (then rebuilt the nation), or the liberation of so many other places around the globe. It is stunning how quickly they forget America's courage (through the Reagan Era), fortitude, and perseverance, which brought an end to the Cold War, thus bringing freedom to many Eastern European nations. It is astonishing how the press never reported the billions of dollars of aid the presidency of George W. Bush provided to the continent of Africa to fight poverty, AIDS, and government corruption. Even more surprising, the Central Intelligence Agency (CIA) is belittled, condemned, and accused of acting immorally. They forget how those men and women operate behind enemy lines and sacrifice the comforts of home with limited pay, virtually no gratitude, and certainly no fame. Why, America, have we allowed the attitude which pervades Europe and other areas of the globe—those attitudes which say America is evil—to pervade our shores? Where, America, is the anti-Americanism coming from? Do you realize your patriots who serve in the armed forces and the intelligence community can only be motivated by love of country because what they endure and sacrifice can only be interpreted within the context of patriotism? Where is this negative sentiment coming from? It isn't factual, and it isn't consistent with our past, our present, and it is certainly at odds with our national character.

Just look for a moment at the United Nations each time the Iranian President arrives in New York to speak to the world. You bet, many nations step out of the room, but there still remain a large number of nations who pay homage to the flagrant words of chaos, hatred, and disorder that come out of this man's mouth. If you go to the root of the Iranian regime, its objective is to usher in the Twelfth Imam of the Shiite faith, which will occur during a period of worldwide chaos. So here is a nation that has divided the world for well over a decade as it pursues nuclear weapons with the ultimate goal to destroy Israel and open the door to worldwide chaos. The world stands idly by, makes empty threats, and slowly Iran inches straight toward her goals. The gridlock from the world governance virtually guarantees Iran's success. With each passing moment, each passing Iranian scientific breakthrough, the world becomes less safe, and our allies (like Israel) come face-to-face with a deadly reality—a nuclear Iran. Come on, America. Shall we sit idly by as a nation insults the world, builds up it's nuclear strength, and moves furiously toward creating conflicts in the Middle East which will affect the United States? Iran already stoked the flames of conflict in Syria, Iraq, Lebanon, Afghanistan, Israel, and Palestine. What exactly do we think they will do when they have even greater regional influence? We have become weak willed, America. We have succumbed to the peer pressures of the world, and we are abandoning our backbone of liberty. America needs to work within the global framework at times, and at other times it requires boldness and allegiance to our flag!

At the root of this anti-American sentiment are two forces, which are both equally destructive. The first is the belief that America is inherently evil and is not a force for good, but a force for evil. There are those amongst us who hold fast to a perception that America is an imperialistic nation that trots around the globe pushing its will upon other nations with the intent to cause harm. Interconnected to the belief that America is inherently evil is an allegiance to the global movement, where people perceive themselves as citizens of the world first, and citizens to the United States second. Just look at the oath a person must take when they voluntarily become a citizen of America:

> *I hereby declare, on oath, that I absolutely and entirely renounce and abjure all allegiance and fidelity to any foreign prince, potentate, state or sovereignty, of whom or which I have heretofore been a subject or citizen; that I will support and defend the Constitution and laws of the United States of America against all enemies, foreign and domestic; that I will bear true faith and allegiance to the same; that I will bear arms on behalf of the United States when required by the law; that I will perform noncombatant service in the armed forces of the United States when required by the law; that I will perform work of national importance under civilian direction when required by the law; and that I take this obligation freely without any mental reservation or purpose of evasion; so help me God.[45]*

It is crystal clear where our loyalties are to remain. This globalized mentality is alive and growing in strength across Europe and the United States. During the recent financial meltdown, we witnessed calls around

---

45   Source: http://www.uscis.gov/portal/site/uscis/menuitem.

the world for global governance structures, global financial structures interconnecting our banking systems under one set of legal parameters, and even the United Nations desires to tax the world at large. We live in an increasingly interconnected world where people born in the United States have freedom of travel and access to virtually anywhere on the planet. When our citizens are not firmly grounded in our *Constitution*, our heritage, and an accurate view of American history, then it is easy to see why their loyalties would shift or fall into doubt. There are many parts around the globe that do not like America, our values, our heritage, or essentially, anything about us. There are some in America who find more in common with Hugo Chavez's and Fidel Castro's view of the world, and their perspective on America. Amazingly, after the tragedy of September 11, 2001, there were citizens—even prominent politicians—who actually believed the United States was the cause of the Jihad (a holy war undertaken by Muslims against unbelievers)[46] declared against our nation. Never could I have imagined our own citizens would possess such contempt towards our nation. There are whole movements within the religious community in America who espouse hatred toward our beloved land. America, we have a problem of the heart. There are no easy answers or quick solutions to convince a group of citizens who have deeply ingrained in their beliefs that America is a force for evil, not good, around the globe.

This is an appeal to every American and any citizen who enjoys freedom, security, and stability as a result of American influence and strength. The hand of America, although imperfect, has reached far and wide across the globe. Our character is clear. We love freedom, we will defend freedom, and we will die for freedom. Equally as crystallized into our character is our willingness to die to bring the gift of freedom to others. Even with such a high calling and noble personality, America is constantly condemned throughout the globe. Europe would like nothing else then to witness the demise of America. Several Middle Eastern nations despise America, and Russia to be sure desires to stoke the memories of the competitive past with America. Most concerning is that within our midst we have had a growing anti-Americanism for decades. There are those who are citizens of *the United States of America* who see us as evil and not as a force for good. Look at many in Hollywood who speak out against America and American capitalism, all the while affording their extravagant lifestyles as a direct result of America and her greatness. Look at some university environments.

---

46   *The New Oxford American Dictionary, Second Edition*, Erin McKean (editor), 2051 pages, May 2005, Oxford University Press, ISBN 0-19-517077-6 .

You would be hard pressed to understand why they affiliate themselves at all with America. Some, including Harvard, are not allowing Army ROTC programs onto their campuses while indoctrinating our young into sentiments inconsistent with history and our accomplishments.[47] We are an honorable people with a heritage to be proud of.

It is time for America and her friends everywhere in the world to stand up to those who spew anti-American sentiments about her. It is time that an American soldier receives a standing ovation when he or she gets onto an airplane, not for their personal accomplishments alone, but for the sentiments and the nobility for which their uniform represents. Several years ago, I met an Iraqi refugee who fled the persecution of Saddam Hussein. The man feared for his life and his family's life under Saddam, and graciously America received this refugee into our land. Over the last several years, the man visited Iraq periodically to see family and friends. This man, who knew the fear of tyranny, was questioned by fellow Iraqis about his allegiance to the United States. These Iraqis possessed a worldview which upheld America as the Great Satan. Person after person, my Iraqi friend confronted their misperceptions and provided examples of American life they rarely heard of or knew about. This Iraqi refugee, who barely had status in America, understood the blessings of America and understood our greatness to such an extent he was willing to confront people, at great peril to his own life, to tell the truth and splendor of this land. How is it someone who wasn't born here and didn't have deep roots in America, arrived, quickly assimilated, and possessed such a patriotic sense for this country to an extent he was willing to risk his own life to be an ambassador for America? He knew what it was like to live under tyranny. He knew how oppressed Iraq was under Saddam Hussein, and he knew how uniquely different the American experience was.

When did we become a bunch of followers? We are Americans. We blaze trails, we go beyond what others ever thought was possible. We are a nation where ordinary people can do extraordinary things. To flirt with the idea of submitting our land to the hands of global governance radicals is dangerous to our national security, and at best establishes America for mediocrity. We are the Wild West. It is in our DNA. We break barriers, we tear down walls, we go places people have never gone, and we do things people never thought were possible. We are Americans, and in the first

---

47   *Brown Criticizes Harvard Leader on ROTC Policy.* Matt Viser, *The Boston Globe, September 24, 2010.* See: http://www.boston.com/news/nation/washington/articles/2010/09/24/brown_criticizes_harvard_leader_on_rotc_policy/

sentence of our constitution it says: *"We the People of the United States, in Order to form a more perfect Union ..."* Did you hear that? We—the "people"—of the what? "United States." No place in the entire text of the document does it say: *"We the People of the World ..."* America first, the world second, and when those two conflict it should be America first, period, end of discussion. There are some in the global movement who believe times have changed. It is a world economy, and we can no longer just think of America. Absolutely, times have changed. The world economy is more tightly integrated, but America is first, because to do anything else robs the world of the beacon of liberty. To deny American sovereignty places the hope and the optimism of the world at risk. It is the direct result of the Declaration of Independence and maintaining its relevance, which is exactly the prescription for moving our nation and this world ahead with hope and prosperity. Make no mistake we have allies. We have international partners, we must be mindful of international economics, but when push comes to shove it must be America, both for our national interests and the interests of freedom loving people across the globe. We were birthed into freedom, and our greatest gift to the world is remaining free! Let that sink in a bit. The single most important contribution America can make to the world is to be the beacon of liberty we were pronounced to be.

Stand up, America. Stand now for America first, and set loose those rugged cowboys who roamed so free!

THE GREATEST HEIST—THEFT
OF THE EDUCATION SYSTEM

꧁꧂

"It has been the error of the schools to teach astronomy, and all the other sciences, and subjects of natural philosophy, as accomplishments only; whereas they should be taught theologically, or with reference to the Being who is the author of them: for all the principles of science are of divine origin. Man cannot make, or invent, or contrive principles: he can only discover them; and he ought to look through the discovery to the Author." [48]

"The evil that has resulted from the error of the schools, in teaching natural philosophy as an accomplishment only, has been that of generating in the pupils a species of atheism. Instead of looking through the works of creation to the Creator himself, they stop short, and employ the knowledge they acquire to create doubts of his existence. They labor with studied ingenuity to ascribe every thing they behold to innate properties of matter, and jump over all the rest by saying, that matter is eternal." Thomas Paine: *"The Existence of God--1810"* [49]

"What students would learn in American schools above all is the religion of Jesus Christ." George Washington [50]

There is a war being waged in American academic institutions each and everyday. Schools, colleges, and universities across this land have become the frontline for the struggle to set the tone and

---

48   Paine, Thomas, *The Age of Reason Being an Investigation of True and Fabulous Theology, Part 1*, The Truth Seeker Co., 1898.

49   Ibid.

50   Speech to the Delaware Indian Chiefs May 12, 1779.

tempo of American culture. There in the midst of arithmetic, reading, and writing, cultural forces are campaigning for the hearts and minds of our young at an age, maturity, and life experience level where many are more willing to place their blind faith and obedience into the hands of teachers, professors, and academics by accepting opinion for fact. Our youth are vulnerable, our youth are naive, and our youth are being indoctrinated from people who do not share the same value system as the parents who are footing the bill. Beyond the indoctrination of our youth, teachers and professors who espouse conservative traditional values are being minimized and alienated. To use the name of God, Jesus, and to have a moment of prayer has become taboo in our public schools. America, we are losing the battle for the hearts and minds of our youth. They are becoming indoctrinated with a world view uniquely different from the faith, family, and country we all hold near and dear. This struggle is happening right beneath our eyes and in plain sight. Many parents are simply too busy to recognize the tragedy which is happening in our midst. America, it is time to stand up to the pollution being poured into our schools and to restore a sense of character back into the academic institutions. These times are perilous, and the academic institutions are the fight for the generations to come.

The Ever Growing To-Do List

How often do you hear a family member, a colleague, or friend say there simply isn't enough time in a day to do everything they need to do? Life has become busy. We work harder, we work longer, and we have longer to-do lists than ever before. The dream of this modern technological era was supposed to be a life filled with less anxiety. Instead, we live in a time where there is more anxiety, more stress, and never ending demands upon our time. Between the two-career homes, the constant demands for our time and attention, and the general rapid pace of life we find ourselves offloading our traditional responsibilities to others. We now pay immense amount of money each month for childcare expenses so we can either maintain our two-income home status or merely support the financial demands of modern life. At best, our children are becoming addicted to the constant onslaught of activities, and at worst our children are having to learn about sexuality, spirituality, emotional intelligence (a term coined by Daniel Goleman), and family structures from everyone but their parents. Parents are frankly stressed, and by the time they hit the pillow at night, they find themselves absolutely exhausted, only to set the alarm and do it all over. America—perhaps the world— has become a nutty place to grow up and a crazy world to attempt to parent a child. America, we must begin to simplify our lives. We are outsourcing the rearing of our children to the Internet, the schools, and the media in areas in which God intended the instruction to come directly through a mother and a father in a home.

Our schools have gladly accepted this responsibility and taken on the role of parent. They are now where most children learn about sexuality, about authority and discipline, spirituality, and about what is to be valued most in life. The culmination of all the cultural issues we have discussed intersect right into the classroom, from the culture of intellectualism over common sense to the environment which prevents failures and consequences for fear of hurting our children's feelings. Look at the moral demise in America. You need look no further than the setting of schools, or perhaps your beef is with authority where the home and the school use to work together, but now appear to be either at odds or never in communication. Many children feel entitled to the diploma no matter how hard they work or what their grades are. Whether or not we recognize it, the cultural battle rages on throughout our schools and across the campuses in America. Look at many universities who value global citizenship over the nationalism of Old Glory. Do the math, America. Once your children go to school, the schools have their minds for the next twenty-two years. You have them for two hours each night. It is like one man with a pistol trying to face down a battalion of tanks. With those odds, we can predict who will win.

Sex Education

Sexual education has moved from the homes and churches to the classrooms. Children no longer have the benefit of putting sexuality into the context of spirituality. Many children in today's culture receive their instruction on sexuality from their friends, the television, Internet, and the schools. We have offloaded our responsibilities to rear and instruct our children. We have become flagrantly irresponsible with what could be coined the most sensitive area of all, mainly sex education. Those who hold traditional values near and dear sit in wonderment at our "anything goes" sexual culture, while our children are outsourced to public institutions for their primary source of information. Our academic institutions are filled with the political agendas of the sexual war going on in America. There exists powerful activist and lobbying groups who desire to indoctrinate children in alternative lifestyles. We are losing the battle, right under our noses, as our children are exposed to the varied views on what constitutes marriage. Our children face tremendous confusion as to sexual roles and sexual identities. The definition of sexually deviant behavior is being redefined right before our eyes, and we are allowing it. The textbooks, the lesson plans, and the instructional staff hold captive our children in an area of life which needs to be handled with care and interpreted in the context of one man, one woman, for life. We are seeing the cornerstone of American society, the traditional family, erode, and with it we are witnessing increasing amounts of chaos and the never-ending re-definition of marriage and family. America, we need to heal these wounds. We need to turn from our ways, and we need to win the battle by taking on the yoke of sexual education. Our families, our communities, and a vibrant nation depend upon each parent.

The Dumbing of America

Look across the American academic setting and you will see school after school that is failing. We keep pouring more money into them, upping the tax dollars, and still our schools face failure. Why is this, America? Why is a nation who has spent so much on the education of our children not seeing a return on our investment? Perhaps, America, the cause is a system which is largely based upon a monopoly where your geographical region mean you have ownership to all those who fall under your fiefdom. There is no competition or reason to strive for excellence when year after year the budget increases and another program is added. Then, we turn toward our students many of whom are passed without merit or for whom teachers have looked the other way, for to tell them they failed would be too detrimental to their self worth. We see this in other areas of life, and we see this in schools where we are trying to raise our children devoid of any consequences or personal responsibility. Failing a test or not making the cut seems harsh and cruel at first glance. No doubt it stings when a child receives a failing grade, but it is in this grade where a child learns, like that little old blue engine: "I think I can, I think I can." Failure induces our children to work harder, to seek help, to exploit their natural born gifts. Failure facilitates our children to become more than they ever dreamed. It is in unearned success where children really fail, for they gain the spoils of victory without knowing its toil. So, America, we must choose to allow consequences to occur or to insulate our children from reality and then wonder why their lives are such a mess.

The Changing Curriculum

A few years ago, I was reading a book that was discussing the change in the language instituted in our textbooks and even in our children's bedtime stories. I didn't think much about it at the time until my wife and I had our first child, and I began reading the stories to my son at bedtime. It amazed me how frequently I would see the word "he" replaced with "she," or "his" replaced with "her." On the surface, this seems benign, but in reality it made me wonder if there was an agenda to marginalize men in our culture. You be the judge. As a few more years rolled by, there was a great eruption over Evolutionism versus Creationism, and then it came to light that many schools across America teach an abridged version of history. This abridged version of history minimizes the heritage and the prominence of the United States while amplifying the global world we live in. Our children will never know the depth of our heritage and the truth which surrounds it unless parents take this mantle up themselves. Many Americans used to perceive home schooling as being for those "odd" people—extremists and the very far right. Suffice to say, in the last five years, parents are having a change of heart. More American parents are turning toward home schooling not out of choice, but out of necessity. That is, parents are faced with the dilemma to either forego their local school or to give up their convictions. It shouldn't be this way, America.

The Shifting Role of Discipline

There was a day in America when a child who was scolded at school arrived home to a parent who presented that child with its second scolding; a time when the parent and teacher worked in tandem to ensure their children received the life lessons necessary to lead a healthy, functional life. Now, there are teachers and parents who still aspire to this idea, but unfortunately there is also a large cross-section of America where neither the parent nor the school believe in the role of authority, discipline, and punishment. Look at most homes in America, where it is considered abusive to spank your child even when it is done in a tempered reasoned manner. This "don't upset the apple cart" culture plagues our schools. Children no longer have fear and respect for authority. Ironically, we have a hard time understanding why the revered policeman is now considered the abuser of force and must endure taunting, insults, and often times physical abuse. Where we decided discipline was bad—whether in the home or in the classroom—nobody can say for sure, but as this trend continues, there will be less learning, more confusion, and generations of kids who live in an altered reality devoid of natural consequences. Pray, America, that something changes, for our land was not meant to work without consequences. It is part of the process for all of us to become our best.

Removing God from the Classroom

Why are we afraid to acknowledge the existence of a creator? Why do public academic institutions refuse to acknowledge God as Creator when the Declaration of Independence refers to the Creator right smack in the preamble? Why have our schools decidedly removed God from the classroom when the first President of the United States, George Washington, stated clearly the importance of teaching the religion of Jesus Christ? Who decided our academic institutions are stronger when they remove the Creator? Have we become so wise or too smart for our own good?

This trend to remove God from all aspects of society, including the academic setting, is sad. It is insulting to the founding fathers, it spits in the face of God himself, and is weakening the balanced development of our children. God created the earth, God created the universe, and God created you and me. There is no room for negotiation, there is no room for compromise, and there is no room to accept the myopic view which excludes our Creator in the creation of the universe. Outright rejection of children being able to pray in the academic settings is wrong. Our heritage has always relied upon the Almighty through prayer before we testify in court, before a session of Congress, before the swearing in of a new president, and before sporting events. Prayer has been and always should be a pillar of our America, and there is no reason why we should demonize children for desiring to express themselves through prayer to Almighty God Himself. Who cares if we offend people? Who cares if we aren't "politically correct", and who cares if we cannot accommodate each and every religious faith on the planet? America, our roots began in Christianity, and to change our roots is to change America. To err on the side of Christianity is to err on the side of our heritage. If people desire a Muslim nation, then feel free to go to Saudi Arabia. If people desire a Hindu nation, then feel free to move to India. If people desire a Buddhist nation, then move to China. This is America. We know who we are. We are a land where the strands of Christianity and freedom are woven so closely together, to tug at one tugs at the other. Therefore, America, restore God to this nation. More specifically, restore God to the schools.

Higher Education

It is very irritating, offensive, and downright wrong what is occurring in American colleges and universities. Our children are supposed to be headed to these institutions to receive an education, and instead they are being indoctrinated by a social progressive agenda. They are attacking our children's morals, and values, and infecting their thinking not just with engineering or mathematics, but attempting to reeducate our young. The general attitude at most universities is allegiance to the world, not to the United States of America; a posture of challenging and changing traditional conservative values in favor of a social liberal perspective; a constant barrage of attacks on capitalism in favor of a more socialist worldview. Our future generations are the targets of constant propaganda in favor of intellect over truth. Parents, spend some time talking to your college-aged children about their professors, the general environment, and the attitudes that are so prevalent on the university campuses. There is an obvious disdain for America, a dislike of traditional values, and increasing one-world mentality, even to the detriment of our nation.

I recall having a conversation with a colleague of mine regarding two of his children who are currently attending a university in the United States. Politically, the man considered himself a conservative and indicated he had raised his children to be conservatives as well. It didn't take long before his two children approached their father with a dilemma they were having at school. These two students quickly learned conservative values were not welcomed, typically dismissed, and even discriminated against at school. They came to their father seeking his advice on how to handle themselves when caught between their conservative values and the liberal agenda being taught. The father told them they really had two choices. They could either confront the professors or go along with the system. If the students decided to confront they would be faced with certain discrimination for internships, research positions, and ultimately have a more difficult time successfully completing their studies. If they went along with the system then the students were going to have to keep their convictions silent and live to fight another day. What a rock and a hard place for a dad and for his children. Here you go son, one path will be littered with trials, suffering, persecution, and hardship, but at least you will have your convictions in tact. The other path is filled with a selling of your soul. Talk about discrimination and indoctrination.

Whoever is attending college or paying one cent to a university in America, begin demanding more from your university. Alumni, before you make those donations, hold the university accountable for making changes in favor of America. Students, when you experience an environment that attempts to rob you of your value system, leave. Student bodies, student officers, and campus political groups, raise support, conduct rallies, and drive change—change that embraces our heritage, embraces allegiance to America first, and embraces God. Stand tall. Stand firm. It is time to take back our universities. No longer can we afford paid parties which indoctrinate our children into a liberal agenda which rejects God, capitalism, and America.

Between the ever growing to-do lists, the liberalization of our schools, the politically correct and entitlement mentality, and the secularization of the classroom, our schools have become the culmination point for all of America's cultural ailments. The battlefront is taking place right in front of those precious eyes, impressionable minds, and sacred ears. Should we wonder why we are losing the battle for the hearts and minds of American children? The pendulum has swung far and swung wide. Now, its time to return the pendulum back to its roots.

Stand up, America. Stand now for justice within the classroom, and set loose those rugged cowboys who roamed so free!

Go Home, America. Go Home.

⌒☙

*"But we had to celebrate and be glad, because this brother of yours
was dead and is alive again; he was lost and now is found."*

Luke 15:32[51]

O ur problems are vast, the chasm is great, and looming over the
horizon is a storm. The great book of old tells us we will reap
what we sow. Now, America, we must begin the hard road
back. I would love to promise you that our journey home will be filled
with comfort and ease, but frankly it won't, for the status of our land has
drifted so far that to make such change will bring sacrifice and suffering to
virtually every American. You see, there are consequences to our actions,
and a land can only spend more than it takes in for so long. Our efforts to
secure our economy from the implosion from the last few years resulted in
the use of the same tactics by our government which created the implosion.
There is much uncertainty, fear, and insecurity in the air due to our choices
and the changes in our culture. So I ask you, America, to brace yourselves
and prepare. The warnings of history are very clear. When a nation makes
great changes, it is accompanied by great pains. Rarely does any measure
of progress come without sacrifice. Truth be told, like the revolutionaries
who gave us this land, they were left with only two choices: either fight
for liberty, or face certain death. Now, over two centuries later, history

---

51 Scripture taken from the Holy Bible, New International Version®. Copyright © 1973,
1978, 1984 by International Bible Society. Used by permission of Zondervan. All rights
reserved.

has chosen to provide us with the same choice to fight for liberty or face its death.

As we begin down this uncertain path, where do we begin to regain our footing? How do we go from this place of immense uncertainty to the process of healing and bringing our freedoms back, like the prodigal son who left home with his inheritance? During his time away, he was reckless, wasteful, and squandered his wealth. When he came to his senses, he got up and went back home to be a slave. The scene plays out as the father rushes to the son and welcomes him back with open arms. The parable ends as the father addresses his jealous brother, who remained by the father's side, and says: "But we had to celebrate and be glad because this brother of yours was dead and is alive again; he was lost and now is found" (Luke 15:32).[52] America, let's go home like the prodigal son. Let's run to the fathers of this land to see what they saw and believe what they believed. As we peel back the years of history in search of paternal wisdom, there are four places we must stop. The first is called the Constitution of the United States[53], where our founders demonstrated to the world how a democracy should work. From there, we need to acquaint ourselves with the first ten amendments, the Bill of Rights[54], which was a contract between freedom, its people, and its government, otherwise known as the guardians of liberty. Naturally, if we are going to acquaint ourselves with the first ten rights, we should go further and look at when liberty was declared. If we are going to sit with our fathers, let's go to the document that began it all, the Declaration of Independence.[55] With three legs of the stool down on the ground, America, we can begin to take a deep sigh. Don't rest for long, now. It's time to get the last leg down on the ground, The Final Branch, where we will sojourn with the Maker of man Himself.

Prayer

Almighty God,

Our nation bleeds. Our homes are a mess, our culture is out of control. We have lost our way as Christians, as Americans, and

---

52 Scripture taken from the Holy Bible, New International Version®. Copyright © 1973, 1978, 1984 by International Bible Society. Used by permission of Zondervan. All rights reserved.

53 See Appendix B – The Constitution of the United States.

54 See Appendix C – The Bill of Rights

55 See Appendix A – The Declaration of Independence

as a nation. We have become prideful, complacent, materialistic, and selfish. We acknowledge our sins and our imperfections before a perfect and loving Creator. We ask, Lord, for You to allow freedom to ring again. Re-ignite the vigor and the fervency in which America was founded upon. We ask to reconnect with our heritage and to unearth those values You so delicately and perfectly wove into the fabric of America. May the heart of each American who reads this book and the heart of America experience repentance, transformation, and renewal. We ask, God, for You to shed Your grace onto America again. Not in materialism, nor wealth, but restoring the foundational truths this nation was erected upon. As we begin the journey to look through our founding documents, we ask for your guidance, and may Your truth lead us home. Grant our supplication, we beseech Thee, through Jesus Christ our Lord, Amen.[56]

---

56   United States of America, Congressional Record, Proceedings and Debates of the 108th Congress First Session Volume 149-Part 3, Senate-Monday, February 24, 2003, Prayer by Chaplain Dr. Lloyd John Ogilvie who recognizes the day as George Washington's Farewell Address and says it is appropriate to recite the "Prayer for the United States of America as it is preserved in the chapel at Valley Forge," page 4198. The last sentence from the prayer was used.

Section III—The Heart of the Matter (The Constitution of the United States)

THE ARMS OF A
PROTECTIVE FATHER

⟋᳗⟍

"Husbands, love your wives, just as Christ gave himself up for her."
Ephesians 5:25[57]

".... and the wife must respect her husband."
Ephesians 5:33[58]

Our quest for the heart and soul of America must include an examination of the Constitution of the United States[59], the authoritative document which took the call of the Declaration of Independence and put some meat around the bones of a shapeless government. No other document in American history finds itself at the center of the American story more than the Constitution of the United States. It is the brains that outline how the United States government will function. The Constitution was written in 1787 after those young colonies had declared victory from the British. With a few years of distance between America and tyranny, the time had arrived to govern the great experiment in democracy. This was a period of time when our young nation was learning what it meant to live free, but even in freedom our founders recognized the need for governance or else they would face even greater chaos than under the king of England. Recall when Moses and the

---

57   Scripture taken from the Holy Bible, New International Version®. Copyright © 1973, 1978, 1984 by International Bible Society. Used by permission of Zondervan. All rights reserved.
58   Ibid.
59   See Appendix B – The Constitution of the United States.

Israelites left Egypt under years of bondage. God knew Israel, even though they were free from Egypt's reach, would not prosper for long without some structure, and then the Ten Commandments were birthed onto stone tablets. At first, the Israelites fell back into old patterns of bondage by remaining slaves to the golden calves, and it seemed they placed doubt on Moses' leadership and direction at every occasion possible. It was time to bring order and structure to the Israelites which would reach beyond the life of Moses. Welcome the Ten Commandments onto the scene, which established the boundaries under which Israel would operate. For the first time, the young nation of Israel had a foundation to guide, direct, and protect their society. Ironically, they were carved into stone tablets, the very material the Egyptians had enslaved the Israelites to mine in the quarries. Perhaps God was trying to tell Israel that the key to its prosperity was to honor those tablets. In the book of Exodus 34:10, when God is speaking to Moses, he says, "I am making a covenant with you. Before all your people I will do wonders never before done in any nation in all the world. The people you live among will see how awesome is the work that I, the Lord, will do for you. Obey what I command to you" (Exodus 34:10–11 NIV). Look at that. All the Israelites had to do was be faithful to the Ten Commandments and they would do, see, and accomplish things which left the rest of the world in amazement.

Doesn't this ring true, America, for us, and the Constitution of The United States of America? When we follow the document in its truest, most authentic form, has America been blessed? America runs afoul when we attempt to divert, manipulate, or turn the Constitution into something of our own making. From the moment the Ten Commandments came into existence, it birthed the laws, rules, and institutions upon which their society was built. Look at the books of Exodus, Leviticus, Numbers, and Deuteronomy to see how the structure, laws, and rule governing this new clan were assembled. Perhaps, like God's promise to Moses with the Ten Commandments, the Constitution was our forefathers' gift to young America. Knowing the times would change and challenges would arise both domestically and abroad, they provided this young nation with the boundaries that would provide America direction during moments of uncertainty. From the Constitution, they derived the shape, span, and scope of our democracy, including the various branches of government and the rights enumerated to each branch, the states, and to the people. This was the moment where the forefathers and destiny collided to produce a document that, when adhered to, America would "... see wonders never before done in any nation in all the world" (Exodus 34:10 NIV).[60]

Do we dare to believe the Constitution was anointed with such authority and foresight to guide America from the era of horse and buggy to the era of supersonic jets? Do we dare to trust the promise, *the pursuit of happiness*, was instilled into the fabric of the Constitution? Only through the lens of faith and the lessons of old can we approach the answer to this question. Look at the nation of Israel. Each time throughout the Old Testament they stepped outside the Ten Commandments, their nation erupted into chaos and confusion, and at times found herself back in captivity. This was the love story of the Old Testament, a God who loved and cared for His people, who brought them out of bondage, and established some essential boundaries, only for the nation to repeatedly find itself back in the deadly grip of tyranny each time they veered outside the Ten Commandments. Throughout Israel's history, there was a constant ebb and flow toward the Ten Commandments and away from them. Ultimately, Israel became divided and split into two distinct nations, where the dream given to Moses slipped away into the winds of history. The Ten Commandments were the essentials that could not be broken or else calamity was sure to follow.

America, in the dawn of the twenty-first century, finds itself with the same problems that plagued the nation of Israel. We live in an era where many subscribe to the theory that the Constitution is relative to the time, the situation, and the particular matter under consideration. In essence, we can bend it to meet the whims of the moment. They subscribe to a theory which views the Constitution as a living, breathing, and evolving document where, for example, the right to bear arms really doesn't apply to modern America, or we live in a global society where international law should trump constitutional law. Frankly, each time the Israelites swayed from the Ten Commandments, the outcomes were usually not pleasant. When Moses handed down those ten rules, nothing contained in them nor the words spoken by Moses indicated an expiration date, and neither did the authors of our Constitution. The Constitution is timeless. It never expires. It should always govern America. If Destiny desired for us to rewrite the Constitution, then I believe Destiny would have ensured we were around during 1787. For most, we weren't even thought of then, so our job isn't to recreate the text. Our job is to preserve its existence.

---

60   Scripture taken from the Holy Bible, New International Version®. Copyright © 1973, 1978, 1984 by International Bible Society. Used by permission of Zondervan. All rights reserved.

Anything else is nothing short of treason against this nation, betrayal to our lineage, and setting America up for certain calamity.

The Israelites and present day America sound eerily familiar, as we live in the day and age where we attempt to redefine, re-create, and challenge every tradition and authority placed upon us. Will we learn, America? Will we learn to return to our greatness? Will we learn to trust the promise given to us from our fathers of old, or will we learn to trust in the wisdom of the moment, to place blind faith in the path of the unknown? I boil it down to a simple analogy. My two-year-old son, Benjamin, loves to be free, and every chance he has to run, he bolts out the door and heads for freedom. There have been several occasions where Benjamin has made it past us and darted straight for an alley behind our home, where the fences are so high you cannot see a car coming from either direction. As Benjamin's father, the ultimate fear of any parent races through my mind as I see our only child heading straight into danger outside my protective care. It never occurs to Benjamin he is crossing a boundary where, once crossed, the consequences are severe and the damages are permanent. There is a war going on within our borders between those who desire to dart for the road and for those who desire to remain within the protection of our forefathers. Unfortunately, both sides appear to be equally convicted, equally motivated, and equally willing to take America down their desired path. This is where America has found herself—frozen, unsure, and at a crossroad of fate. This nation, once united by common ideals and common values, has grown into two camps—those who desire to preserve and those who desire to progress. If you are one who desires to preserve the Constitution, then you might find more comfort than challenge in the section that ensues. For those of you who desire to progress, my goal is to take you back to the words themselves to provide challenges to your current pretenses.

Shall we, then, for the few brief moments of pages, discover what it means to jump into the arms of our forefathers? Will you soak up the fragrance of *love* of a people born out of servitude straight into *liberty*? As the vibrations of divinity inspired the American plan, may our land breath deep and allow our lungs to expand as the state again reveres the people of this land. May civility be restored as *love* takes root and our need to mandate morality withdraw as the era of the state faces its final curtain call. Let's pull back to the year 1787 and pretend as if we are reading and hearing this for the first time. We no longer have two hundred years of history, for we are right back in time. Sit by the fireside, America. Take your rightful place as the sons and daughters of liberty so we can listen to the greatest story ever told, not on satellite, television, or phone, but from the arms of those men who stood up for liberty and grabbed hold of their destiny. It is now time for us, America, to quiet, to pause for an instance, and find the pulse of the greatest society ever known encapsulated into the Constitution of the United States of America. This, America, is where the cowboy will ride again. This is where he can stand tall in his saddle and roam the range again. Let's go! Let's return to the place where the West was won, and once again, let's live to ride, and ride to live!

WE THE PEOPLE OF THE UNITED STATES

─────────────── ⸎ ───────────────

*"**We the People of the United States**, in Order to form a more
perfect Union, establish Justice, insure domestic Tranquility, provide
for the common defence, promote the general Welfare, and secure
the Blessings of Liberty to ourselves and our Posterity, do ordain and
establish this Constitution for the United States of America."*

- The Constitution of the United States (September 17, 1787)

The year is 1787. America is free of England, knows the victory of war, and the toils of birthing a nation. The colonies are now the United States of America, but are attempting to govern themselves without an established, agreed upon, and subscribed method. There exists a tension between the colonies' desire to remain autonomous and the need to operate as one nation. The fears of giving up autonomy to a centrally declared government bring flashbacks of the Revolutionary War. There are enemies abroad, mainly the British, who still desire to see America fail, and there are threats within who also desire to see the dismantling of this new nation. So, they find themselves amidst a time of great change, great national pride over their victory in the Revolutionary War, great fear over their enemies, and grave concern for repeating the lessons of history. This was a place of such enormous uncertainty, where each state held to its sovereignty, but also knew they were weak alone. So, within this context, the drafting and acceptance of the Constitution of the United States[61] occurred, creating a balance between the rights of the people and the

───────────

61   See Appendix B – The Constitution of the United States.

powers of the government, rights of each individual state and the rights of the collective nation, and the rights between freedom and security. The Constitution, as we are about to discover, is a document with which our founders attempted to guard the rights of the individual, ensure our national security, provide the basis for prosperity to follow this nation, and strive forward towards *love's* call.

The balancing act begins with the first three words in the Constitution, *"We the People ..."* Here, we get a glimpse of the heartbeat of the manuscript, which every other enumerated power found itself bound and built upon. In truth, there wasn't much of a balancing act, since all the authority for each article and each amendment found roots in this opening line. Our forefathers found it fitting to endow the citizenry with ultimate power and denied this right to a central king, ruler, or government. At our core, our founders discovered great strength in great numbers, thereby making the strongest branch of the United States government, often referred to as the fourth branch, *the people.* This was precisely the opposite of anything the world had seen up to this point in history, and precisely the opposite of the tyrannical rule of the king of England. It must have sounded foolish. I can only imagine the naysayers, the elite, and the nobility who couldn't fathom how a group of uneducated, untrained, and non-pedigreed people would be able to govern a nation. This would have been nothing less than bizarre, and bordered on crazy. Think about it. What is the likelihood a rag tag, ill equipped, ill supplied, and ill trained group of colonists would defeat the British, the most powerful military in the world? Pretty darn low. Okay, they got lucky. What is the likelihood the same group of rag tags who defeated the British were about to establish a government where the least educated possessed the same rights as the most educated, and the system of government would look radically different than anything the world had known? They must have looked like Noah when he built the ark and prepared for the greatest storm the earth had ever witnessed. Imagine the ridicule Noah endured while building the Ark when there was absolutely nothing indicating a need for an ark. Calling him a laughing stock would be putting it lightly. America must have experienced the same ridicule across the globe as it erected the unimaginable by placing its faith and confidence into *We the People.* Nonetheless, we now know the rain came, vindicating Noah. Like Noah, the past two hundred years of American history have demonstrated our *"We the People"* approach to governance is a smashing success. Got it, America? *"We the People,"* is our core, our default, and where all authority is derived from. It is the foremost building block in the Constitution. Nothing done within the context of the United States of America shall be done against the will of the people.

A Mysterious Union

Where did the inspiration come from as our forefathers formulated the magnificent Constitution? Where would these men have looked for wisdom into the design of the sacred bond between the government and newly anointed citizens of America? Sure, they would have had the benefit of history, the lessons of other attempts at democracy, and countless precedents from English life to draw upon, but America had to be different. The Revolutionary War was nothing less than stunning to the global audience. Therefore, America's approach to governance would need to match the level of expectation established through the Revolutionary War and the Declaration of Independence. The Constitution exceeded the expectation by outlining a mysterious union where the will of we, the people, would guide and direct the affairs of the state.

I can think of no other union, equal in mystery, which parallels the Constitution, than that of a marriage between a man and woman, or between Christ and His Church. In all three unions there exists exacting blueprints which delineates authority, and provides an optimal architecture to be followed. We are told in Ephesians 5:22–25:

> *Wives, submit to your husbands as to the Lord. For the husband is the head of the wife as Christ is the head of the church, his body, which he is the Savior. Now as the church submits to Christ, so also wives should submit to their husbands in everything. Husbands, love your wives, just as Christ loved the church and gave himself up for her.*[62]

The Bible tells us through these passages that there is an order to the Christian marriage and to Christ's church. It is the role of the husband and the role of Christ to be the head of the relationship. The headship brought order to chaos and established clear roles and patterns for authority for both the church and a marriage. Headship (or leadership) exemplified its love by laying down his life for his bride. The wife is commanded by Scripture to submit to her husband's authority and, in the process,

---

62 Scripture taken from the Holy Bible, New International Version®. Copyright © 1973, 1978, 1984 by International Bible Society. Used by permission of Zondervan. All rights reserved.

submission would demonstrate respect to his headship. There exists a mysterious union between God and a man and a woman who enter into matrimony when they follow His intended design. In twenty-first century America, it is no longer fashionable, but where order exists, lines of authority are established, and the unique combination of love (husband) and respect (wife) in the marriage produces stability, peace, and security. Unfortunately, the tolerance culture dominates America and prevents us from honoring our heritage and following God's blueprint for the home, for His Church, and for this nation. It has often been said that the family unit is the building block to the American society—as the family goes, so goes America. The view of a Christian marriage would seem more compatible with the Constitution than a more liberal view, pushing any number of combinations for marriage. This rebellion to an ordained order for marriage has also taken root within our union as we witness the arm of government operating outside the boundaries of the Constitution. The union established in the Constitution between *We the People* and the government of the United States provides a similar order to America. Contained within the Declaration of Independence is a submission of America to Almighty God. Fast forward to the creation of the Constitution and we witness a government placed into submission to the people.

We, the People, were placed in a position of authority over all other powers in America. This is the heart of the Constitution, the lifeblood where nourishment is supplied to every article of the Constitution and each right enumerated under the Bill of Rights. America works when our nation places great deference to the ordained order of this land. When a branch of our government severs its ties with *We the People,* and attempts to operate beyond its grasp, certain calamity is sure to follow. With each step taken beyond the boundaries of the people, the sacred bond of trust established between the governed and its state is undermined. America is a mysterious union between the people and its government, based upon *love* and *respect.* We, the people, are held to the former standard, while the powers of the state are called to the latter. So it is with the adulterous gestures of an overreaching state that we, the people, are betrayed and must formulate our response to simply choose the path of long suffering, the road of separation, and God forbid, the most dreadful of all—divorcing the state. Our founders warned us in the Declaration of Independence that we should not choose the most severe course of action based upon transient causes, but when, over the course of generations, our state grows more rebellious and *We the People,* grow less patient, let it be said it wasn't the people who created the crisis. The blame would most certainly be placed on the back of a wayward state!

With *love,* America, we must love our land. We cannot advocate violence for this cause. For a state run amuck to change it must start with Americans exercising their greatest authority, from their position under God. Our founders placed this great land under His authority so clearly and plainly through the Declaration of Independence that America must begin by praying for His divine hand. It is with hearts filled with *love* where we, the people, will find a pure heart and clear conscience to determine the steps required to discipline our state. There are no easy answers when the state has run astray, when the political parties are found corrupt, and our branches of government are inept.

Our forefathers made it clear that when we begin sensing a chasm growing between our will and the actions of the state, the fight to repair it shouldn't be easy. It should be an all out holy struggle. So from our knees, America, as a nation united through the bonds of peace, is where we will find the strength to resurrect our land. This nation placed *firm reliance on the protection of Divine Providence,* so let's join our fathers to seek this invisible hand. The authority has been granted, our position secure. We must resubmit ourselves to the *Painter's* brush, for it is His masterpiece which began this nation, and it will be His stroke which will restore it. We are not advocates of a position of silence or recluse. Rather, quite the contrary, we who know the title of *"We the People"* are being called to a fervent action. For many, you have been steadily learning how to use this armor from the ages. Your feet are steadied, your weapons secure, your defenses prepared, but for others, you have been floating with every doctrine in the wind. You are still drinking milk, and are far from ready. So it is with a call to *"We, the People",* that those who are considered strong must find the weaker sojourner, and like the good Samaritan, build them up and bring greater grace to all. For when our roots are firm and our hearts are firmly planted, then America will be able to reclaim our land and shout *"Liberty for all!"*

We, the people, have been called to steward this great land, to provide for her protection, and to allow the world to see what happens when ownership is taken from a central authority and dispersed to the masses; a watershed moment in the history of civilization where all assumptions were shattered. Recall Jesus, who came to this earth not to be served, but to serve. With all authority granted to Him from heaven above, He chose the fate of humility. The forces of evil tried to claim victory because

Jesus never sought to sit on a throne, but it was through His death, a transformational moment, that one calendar closed and another began. When America was birthed and our Constitution ratified, the world saw a dividing line between a world where liberty had to hide and a world where liberty was placed up high. By no means was the birth of this nation or the Constitution on par with the death and resurrection of Christ, but there are few moments where the records of history have such a line of demarcation.

We the People of the United States

We are forever connected to one another through the preposition "of." This linkage is where aliens in a foreign land became heirs of this new nation. No longer orphans unsure of where we belong, this country, known as America, just became all of our land. For some they received citizenship through birth and for others through naturalization, but when this is your land you are every bit as equal. The rights of adoption were conferred upon every citizen who could rightfully claim status as a United States citizen. Often times, Americans who are three, four, or even five generations from first generation ancestors who immigrated to the United States forget what occurred during the moment when citizenship from one land was renounced and the adoption into the American family pronounced. This is profound. The moment a person becomes a United States citizen all legal rights of their country of origin are broken, severed forever. Not only are the requirements of their former country broken, they now are entitled to receive the full inheritance and rights of a citizens of the United States. In America, there is no king, no czar, or supreme leader. This land is yours, this land is mine, this land is our gift from heaven's hand. Like our Christian heritage of old, when we begin following Christ, we receive our sonship to God and our status as co-heirs with Christ (Romans 8:15–17)[63]. When we are considered co-heirs, we have all the rights God conferred to His only Son, Jesus Christ, to share in His glory! Back in the days when Jesus walked the earth, the culture dictated that only the first-born son was entitled to a double portion of the inheritance. This is no longer the case. Christ died to radically alter how we related to our heavenly father. There is no preferential treatment, and no longer does birth order matter. He, Jesus, disrupted how it had always been done. As citizens of this great land,

---

63   Scripture taken from the Holy Bible, New International Version®. Copyright © 1973, 1978, 1984 by International Bible Society. Used by permission of Zondervan. All rights reserved.

we all become co-heirs to the United States of America, where we have the same relationship with every other citizen and every citizen has the same inheritance as every other citizen. There were no favorites in God's family, and there are no favorites by the pure definition of *the Constitution*!

This is exactly why citizenship in the United States must be prized. It must be valued, and it must be kept sacred. It is a lofty goal and unbelievable privilege, and the rights and inheritance we lay hold of is beyond what any other citizen in the world has, and will ever experience. Lay hold of this, America. Your status as sons and daughters of liberty is secure. It is majestic, and you are wealthy beyond your comprehension. This process of sonship breeds humility into our America, humility that all of us were created equal. Just travel the globe a while and you will see class systems alive and well in the world, nations who treat women as mere property and countries who rely upon genocide to propel one race's superiority over another. Yes, America has her ailments. We have our faults. We haven't always been perfect, but in America the ideal was implanted into the root of our society where we've become co-heirs, no matter our religion, race, sex, age, or social economic status. The ideal is America. The ideal is the cornerstone from which our nation was built upon, and the ideal is what we need to keep sacred.

This almost sounds harsh, that our nation shall only grant citizenship to those who are legally entitled to it through birth or naturalization and not the rest of the world. Why? To do otherwise would be to violate the rule of law and undermine *the Constitution* itself. Brilliance if you ask me, just brilliance. It is a document that provides a check and balance to itself. Think about God's family for a moment. Jesus says: "I am the way and the truth and the life. No one comes to the Father except through Me." (John 14:6)[64] Sounds almost elite, arrogant, or rigid, but in fact it is the absolute opposite. You see, God provided people a path into His kingdom, but it had to be done on His terms and in His way, or those privileges would not take affect. He tells us over and over through Scripture if we obey Him, then we will be blessed. We receive the blessing because we respect the way He has ordered for things to be done, and we submit to His hand of authority. It's simple to understand, and harsh for those who cannot find the humility to submit to God's way. This is absolutely true for citizenship in the United States. It begins with recognizing the Constitution, which

---

64 Scripture taken from the Holy Bible, New International Version®. Copyright © 1973, 1978, 1984 by International Bible Society. Used by permission of Zondervan. All rights reserved.

(as we will see under the chapter *Establish Justice*), establishes the rule of law as just and impartial. All citizens must obey it because it creates an orderly society where tranquility and prosperity are made possible. That is how America was ordained. My heart at times goes out to all those illegal immigrants in the United States who desire to live under the shelter of America. At the same time, every time we propagate illegal immigration, we undermine the very thing they desire and inject chaos and disorder into our nation, which ultimately leads to confusion and a weakened dream of *liberty*. Sons and daughters of liberty, catch hold of how wide, long, high, and deep is the inheritance of America. Sure, we desire to go out into the world and crown others with the right of citizenship, but there is one way—by respecting the Constitution and upholding the rule of law.

Could you imagine the disciples who were given the great commission of going out and baptizing people, but then having them tell you that you can become a Christian by following anything and doing anything you like? It sounds crazy. Instead, the disciples were commissioned to "... make disciples of all nations, baptizing them in the name of the Father and of the Son and of the Holy Spirit, and teaching them to obey everything I have commanded you" (Matthew 28:19–20 NIV).[65] There are two central tenets here. First, baptize them in the name of the Father, and of the Son, and of the Holy Spirit, whereby they would have to make a public profession and commitment to follow God. Said another way, they swore allegiance to Christ. Conceptually, becoming a citizen of the United States must include swearing allegiance publicly (and the citizen makes this a reality), which recognizes committing to the new vow instead of the old. Furthermore, those disciples were told to teach the new converts to obey everything God had commanded. In other words, they must uphold God's rule, laws, and ways. As anyone who is about to receive citizenship, there must be a process of education, a clear indication of desire and willingness to swear allegiance and obedience to the rule of law established by we, the people. One last note, then onward we will move. The process to receive citizenship is lengthy, sometimes costly, and at times, exhaustive. In the end, both the United States and the person applying for citizenship are both informed, and the person knows if they are committed to becoming a citizen of the United States. Whether by design or not, it works, and thousands of people are bestowed with this honor each year.

---

65   Scripture taken from the Holy Bible, New International Version®. Copyright © 1973, 1978, 1984 by International Bible Society. Used by permission of Zondervan. All rights reserved.

United States

Let's break the words "United States" down even further. The word *united* means to come or bring together for a common purpose or action[66]. The origin of the word *united* is derived from the Latin word *unitatem*, which means oneness, sameness, or agreement[67]. The word *state* denotes a nation or territory considered an organized political community under one government[68]. At our root, we are a collection of territories considered organized political communities that have decided to come together for a common purpose. Now, that's a mouthful! The people who belong to the United States have come together as separate territories for a common purpose or action. So, if you are a citizen of the United States, you are forever linked to every other citizen past, present, and future for the common purpose established for the United States. It is in this purpose that the depth of America's call to liberty can be felt. It is at this point of the document where our sense of belonging, ownership, and unity awaken as our ears receive destiny's call. It is between the words that bring the people together and the *United States* where we receive our purpose. This is where oneness is birthed, our political affiliations lose their grip, and those items that separate us are removed. Have you ever noticed when there is a crisis how well people pull together? The fighting dissipates and the job just gets done. Well, our founders were about to announce the crisis facing America and confounding the world. The comma applied after *United States* is where we pause, catch our breath, and prepare ourselves to receive our purpose.

Traditionally in American society, when a husband and wife are married, the wife takes the last name of her husband. This tradition, which is centuries old, communicates to their family and friends that the man and woman were once separate, but now united through matrimony. A change occurred in both of their lives and from that point forward their goal in marriage was to strive for oneness. This tradition places both the husband and wife under a single name with a single purpose. In today's post-modern era it is becoming unfashionable to maintain this tradition, but the tradition symbolizes a seismic event in someone's life. A permanent

---

66 *The New Oxford American Dictionary, Second Edition*, Erin McKean (editor), 2051 pages, May 2005, Oxford University Press, ISBN 0-19-517077-6.

67 *The Barnhart Concise Dictionary of Etymology*, Robert K. Barnhart (editor), 916 pages, 1995 H. W. Wilson Company, ISBN 0-6-270084-7.

68 *The New Oxford American Dictionary, Second Edition*, Erin McKean (editor), 2051 pages, May 2005, Oxford University Press, ISBN 0-19-517077-6.

change has occurred for both the husband and the wife. The husband, through the acceptance of his role, takes on the servant based role as the leader of the marriage, and the wife, with acceptance of this, is afforded the security of the marriage and becomes a permanent part of a new family. Similarly, when *"We the People,"* are connected to the words *United States,* the people and the land are permanently joined. Like the name of the husband, the United States of America does not change. It is us who are joined to this nation as her citizens. It is us who must leave behind our heritage of old, take on the security of this land, and accept our civic duties. This is a critical reason why citizens of this nation must leave their heritage of old behind when they accept the privilege of becoming a citizen of America. You cannot have a fully functioning marriage where both parties have different goals for the relationship outside of oneness. When Americans continue to carry labels and identify themselves as Italian American, African American, or Iraqi American, it is a form of adultery upon the national character and tears at the fabric of oneness and unity to our nation. We are all Americans! We are told in Scripture *"... no one can serve two masters. Either he will hate the one and love the other, or he will be devoted to the one and despise the other" (Matthew 6:24).*[69] When we take on this right to be citizens of this land, a choice must occur. Otherwise, we dilute America and we lose our national pride. There is great strength in America's diversity, but we all must become Americans first, or we will limit our nation's ability to fulfill our purpose *in order to form a more perfect union.*

---

69   Scripture taken from the Holy Bible, New Internationl Version®. Copyright © 1973, 1978, 1984 by International Bible Society. Used by permission of Zondervan. All rights reserved.

IN ORDER TO FORM A
MORE PERFECT UNION

⸙⸙⸙⸙

"We the People of the United States, in Order to form a more
perfect Union, establish Justice, insure domestic Tranquility, provide
for the common defence, promote the general Welfare, and secure
the Blessings of Liberty to ourselves and our Posterity, do ordain and
establish this Constitution for the United States of America."
- The Constitution of the United States (September 17, 1787)

So, here we are, America. The year is 1787 or so. We are a restless group of people who have known the victory of war and the struggles of birthing a young democracy. We are excited over our accomplishments, yet anxious over where to go from here. Our forefathers knew they needed to unite this land around a central purpose and structure or face the possibility of thirteen mini-nations. Our states knew they needed to unite to endure times of national testing. The time was ripe for the arrival of America's purpose, but it couldn't be just any purpose. It had to be timeless. It had to encapsulate the sentiments of the Declaration of Independence, strike the right balance between the people, the individual states, and the collective nation while grabbing the hearts of all generations of Americans. This was no small task. It was extraordinary! Can you imagine the weight of destiny that must have been on the shoulders of those men while they wrote the document? Can you imagine how ill equipped they must have felt to create a governing structure which could foresee events well into the future? Could you imagine producing the document required to heed liberty's call? This was a tall order the scale of which none of those men had known in their lives. There were no playbooks or "how-to" guides. This was completely new. Sure, there were Old English laws and other things to draw upon, but this was a democracy built upon *"We the People."*

Those men must have been humbled and drawn toward the Almighty to bear up under the weight, for they realized if they succeeded, then *liberty for all* would make its rounds across the globe and throughout time. If they failed, they also understood that all the suffering endured by this young land was for naught, and the fate of the world rested in the strokes of their pens. Outside of the Bible, I cannot think of any other document written which was so consequential to world events. The Bible itself contains some sixty-six books written over thousands of years by multiple authors, and somehow it has stood the test of time. We know for sure the Bible was divinely inspired, divinely crafted, and has been a light for all to see since its completion in the first century. We cannot explain how the Bible was seamlessly woven together across thousands of years. It had to be God. Perhaps the Constitution is of the same vein. No, it doesn't supplement the Bible. Rather, the enormity of the task, the complexity of its design, and the variety of the delegates involved most certainly would push these men beyond their own capacities. George Washington thought it was "little short of a miracle," that the delegates could agree on such a document.[70] The invisible hand of Liberty was at work then as He is now. These may not be divinely inspired words, but it is a divinely inspired set of events in response to America's rendezvous with destiny.[71]

America's purpose begins with *"... in Order to form a more perfect Union."* With *firm reliance on the protection of Divine Providence*[72], America had accepted her call to Liberty, but recognized the journey had just begun. Our forefathers were well aware of the nobility of our calling and the shortcomings of our character. They knew the goal of America—the goal to strive toward a more perfect union, or one free from any flaw or defect

---

70 Sparks, Jared, *The Writings of George Washington; Being His Correspondence, Addresses, Messages, and other Papers, Official and Private, Selected and Published from the Original Manuscript; with A Life of the Author, Notes, and Illustrations, American Stationers' Company, Boston, 1837.*

71 Source: Taken from Ronald Reagan's 1964 speech in support of Barry Goldwater's presidential campaign.

72 The Declaration of Independence: taken from U.S. National Archives & Records Administration, 8601 Adelphi Road, College Park, MD, 20740-6001,• 1-86-NARA-NARA• 1-866-272-6272; taken from http://www.archives.gov/exhibits/charters/declaration_transcript.html.

in condition or quality[73]—was neither static nor ever complete. This young nation had accepted the grace of the Supreme Judge of this world[74], but now America must strive to brighten the beacon of liberty. As anyone amongst the ranks who call themselves a Christian understands, our acceptance by faith is but the first step. The more arduous challenge is the working out of our faith with fear and trembling so that we become blameless and pure, children of God without fault (Phil 2:12,15).[75] So here America has it. We have accepted our call to liberty, and now the real work would begin as we attempt to remove any defect which may lie in our national character. This call to form a more perfect union was a call to *oneness*, where two parties put their individual desires aside for the betterment of the nation. Think about it. Our forefathers were asking a land full of immigrants to place their interests beneath the interests of America. They knew it was in this place where selfishness dies and selflessness is birthed, where divisiveness withers and oneness is harvested.

The word *order* means the arrangement or disposition of people or things in relation to each, according to a particular sequence, pattern, or method.[76] By utilizing the word *order* and placing emphasis on the word through the capitalization of the letter *O* in the text of the Constitution, the reader must conclude that the forefathers were intentional about how America would be organized. The word *order* denotes that there was a preferred method or sequence of forming a more perfect union. In other words, our forefathers preferred a particular method at the exclusion of other methods. Sadly, in postmodern America we find ourselves having to accommodate virtually all views and all methods—a term known as *tolerance*. To be intolerant in America is countercultural and considered offensive. Ironically, the historical truth (from the text of the Constitution) indicates that our forefathers preferred order, sequence, or a particular method to arrange our civilization. They too would be labeled as intolerant.

---

73 *The New Oxford American Dictionary, Second Edition*, Erin McKean (editor), 2051 pages, May 2005, Oxford University Press, ISBN 0-19-517077-6.

74 The Declaration of Independence: taken from U.S. National Archives & Records Administration, 8601 Adelphi Road, College Park, MD, 20740-6001,• 1-86-NARA-NARA• 1-866-272-6272; taken from http://www.archives.gov/exhibits/charters/declaration_transcript.html.

75 Scripture taken from the Holy Bible, New International Version®. Copyright © 1973, 1978, 1984 by International Bible Society. Used by permission of Zondervan. All rights reserved.

76 *The New Oxford American Dictionary, Second Edition*, Erin McKean (editor), 2051 pages, May 2005, Oxford University Press, ISBN 0-19-517077-6.

The *tolerance* movement in America starkly contradicts the letter and the spirit of the Constitution.

This is no different than when a man and woman are thinking about marriage. In its most Christian form, marriage could be defined as the bringing together of one man and one woman for the purpose of growing in oneness. As discussed in the previous section, the mysterious union in marriage has a particular order, where the husband is the selfless, servant-hearted leader and the wife is the respectful mate willing to submit to the man's authority. When America decidedly went away from an ordered view of marriage, we injected chaos into our society. The traditional Christian view of marriage is more compatible with the text of the Constitution than the tolerant view being popularized in our culture. This is how God defined marriage and how our founders designed America. As America redefines marriage, it will redefine the order of the land and it will reverberate to the core of this nation. To redefine marriage moves America further away from God's design and the intentionality and exclusiveness of the Constitution. To strive toward a more perfect union, it hinges upon our acceptance of two traits: *love* and *respect*, which somehow are the heart and soul of any union, especially one as grand as this nation.

Constitutional Love & Respect

Let's set the stage with a bit of context from the hearts of our dear forefathers. By this time they had written the Declaration of Independence, and victory against England was complete. With great joy, America finds herself in a position of liberty with an uncertain future. It is within the great text of the Declaration of Independence where we find four distinct references to God: *nature's God, Creator, Supreme Judge of this world, and Divine Providence*[77] (of which we will have more to say in another section). Suffice to say, our forefathers submitted the creation of America to Almighty God, both in print and in deed. It is within this context of a nation submitted to God Himself, as its chief cornerstone, where we pick up the linkage to the Constitution, where America was provided a framework to govern her citizens. The concept is not unlike the Israel of old, a nation God brought out of tyranny and then decided to provide boundaries (the Ten Commandments) within which God would pour out His blessings and love upon His chosen people. The Constitution is a document of *love* in its highest form. It is within the boundaries of *love*

---

77   See Appendix A - The Declaration of Independence.

where America will find her most certain blessings, path to liberty, and longevity of prosperity.

The Constitution provides a roadmap for our nation to discover the depth, the breadth, and height of *love* like no other nation in the history of civilization. A recipe is only as good as how well the chef follows the directions. Our founders knew that this union, if administered in the context of the time, would see a marriage occurring between we, the people, her government, her states, and each of their respective rights. America's radically different approach to governance placed we, the people, in a position of authority over America, her government, her states, and her laws. Not just any authority, but a *love* filled authority where we, the people, would love their nation with a willingness toward sacrifice and service, the highest of callings. *Love* is the stage at which we arrive as our forefathers agree on how our nation shall be governed, protected, and preserved. If *love* is the ultimate charge of we, the people, then to complete this union it must also include *respect.* Respect is the willingness of a government and her states to humbly submit to the authority of we, the people. Just for a moment, let's explore in more fullness what is meant when we, the people, receive the high call of *love* and a government accepts its perfectly placed position of humility by granting the *respect* accorded to the ordained order of this nation.

Love, the origin of this breathtaking word is Latin and denotes a kind of Christ-like love for one's fellows[78]. What better place to find a definition of *love* than Scripture itself? In the book of 1 Corinthians 13:4, we find a definition of love:

> *Love is patient, love is kind. It does not envy, it does not boast, it is not proud. It is not rude, it is not self-seeking, it is not easily angered, it keeps no records of wrongs. Love does not delight in evil but rejoices with the truth. It always protects, always trusts, always hopes, always perseveres.*
>
> *1 Corinthians 13:4–7 (NIV).*[79]

---

78 *The New Oxford American Dictionary, Second Edition,* Erin McKean (editor), 2051 pages, May 2005, Oxford University Press, ISBN 0-19-517077-6.

79 Scripture taken from the Holy Bible, New International Version®. Copyright © 1973, 1978, 1984 by International Bible Society. Used by permission of Zondervan. All rights reserved.

This is a high calling, and we are called to it as Christians and as patriots of the Constitution. It is in this breadth of *We the People* where we find the lifelong commitment between a people, her nation, and civility herself. Look deeply at the words in the Scriptures written by the Apostle Paul. He seeks to rouse in us something entirely opposite of selfishness and self-interest. Rather, he seeks to stir a sense of deep civility rooted in Christian love. There are numerous individuals many times my senior who can recall the days when our character was marked with such depth, such virtue, and such honor. Look no further than the rules of dignity written by George Washington himself, which resound so closely with the harmony of those Scriptures. The founders possessed a deep sense of duty to country over duty to self. Our duty, to form a more perfect union, is to strive towards oneness or unity. The Bible instructs a man to leave his father and mother and be united to his wife where the two will become one (Mark 10:7-8).[80] The secret to oneness contained within scripture is when each party to the marriage places their needs and interests below their partner's needs and interest – death to self gives birth to love, joy, peace, security, and blessings.

When the Constitution was complete, the union between we, the people and this nation were forever linked and the vows were taken, just like when a husband marries his wife. As we know, what God puts together let no man pull apart. We are a people like no other on earth, who have been called by our forefathers to express a *love* to the world motivated by our Almighty. This is no small task, nor a destination that can ever fully be achieved. As Americans, we will know we have arrived when the majority of citizens willingly lay down their self-interests for their country. This *love* should not be confused with weakness, as we find so often the case when the meek are perceived as fragile, for it is in the humility of *love* where America finds her great strength. It is our duty to return this expression by pouring ourselves out and leaving nothing for ourselves as we continue the great journey of forming a more perfect union. It is here, America, the place where sense of duty to country rises above our individual interests. It is here, America, where we will find our roots renewed. It is here, America, where our posture will be readied and our nation restored. The fathers of this land did not place an expiration date on our ability to find this path. They knew from history that we might wander, but as we find our land in

80   Scripture taken from the Holy Bible, New International Version®. Copyright © 1973, 1978, 1984 by International Bible Society. Used by permission of Zondervan. All rights reserved.

the twilight of the evening, we need look no further than to the bright star in the sky. It is the same constellation that inclined those wise men of old to travel the road that lead to the birth of the great Savior we have come to know. This great Savior took selflessness to an entirely new level, placing the interests of mankind (His church) above His personal comfort as He faced a gruesome death upon the cross. Look up, America. Look toward the sky. We are being led by up high. It is time to take our steps, to be on our way, to leave selfishness behind, and restore America's great name!

Love is but one aspect to this great equation. It is the call of *respect*, where a nation's government accepts her proper place under the *charitable* authority of the people. It isn't enough when one party to this union is filled with *love* and the other has turned her back. It only works well when we all fall into our rightful places. As a nation, a government, and a collection of states, our whims, wishes, and dictates are a cause for concern when the state becomes the head and its people become the tail. America was called to something more grand. We were called to inspire a government which possessed a sacred submission towards the will of the people. We dare not reverse the ordained order from above, because those boundaries were built with wisdom to position us for far greater blessings. There is an invisible line in the sand where the will of the people is circumvented by the will of the state. This was never the plan for this great land, for the government need not love its people, but it certainly must respect their authority. It is at this key juncture of the Constitution where each branch of government, every article written, and all amendments enacted will all find unity in the will of the people. In unity there is great peace, and it breeds such strength. It is in this aspect of the great Constitution that America separated herself from every other land. We dare not change the framers' plan, for we were never called to this great moment when our nation was born. Our responsibility is to carry out the duties outlined in the Constitution, not to rewrite the text itself. Imagine going to war when the soldiers do not have a clear chain of command, where everyone can issue dictates. It would be a recipe for certain disaster. There are many things our military could teach our land, but most of all, knowing the structure of its command has brought order to chaos, victory through death, and love through war. Look at Scriptures in which we are commanded not to seek our will, but the will of Him above. The Father promises us a life well after this one when we accept and follow His will, His order, and His divine way. America will prosper as long as we follow the ordained order of our union set forth in the Constitution through the lens of one nation under God.

ESTABLISH JUSTICE

--- ∽⊙⊙∼ ---

*"**We the People of the United States**, in Order to form a more perfect Union, **establish Justice**, insure domestic Tranquility, provide for the common defence, promote the general Welfare, and secure the Blessings of Liberty to ourselves and our Posterity, do ordain and establish this Constitution for the United States of America."*

- The Constitution of the United States (September 17, 1787)

"**W**e the People of the United States," those words are not just historical, they are soul gripping. They usher thoughts of a new beginning, a new nation, a new democracy, and also place both responsibility and purpose onto the bedrock of the American government, *we, the people.* Our founding fathers could have said "We, the executive branch," or "We, the legislative branch," or even "We, the judicial branch," but they decided to say "We, the people." There is inherent accountability and a sense of urgency for each American when you read those words, for they called this nation to action back then, and they are calling Americans to action today. Grab hold, America. Grab hold of your purpose. It isn't your parent's purpose, the founders' purpose, or even your grandparent's purpose. It is your purpose. It is each person's purpose who stakes claims on being called a United States citizen. We are first called to *form a more perfect union,* and then to *establish justice.* Here it is, America— the people, a perfect union, and the establishment of justice. Let's move to seize our moment and discover what it means to establish justice.

The word *justice* is defined as the quality of being fair, just; borrowed from Old French *justise, justice,* which was borrowed from the Latin *justitia,* meaning righteous, equity.[81] Our forefathers recognized the need for the fair and impartial administration of law and justice in the United States. In fact, justice was mentioned first out of a list of action imperatives given in the preamble. Our forefathers knew our society must place preeminence upon justice and the rule of law. There were no favorites, special deals, or partial treatments. All citizens received the same impartial response from the voice of justice. Law and justice provide order to a society by informing the citizens of societal boundaries. It makes sense in this context why justice would precede the establishment of tranquility. In America, there were no surprises or unjustified raids in the middle of the night. Think about this for a moment. The people knew the rules in advance, and knew exactly what would happen if they didn't follow those rules. It was pretty simple stuff. Obey and you will reap the benefits of living in peace. On the other hand, the people must perceive justice as impartial otherwise the tentacles of tyranny begin to grow. There were two aspects to this equation. The people had to obey the law, and the law had to be impartial. The Ten Commandments were static once God gave them to Moses, literally written in stone. God knew the Israelites needed boundaries, but even more importantly, God knew those boundaries would produce trust, order, and ultimately, peace. Our forefathers understood the same delicate relationship between justice, accountability, and trust. This is a critical aspect to our Constitution and to the judicial branch of government. When the judicial branch steps beyond the role of impartiality by adding to or subtracting from laws, they are going against the will of the people. This act alone is horrendous, but even worse they are injecting chaos into our society by not allowing the people to know the laws ahead of time and by removing the judicial branch's ability to be impartial. Operating beyond the boundaries of the people breaks the sacred trust and makes tranquility a less attainable goal.

Unfortunately, in America today, the debate over our justice system usually gets politicized and polarized, so the average person is left in a windstorm of confusion with little explanation of the heart of the matter. *"We the People"* is at the core of everything written into the Constitution. This is the strand which binds the Constitution together and provides a link to the Declaration of Independence (of which we will say more on later.)

---

81   *The Barnhart Concise Dictionary of Etymology*, Robert K. Barnhart (editor), 916 pages, 1995 H. W. Wilson Company, ISBN 0-6-270084-7.

This goes for each article and amendment of The Constitution. Therefore, to chip away at this strand is to chip away at the Constitution itself. Some may disagree with this analysis. Others may argue it doesn't meet the theology being taught in our law schools. All I can say is read the document. It is the brushstroke of those artists in 1787. In high school physics, we were taught Newton's law of motion: every action has a reaction equal in magnitude and opposite in direction. Each time the justice system oversteps its boundaries, even when the action is subtle, there is an equal reaction upon the trust the people have in their government. It has to, because they are writing the rulebook as they go along. Imagine attempting to play a football game where the referee makes up rules as the game progresses. What was a fumble in the first quarter is now different than a fumble in the second quarter. Oops! A touchdown in the third quarter is worth only three points. It would be utter chaos, absurd, and it would most certainly disrupt the ability to conduct a game in an orderly manner. Spiritually speaking, imagine God changing the conditions for guaranteeing our entry into heaven. Imagine you spend your entire life living by the Bible, and then He decides to change the rules. The average Christian would lose complete trust and confidence in their personal faith. Fortunately, we live for a God who has gone out of His way to maintain the integrity of His Holy Word. God wants His rule of law and the character of His behavior to remain firm, because He knows firmness breeds stability, predictability, reliability, and ultimately, peace. The book of Hebrews tells us Jesus Christ is the same yesterday and today and forever (Hebrews 13:8).[82] Personally, the unchanging nature of God's character brings great comfort to my soul. Obviously, the Constitution has an established provision to amend and to create laws, but the spirit of the document was intended to remain intact. Laws are to be created through the will of the people with a semblance of stability. Look at the large columns erected in front of the Supreme Court building, the architecture projects strength, wisdom, and stability. At times, friends of mine have accused God of being mean, unforgiving, or unjust for not allowing everyone entry into heaven. In fact, it is quite the contrary. Justice is providing in advance the rules and the consequences for not obeying. The rule of law and the establishment of justice in America must remain within the bounds of the will of the people. It is within this tapestry where strength, stability, security, and predictability are woven into the American way of life.

---

82 Scripture taken from the Holy Bible, New International Version®. Copyright © 1973, 1978, 1984 by International Bible Society. Used by permission of Zondervan. All rights reserved.

The second aspect to this equation belongs to the people. Justice is bound by the people and in turn, the people are bound by the rule of law. This is what distinguishes America from every other nation on earth, and further establishes the roots of strength, stability, security, and predictability. Imagine a society in which people did not have to follow the rule of law. Look at Russia or other underdeveloped nations that do not uphold the rule of law, where corruption and bribery plague their legal system. This is why bribery and public corruption are damaging to our success and longevity in America. They strike at the heart of a nation's ability to bear good fruit. I love the passage in the New Testament where we are instructed to treat the rich the same as the poor (James 2:8).[83] In theory, America was established to remove any favoritism and to encourage people to follow the laws that were created ultimately by the authority they voted into the legislature. Obviously, even in our system, there are those who can buy their way around the law or those who operate beyond the boundaries of the law. We should have pity for them. At some point they too will have a reckoning with the Supreme Judge of this world! Just as the government must remain within the bounds of the people, the people must remain within the boundaries of the rule of law. You see, *"We the People"* makes it work. It binds us together and bears the fruit it promises, not to mention it guarantees the forces of tyranny will not have their way for long.

The call to establish justice is a two-part equation where both the people and the government must operate within the protective arms of *"We the People."* The government must resist the temptation to move beyond the laws of the land, and the people must submit to the rule of law. Those are the ingredients to produce the stability that has guarded America for over two hundred years, and to create the conditions to *insure domestic tranquility.* Our forefathers were not naïve enough to think we would not have differences, nor would America always have just laws or perfect citizens, but they did establish a nation where the invisible hand of the people was the great equalizer. Have faith, America, in the wisdom of the ages and Providence's call to those great authors of the Constitution. They not only breathed life into America, they provided her with a call to every generation and a prescription of faith designed to ensure the momentary trials of a nation are overshadowed by enduring tranquility.

---

83 Scripture taken from the Holy Bible, New International Version®. Copyright © 1973, 1978, 1984 by International Bible Society. Used by permission of Zondervan. All rights reserved.

INSURE DOMESTIC TRANQUILITY

$$\text{~~~~~~~~~~~~~~~~}$$

*"**We the People of the United States**, in Order to form a more perfect Union, establish Justice, **insure domestic Tranquility**, provide for the common defence, promote the general Welfare, and secure the Blessings of Liberty to ourselves and our Posterity, do ordain and establish this Constitution for the United States of America."*

- The Constitution of the United States (September 17, 1787)

I recall driving to work in my 1977 Ford pickup truck in Montgomery, Alabama when the news broke on September 11, 2001. A large airplane had struck one of the twin towers in New York City. As I drove, I learned that it appeared a second plane had struck another tower. My thoughts raged with suspicion that this was not an accidental type of crash. Something was very wrong in America. I arrived at work, and my co-workers and I quickly huddled around a television in the break room as we witnessed the tragedy unfold. Words were not sufficient for those dark moments, and as Alan Jackson so eloquently put to music "... the world stopped turning that September day ...". The grief endured by the families who lost loved ones in the collapse of the twin towers, on the plane that went down in Pennsylvania, and on the tragic collision of the airplane into the Pentagon is hard to fathom. The day known as 9/11 is indelibly carved into the American psyche. We lost something that day, something precious to a young nation. We lost our innocence. Yes, Pearl Harbor was huge, but this attack struck at the heart of our financial sector, the heart of our government (with the apparent plans to strike the White House), and the heart of our military might. The devastation and loss of life were paralyzing as we watched our skies cleared of planes, our President shuttled off to an unknown location, and the collapse of the twin towers. During those moments, a cloud came over America. We knew we were at war, we were vulnerable, and the world would never be the same. The protection those oceans had provided to the homeland for over two hundred years had just been removed. The scarce memories of the Revolutionary War, the War of 1812, and the Civil War, where our homes, businesses, and communities were the battlegrounds, were just that—distant memories. We read about these events in history books and saw them in movies, but we never dreamed this would become our reality. An arrow of fear drove deep into the American heart. Our security was threatened, and the blanket of tranquility removed.

Imagine what it was like during 1787. The smell from the barrels of those English guns was still fresh. Our economic security was uncertain, our government virtually nonexistent, and the threat of war from enemies abroad very real. The peace and security of young America was vulnerable and far from a guarantee. There may be over two hundred years of history separating us from this moment in history, but as the events of September 11, 2001 unfolded, we were forever connected to our forefathers by our plight. Those forefathers knew that in order for America to survive, there must be tranquility. To have tranquility, our nation must have security. This is exactly why the third call to America, to insure domestic tranquility, finds itself securely sandwiched between the call to establish justice and provide for the common defense. You see, America, peace was a gift born out of war, and now it was up to this nation to guard the gift of peace. Tranquility was the exact condition necessary to allow the light of liberty to beam across the globe.

Our forefathers were quite familiar with the differences between authentic peace and peace for the sake of peace. They had just broken ties with England, a country that provided a perceived peace not based in freedom, but grounded in tyranny, as they ushered this third call to our great land. Tranquility rooted in tyranny is a one way street. The founders were not advocating peace at all cost. They had limits. After all, the entire purpose of the Revolutionary War was not to bring peace with England. Rather, the purpose was to bring the sword and sever our paternal ties. With this separation, the conditions were now ripe to form a uniquely different relationship between the government and its people, a relationship that was based in life, liberty, and the pursuit of happiness.

Therefore, tranquility must be seen through the prism of those unalienable rights and through the lens of the people. When any of those rights are violated or the government steps beyond the boundaries of the people, then by the powers vested in the Constitution and the Declaration of Independence, each of us are called to stand up to the forces of tyranny no matter where its tentacles arise, even if it means risking our perceived peace for enduring tranquility. This isn't to suggest the citizens are to resort to violence, because the people also have a check and balance in the Declaration of Independence where we are not to remove a government for transient causes. The bottom line is that in America, we are called to seek peace, unity, and tranquility. It is our duty and destiny's third call to each American. However, we are also called to ensure we are seeking *authentic tranquility* bound by the people and those unalienable rights.

The Civil War is an excellent example of what happens when a nation allows tyranny to exist in its midst, where one race dominated another. Yes, there were many other issues which formed the basis for the Civil War, but the Emancipation Proclamation most pointedly addressed the need to bring freedom and liberty to a race that found themselves in slavery. In a sense, before the Civil War there was a false sense of peace, a peace based in tyranny, not based in liberty. There was a long history of events that ultimately culminated in the Civil War. Go back as far as the creation of the Declaration of Independence and you will find heated discussions over slavery. The issue continued to build up over a generation or two, and then America, the land of liberty, had to stand up to the forces of tyranny and bring freedom to the captives. This resulted in brother against brother, father against son, but after the dust settled, America found herself better fit to be called the land of liberty and sat on a firmer foundation of tranquility.

Even during biblical times, there were accounts where God had to use extreme measures to bring liberty and peace to a people. Look at when the Israelites left the grasp of the Egyptians. God brought the Ten Plagues to Egypt, including the most extreme—the killing of the firstborn of every household. Ultimately, God's purpose was to liberate His people and to bring freedom from the bondage of a terrible tyrant. This is the great love story of God's Word. There are stories where God's people find themselves in bondage, and before you know it, our white knight comes to rescue His sheep. Fast forward a bit into the New Testament, and you will see an account where Paul points out we can either be a slave to sin or a slave to righteousness (Romans 6:6).[84] When we enter into a relationship with Christ, we are freed from the evil desires of sin (Romans 6:11).[85] Look at Jesus, the Prince of Peace (Isaiah 9:6) who in the Gospel according to Matthew tells us he did not come to bring peace, but the sword (Matthew 10:34).[86] You see, this is how the story goes. First the tentacles of tyranny, then the battle cry for liberty, and ultimately the great white knight liberates those who are in bondage to slavery. This is the cry of every human heart—to find truth, to find liberty, and to find peace. Therefore, when I place the writing of the Constitution into the worldview in which these men were rooted, they too heard the voice of liberty. They too knew once they moved beyond the boundaries of slavery, they would experience a peace which transcended all understanding, an authentic tranquility. With those bold steps there was certain suffering, for nothing great in life comes without great sacrifice.

This is our story, America. This is our call, to heed the voice of liberty, for the path of liberty brings freedom, defeats the bondage of tyranny, and breaks the strongholds of fear that withholds the gift of peace. This isn't an artificial peace, it is a peace which is birthed out of liberty and protected by *the people*. It is when the government moves beyond the ancient foundry stone, the people, that we Americans hear the voice of liberty which calls us up, calls us to suffer for her cause, and calls us to break free from the bondage which so easily entangles a nation. We are called, America, to form a more perfect union, to establish justice, and to insure domestic tranquility. This may be our third call from those great men of old, but it isn't our last. There is a vast world out there, beyond the shores of America, where the battle between good and evil wages onward. Our founders were neither naïve nor ignorant to the external threats to America and the existence of evil in the world, the likes of which would love for America to fail.

---

84 Scripture taken from the Holy Bible, New International Version®. Copyright © 1973, 1978, 1984 by International Bible Society. Used by permission of Zondervan. All rights reserved.

85 Ibid.

86 Ibid.

PROVIDE FOR THE COMMON DEFENSE

———————— ✑◯◐◯✑ ————————

*"**We the People of the United States**, in Order to form a more perfect Union, establish Justice, insure domestic Tranquility, **provide for the common defence**, promote the general Welfare, and secure the Blessings of Liberty to ourselves and our Posterity, do ordain and establish this Constitution for the United States of America."*

- The Constitution of the United States (September 17, 1787)

Out of this fourth call to the people, the text provides a place and a purpose for the purest of patriots, those men and women who have loved their country enough to have fought and to have died for her cause. Our hearts weigh heavy for the men and women who consider service in defense of our flag more worthy than life itself. There is perhaps no greater measure to a man's character than his willingness to place the cause of liberty above himself.

Our blood, their freedom! Chew on that sentence for a few moments. That's correct. Over the few centuries of American existence, we have shed more blood of our young to usher in freedom all across the globe than any other nation. This is American exceptionalism at its best! We are a nation who willingly places our young into combat for the hope of freedom. Our magnificent country was given this high honor by Providence itself as it took root during the Revolutionary War. Our history has matured us as a nation. We witnessed America's role in conflicts across the world, from the Revolutionary War, to the War of 1812, to the Mexican-American War, to the Spanish-American War, to the Civil War, to World War I, to

World War II, to the Korean War, to Vietnam, to the Cold War, and the present day war, the War on Terrorism. The thread of liberty weaves our history together, and when the horizon of destiny looks cloudy, America need look no further than the strands of freedom for direction. We are an awesome, divinely inspired nation with a purpose so grand it transcends the momentary existence of individuals to a land willing to sacrifice and suffer for the cause of freedom whenever and wherever we hear her voice call. We established liberty, we are drawn toward liberty, we embrace liberty, we defend liberty, and we promote liberty. After all, we are Americans! Stand strong, Americans! Stand united, and stand proud of our past, the present, and the high calling of our future. We are the greatest nation on earth. We will prevail, and liberty once again will reign!

What would motivate a nation to expend its most precious resources for the benefit of others? Why would a country so rich in so many different ways willingly die for the possibility of bringing freedom and liberty to oppressed nations? Why does history keep placing America between liberty and tyranny? Are these just random events, or has America perhaps had a clear and purposeful direction for its existence? Is freedom so deeply ingrained into the American psyche that it is a natural expression of our national character? How has America been so blessed to have men and women voluntarily die for freedom?

The American Psyche

Deep within each Americans' soul is the aptitude, the desire, and the need to live, eat, and breathe freedom. Our souls know all too well the sustenance which comes from freedom. It is a part of our individual character, and a characteristic of our national personality. Therefore, to take up the cause of liberty is a natural expression of what it means to be American. The determination of those forces which desire to reshape freedom can be tolerated for a brief period, but at some point we inherently know liberty costs. Throughout our history, we are well aware of the costs and know the familiarities of sacrifice. In recent years, we have witnessed the attack on the bells of freedom across the globe and certainly here at home. Most notably, the terrorist attacks of September 11, 2001 left the American psyche indelibly changed. It made the world stop on that dark day in American history, and made each American less secure than one day prior. September 11, 2001 was a watershed moment to this nation and to the world. It was the moment where history beckoned America to return to the epic struggle of good versus evil, of liberty versus tyranny.

Call it what you like, radical Islam or Jihad, the roots lead to a tree of tyranny with the desire to spread its version of control and domination across the globe at any cost. Our nation grieved deeply over the loss of life, and probably more collectively, we grieved over the attack on American freedom. You see, the terrorists on September 11, 2001 were not satisfied to inflict terror and death the likes of which American soil has never seen. No, their inclinations were much more grand. Beyond the immediate death and destruction, the devious plot was to combat freedom with fear. Their goal was to strike an arrow of fear at the heart of the American psyche and demolish the American way of life. Recall where you were and what you were doing at the moment you first learned of those attacks. Remember the emotions that flooded your mind, the insecurity you felt, the fear for the future, and the fear of our invincibility being taken away. It reminds me of the first time a child is exposed to the harsh realities of life. For most, we took it for granted that we would be a free and prosperous nation. On that day, our innocence was robbed, and we all felt the call to defend liberty. Look at the events immediately following September 11, 2001. There was an outpouring of patriotism, support, and the rising tide of war had found its way to each American. Truth is, we all knew war was coming well before the formal declaration came from the President and Congress. For just a moment, our intimate walk with freedom had been disrupted. With crystal clarity, we saw the possibility of a world without liberty, and it felt dark, cold, and harsh. We didn't like it, and instinctively we all knew we were at war!

War Hurts

When America decides to send her blood and treasure into war, there is no higher calling and no higher cost. War is tough. It strains, it stretches, it grieves, it transforms, and it hurts. There is no greater responsibility given to the President of the United States than the Commander in Chief of the Armed Forces. The decision to send our men and women into armed conflict comes with the foreknowledge that many will never return home. Again, I am reminded of the film *We Were Soldiers.* Colonel Hal Moore, played by Mel Gibson, gives the troops a speech right before they are about to deploy into combat. Colonel Moore tells the young officers he cannot guarantee he will bring everyone home alive, but he can guarantee he will not leave anyone behind. In this moment, we get a glimpse into the soul of Colonel Moore and the eyes of war. We see the pain of war, the triumph of victory, the profound responsibility of courage, and most of all, with the slight shed of a tear, the inevitable grief which will accompany these men, women, and their families in the days to come. Colonel Moore knew war was hell.

The costs of war are profound, and leave generational scars. War changes the men and women who are in the foxholes and changes the loved ones left behind. War changes the nations where the battles are fought and the lands that send their own into battle. War changes the present, tries to correct the past, and attempts to redirect the course of the future. Even the prevailing side knows the grief that accompanies victory. The effects of war have permanently altered the American character. At times, the change in personalities was positive, and at other instances, negative. War brings out the best in America, and has the unique ability to spotlight the fissures in our society. War hurts. War is hard, and war changes those touched by its tentacles.

America is no stranger to the toll of war on our nation. Look at World War II, when America sent our young and our brave to combat the evil forces of Nazi Germany, who were attempting an overthrow of Europe. The United States lost several hundred thousand men and women in that war alone. The world at large lost several million people to the casualty of war. Can you imagine losing hundreds of thousands of American men (and women) during this campaign? Thousands of men who never returned home, who left wives as widows, children as orphans, and left a void which affected the American personality for many years after. No doubt, the Allied Forces beat back the evil German war machine and triumphed against the latest form of tyranny. We were victorious, and we restored peace and civility to the free world. However, the plague of such death and the absent seats at the dining room table altered America.

Why is it during our greatest moments of national suffering, our character is placed on center stage? Yes, war is filled with death and destruction, which should not be minimized. By definition, to enter into war means the nation has exhausted other possibilities and is at a point of desperation, with no guarantees as to the outcome. The victor shapes the direction of history, and history shapes the formation of the nation. However, it is in these moments, when America has been called to the battlefield, when all else fails, that we see the best of America. No, it isn't under the stone of politics or the fleeting public sentiments where we must look. It is directly in the eyes, the stories, and the character of the men and women who leave the comforts of our soil to go into foreign lands to defend the ideals we hold so dearly. They are America. They are our heroes.

They are what separates us from all else. The willingness to go into combat, with all of the ugliness of war and put everything this life has to offer at risk for liberty's sake.

A patriot is not motivated by politics or public opinion. A patriot is motivated by the call to liberty. He may not be conscience of the inmost motives, but at the core of our great warriors is something that transcends politics, public sentiments, and the inevitable scars. Their sense of duty to liberty, duty to their nation, and to one another directs them beyond the immediate to a higher nobility. Recall Pat Tillman, a professional athlete in the National Football League, who gave up fame and fortune to serve in the Iraq War. Pat was making millions of dollars playing for the Arizona Cardinals. He had a bright future ahead of him. Pat gave it all up to serve. Why? Pat understood the call of liberty, the sense of duty, and the heartbeat of the American character. Pat Tillman gave the ultimate sacrifice, and in his sacrifice we witness the greatness of America.

Our Blood Their Freedom: A Force for Good & Stability

What nation in the history of the world has sacrificed more blood on every continent, stationed more troops in foreign lands for decades, and has been the greatest force for good and stability throughout the world? No, not China. Not Russia, not the United Kingdom, and certainly not any Western European nation. It is the good old red, white, and blue—America, the beautiful. In return for our goodness, our sacrifice, and our treasure, Europe berates us, Russia attempts to undermine us, nations in the Middle East label us as the Great Satan, and the Hugo Chavez and Fidel Castros around the globe spew anti-American sentiments at every opportunity. Yet America, in her majestic character, continues to place troops in Germany and Japan for the last sixty years, in South Korea for decades, and now we've risked our young in the Middle East. They will likely be there for decades to ensure the security of the region. Believe it or not, we are quickly approaching a decade of our blood, sweat, and tears in Iraq and Afghanistan. Can you believe it? We risk life and limb so millions around the world have security, stability, and an opportunity to find the gift of freedom for themselves. I am not aware of any other nations who have sacrificed to such a degree and given so much to other nations. America, although imperfect, we have upheld that value more so than any other country on the globe, and more than any nation in modern history. For that, the world should be grateful. For that, the world should be looking up to the United States of America. For that, we should take great pride in the fact that we are different than other nations around the globe. We give our blood for their freedom. This Christ-like quality was forged at the inception of America and has defined us ever since. America is great, our causes are just, and we have brought freedom, equality, and justice to more oppressed people than any nation on earth. The men and women of the United States Armed Forces are at the tip of this spear, and should be memorialized as heroes not just in America, but for every nation where America has shed our most precious possession, the blood of our young, for their freedom.

Our Blood Their Freedom: Ambassadors for America

For all of you who call yourselves citizens of the United States of America, and all of you across the globe who have been touched by the hand of American's influence, mainly our armed forces: it is time to stand up and be counted as a voice of freedom. It is time for Americans who deeply love their nation and understand the fullness of our character to wear the banner of patriotism in our hearts and to stop being minimized into silence. We are not perfect, but there is much to be celebrated. We have done great and magnificent things over our short history. We have died to be free and to bring the gift of freedom to others. For those of you across the globe who do not consider yourselves American, but have experienced the benefits of American character, stand up and be counted. It is time for true Americans, whether in title or spirit, to stand up and be counted. For those Americans who despise our past and desire to remake this nation into something it was never intended to be, perhaps it is time to part ways with America and find a nation which represents the Utopia you believe exists out there. My guess is you'll be back. Parents, raise the flag at the house. Say the pledge before breakfast, and when a soldier crosses your path, go up and thank him so your children understand the extent of sacrifice required from our men and women in uniform. Teachers of history, teach it straight and teach it true, for our men and women who have died and will die depend upon the accuracy of historians to know their cause was just and that they didn't die in vain. For those of you new to America, who came from Communism or perhaps lived under the rule of a dictator, talk to your friends and your family members here and abroad about the wonder of America and the security you feel in this land. You perhaps are our greatest ambassadors, because you have the freshest eyes. Many of us only know life in this land, and can often times get lost in our imperfections. America, we are a beautiful nation. We have the greatest military and intelligence agencies made up by volunteers. We need not be ashamed of our nation, our heritage, and our accomplishments. We are the greatest nation on earth, and it is time to drown out the critics who see none of America's greatness with overwhelming affection and pride. It is our land, it is our country, and it is our future. Take care of her, America, for this is a gift, and as quickly as it was given to us, it can be taken away. God bless each soldier, sailor, and individual who has put their life on the line to defend our ideals. They are our heroes. They do their job when they sign up to defend and protect this nation. Now, America, it is time to do our duty. They are motivated to fight and willing to die to ensure domestic tranquility, to promote the general welfare, and secure the blessings of liberty to ourselves and our posterity!

PROMOTE THE GENERAL WELFARE

— ❧ —

*"**We the People of the United States**, in Order to form a more perfect Union, establish Justice, insure domestic Tranquility, provide for the common defence, **promote the general Welfare**, and secure the Blessings of Liberty to ourselves and our Posterity, do ordain and establish this Constitution for the United States of America."*

- *The Constitution of the United States (September 17, 1787)*

The fifth call to the people, to promote the general welfare of America, her citizens, and her children, is one of the most difficult concepts to distill through the cultural guilt that has come to cloud the eyes of most Americans. It is easy to grab hold of forming a perfect union, establishing justice, creating a tranquil society, and even providing for the common defense of our land. When we speak of *promoting the general welfare,* it touches upon the sciatic nerve of our society. No other aspect in our Constitution creates such division amongst the ranks of American citizens. Shamefully, our political establishments play to the sympathetic ears of each side. Truth be told, America was a nation called to liberty through the Declaration of Independence. It stands to reason then, that in the spirit of our birth, America's goals shall be to maximize liberty and to promote independence. Anything less would not be consistent with the fabric of freedom and is counterproductive toward promoting the general welfare of our citizens. By definition, general welfare and freedom go hand in hand in America.

America, we were not set free from the bondage of tyranny to create a government that would nullify the sacrifices of old. We were created to be free and commissioned to take the cause of liberty across the globe. Can you imagine how easy it must have been for the citizens of early America to desire to return to the familiar land of tyranny? It wasn't pleasant, it wasn't liberty, but at least they knew what was expected. Remember how often the children of Israel would complain to Moses when God broke their bondage to the Egyptians. They claimed they were better off under the tyranny of Pharaoh. Tyranny promises instant relief from a societal ill in the name of general welfare, while prowling around and creating dependency. At the root of tyranny lies the desire to control, and at the root of liberty lies *love,* the desire to choose. One desires to dictate, the other desires to relate. One attempts to diminish while the other attempts to strengthen. Think for a moment about raising children. The healthiest of children are those who leave home free from the dictates of their parents, but desirous to maintain a strong relationship with them over the years, a relationship of friendship, openness, trust, and most importantly, the freedom to come and the freedom to go. That is how liberty works. It doesn't will itself or thrust itself upon us rudely. It allows us to choose. In essence, with the birth of liberty we find the birth of choice.

On the other hand, tyranny is luring. Its preferred method of operation is through compelled participation. It seeks to eliminate choice, to undermine trust, and ultimately to reduce individuals to property. There is dignity in freedom, dignity for the individual, dignity for what it means to be human, and dignity that man was created in the image of God with certain unalienable rights. Those forefathers who signed the Declaration of Independence were not compelled by force. They chose to support it upon the ideals of liberty. So, the general welfare of Americans must be rooted in *liberty.* It must contain choice, because we adhere to the belief that liberty is a gift given to men from God, and to chip away at that gift is nothing less than tyranny born again.

In modern America, we find ourselves at a crossroads of our existence, where we must select liberty and choice or the dictates of tyranny. It is tempting to fall prey to the seductive handouts of a government that masquerades as a saint, or to allow the emotions of the moment to incline us to let go of liberty for relief from the discomfort of society. As a government initiates its role as parent, provider, caretaker, and decider, it removes the need for strong families, the role of faith, the need for friends, and the reliance upon the individual to choose. The larger the government, the greater the encroachment upon liberty and our freedom of choice. A large and expanding government begins its journey to solve societal ills but somewhere in the process inadvertently destroys societal structures which creates a greater need for more government intervention, less confidence in the individual, and eliminates the dependence upon the faithful community where lasting solutions are found. It would be hard to conclude this is promoting the welfare of our land.

Rather, America is different from any land on earth. We affirmed our citizens with confidence as they caught the spirit of America, where men and women could dream to be whomever God desired them to become. There were no mountains too high or dreams too lofty to scale. This was America, where a mystery existed between liberty and the promotion of the well being of our countrymen. As men and women reckoned themselves to succeed or fail based upon their individual efforts and contributions, we witnessed an explosion upon the world scene where the impossible became possible, when men began to unleash liberty's call. This is where the purest will find solace in the promotion of our land, where government retreats, and faith, family, and freedom invade. It is in this place, where enough liberty exists, that people can embrace their destiny with liberty! Many may argue for greater confidence in government. Our founders would say that faith in government over the individual is the beginning of tyranny, and the end of the blessing of liberty to ourselves and our posterity!

SECURE THE BLESSINGS OF LIBERTY

*"**We the People of the United States**, in Order to form a more perfect Union, establish Justice, insure domestic Tranquility, provide for the common defence, promote the general Welfare, and **secure the Blessings of Liberty to ourselves and our Posterity**, do ordain and establish this Constitution for the United States of America."*

- The Constitution of the United States (September 17, 1787)

The most solemn duty of any holder of public office is to preserve, protect, and defend the Constitution of the United States of America. Above all and beyond everything else, the holders of public office must preserve this document, protect this great nation, and defend the Constitution of the United States of America. The oath found in Article II, Section 1 of the Constitution says:

> *I do solemnly swear that I will faithfully execute the Office of the President of the United States, and will to the best of my Ability, preserve, protect and defend the Constitution of the United States.*[87]

Let's dwell on that for a while: preserve, protect, defend; preserve, protect, defend; preserve, protect, and defend. The word *preserve* is central to the oath taken by the President, the Supreme Court justices, and members of Congress alike. The definition of *preserve* is to maintain something in its

87 See Appendix B – The Constitution of the United States.

original or existing state.[88] There isn't much latitude here. The oath never states the intent to change, to reinterpret, to bring up to modern age. It says the intent is to preserve, which is to maintain it to its most original state. To change it or to impose our views upon it goes against the very oath our politicians take upon entering public office.

The oath is typically followed up by four words: "so help me God." We know from our Christian heritage oaths made before God are to be taken seriously and can be considered breaking the third commandment of taking the Lord's name in vain. We see this throughout the Scriptures of the Old and New Testament "... *Do not break your oath, but keep the oaths you have made to the Lord ... Simply let your 'Yes' be 'Yes,'' and your 'No' be 'No'; anything beyond this comes from the evil one"(Matthew 5:33,37).*[89] Perhaps, through these various oaths, America was attempting to place accountability between the elected official and the citizen, but more reverently between the elected official and the Supreme Judge of this world (referred to in the Declaration of Independence). It is reckless to remove the accountability of our leaders to God in favor of something less transcendent.

Beyond preservation is the call to protect the United States and the Constitution of the United States of America. Protection is defined as keeping something or someone safe from harm or injury. When someone experiences an injury, their body is typically permanently (or at least temporarily) changed from its original state. Likewise, when our elected leaders take an oath to preserve the Constitution in its original state, he or she is also supposed to ensure no harm or injury comes to the nation or its constitution. They say we can learn much from animals, but look at the average family dog. Most dogs are loyal, loving, and protective. You see, dogs understand their role in the family, and for the most part, they do a good job of following the flow of the home (outside of the occasional garbage run). Dogs are constantly on the lookout, scoping the horizon, and alert for any threats. They are rarely aggressive to any members of the family, but they are ready to jump to the family's defense from outside intruders, no questions asked. The average family dog understands their job: to preserve their home, its owners, and its contents, to protect any and all family members from harm, and if necessary, be willing to use

---

88   *The New Oxford American Dictionary, Second Edition*, Erin McKean (editor), 2051 pages, May 2005, Oxford University Press, ISBN 0-19-517077-6.

89   Scripture taken from the Holy Bible, New International Version®. Copyright © 1973, 1978, 1984 by International Bible Society. Used by permission of Zondervan. All rights reserved.

force to defend the home from those who intend to bring harm. Dogs never question the order of things. They simply see their role as shepherds, to preserve, protect, and defend their beloved family. No, this is not an attempt to equate politicians to dogs or the moral equivalent. Rather, it is to demonstrate the loyalty and keen attention our leaders should pay to their most critical duties if we are to secure the blessings of liberty to ourselves and our posterity.

At the core of securing the blessings of liberty is to ensure the preservation of America, her heritage, and our constitution. In early colonial times, our flag *"Don't Tread on Me,"* captures the essence of ensuring the blessings of liberty. We must not attempt to reformat our beginnings, recreate our heritage, or rewrite the Constitution. In doing so, we place the security of our known prosperity and the blessings of future generations at risk. It is through the preservation of America, our heritage, and our constitution where we solidify the blessings of liberty. Our founders were men of absolutes and men of convictions. They believed in the absolute call of liberty. They believed in the absolute right of each man to those unalienable rights of life, liberty, and the pursuit of happiness. They believed in the absolute involvement of God, or else they would not have made four references to the Almighty in the Declaration of Independence. These were uncertain times, but these were not uncertain men. Preserve this document, America, like our forefathers who ordained and established this Constitution for the United States of America.

Do Ordain & Establish
This Constitution for the
United States of America

—————————— ⚜ ——————————

*"**We the People of the United States**, in Order to form a more perfect Union, establish Justice, insure domestic Tranquility, provide for the common defence, promote the general Welfare, and secure the Blessings of Liberty to ourselves and our Posterity, **do ordain and establish this Constitution for the United States of America."***

- The Constitution of the United States (September 17, 1787)

The call to America is about to conclude. Our nation began by placing the people into the position of authority over their government, a radical concept for the ages. We joined together as *the United State*s, brought together to form a more perfect union where our citizens are commanded to act with *love* toward their land. The governing state may never love her citizens, but must respect the will of the people. From there, America was called to establish justice by promoting a judicial system which upheld the will of the people, dispelled favoritism, and lived up to the calling of equality for all. With order well in tow, we found our quest for domestic tranquility neatly sandwiched between the call for justice and for a nation to provide for the common defense. As we have seen through the hindsight of history, America has shed more blood for others to be free. With internal and external columns of strength erected, America must promote the general welfare of her citizens by extending liberty and protecting the individual from a burgeoning state. At last, we arrive at the final call, to secure the blessings of liberty to ourselves and our posterity by nothing less than through the *preservation* of America, our heritage, and our Constitution.

Then the document was ordained, decreed from the hearts and souls of anyone who finds a home in the people either by birth or through immigration. The results are the same. America was given to a group of foreigners, in a foreign land, who were no longer aliens, but fellow citizens, joined together through all generations to become a temple in which liberty could dwell. To *ordain* means to confer holy orders, to order or decree officially.[90] The second verb following *ordain* is *establish*. To *establish* means to set up on a firm or permanent basis.[91] The word *constitution* finds its origins in Middle English, denoting a law or a body of laws or customs.[92] Therefore, taken to its logical conclusion, the Constitution is a permanent body of laws and customs conferred upon the people of the United States of America by the representatives who signed the document. Did you hear that, America? Our foundation to our nation was intended to be firm, permanent, and fixed. When America attempts to redefine the Constitution, it is like pulling the foundation out from under a skyscraper and expecting it to remain standing tall. Simply put, it can't. The building was designed to work with its foundation, and once removed every floor ever built will come crashing to the ground. Our foundation, America, is strong and paved the way for a nation who has mesmerized the globe. The more we mess with our firm footing, the higher the propensity for American demise in the world. Therefore, America must stand tall and strong against those forces who desire to remove the bedrock of our country. We are the greatest nation on the face of the planet, because we have the greatest foundation ever ordained—the Constitution!

As if a firm foundation was enough. Well, truthfully, for many nations this would be considered monumental, but our forefathers were overachievers who chose to compliment the Constitution with the Bill of Rights. Where the Constitution established the relationship of the people to their government, the Bill of Rights provided citizens of each generation an inheritance from the founders of this land. The inheritance was the realization of the ideals of life, liberty, and the pursuit of happiness.

---

90 *The New Oxford American Dictionary, Second Edition*, Erin McKean (editor), 2051 pages, May 2005, Oxford University Press, ISBN 0-19-517077-6.
91 Ibid.
92 Ibid.

Prayer

Lord,

We acknowledge the rights, the blessings, and the responsibilities that have been passed onto us simply by being citizens of the United States of America. Our forefathers, through Your sovereign hand, embraced the promise of faith and established a more perfect union so each of us would know the right to life, liberty, and the pursuit of happiness. It is through the promises handed down through the Constitution of the United States that hope is breathed into our nation and the world. May You motivate us to recognize the magnitude of this, change our hearts so we place our country above self, and give us the fortitude to unleash our rugged individualism so that collectively, America's reckoning with liberty may move forward. Lord, may You help us to preserve, protect, and defend America, our heritage, and our Constitution. May You, Lord, grant each of the citizens of this land a fresh insight into the majestic call you placed upon this land. Grant our supplication, we beseech Thee, through Jesus Christ our Lord, Amen.[93]

---

93   United States of America, Congressional Record, Proceedings and Debates of the 108th Congress First Session Volume 149-Part 3, Senate-Monday, February 24, 2003, Prayer by Chaplain Dr. Lloyd John Ogilvie who recognizes the day of George Washington's Farewell Address and says it is appropriate to recite the "Prayer for the United States of America as it is preserved in the chapel at Valley Forge," page 4198. The last sentence from the prayer has been quoted above.

Section IV—Our Inheritance
(The Bill of Rights)

ARTICLE V—THE BILL OF RIGHTS

—— ❦ ——

"Love is patient, love is kind. It does not envy, it does not boast, it is not proud. It is not rude, it is not self seeking, it is not easily angered, it keeps no records of wrongs. Love does not delight in evil but rejoices with the truth. It always protects, always trusts, always hopes, always perseveres. Love never fails ... And now these three remain: faith, hope, and love. But the greatest of these is love."

1 Corinthians 13:4–6, 8, 13[94]

The Bill of Rights[95] of the United States comprises the first ten amendments to the Constitution of the United States. The Bill of Rights ensures certain protections to American freedoms and lays the foundation for a young democracy. These rights were not just a set of rules, rituals, or laws. They defined the relationship that was established between America and her citizens. They were the expression of *love* found in the text of the Constitution, where the fruits of her blessings were birthed to the sons and daughters of liberty! This document, known as the Bill of Rights, enables America and the world to see the complete inheritance provided to each child who can legally claim status as a citizen of the United States of America. The breadth, depth, and width of these first ten rights were beyond the comprehension of the world back then, and to some extent they are beyond our comprehension today. There is a mystery tucked into the very fabric of these first ten rights, a mystery

---

94   Scripture taken from the Holy Bible, New International Version®. Copyright © 1973, 1978, 1984 by International Bible Society. Used by permission of Zondervan. All rights reserved.

95   See Appendix C – The Bill of Rights.

known as *love*, where without regard to self interest our founders placed into action a nation which would love her people in a uniquely different type of relationship than the world had ever known. America, go with me for just a few more thoughts on this one. Our founders, in the effort to form a more perfect union, created vows between a nation and her offspring. As a man who takes his wedding vows with the noblest of promises, "... in sickness and in health ... until death do us part." Those vows are sacred, and those vows for most were taken before God, family, and friends. The ring, we are told, is in the shape of a circle to symbolize permanency of the union of marriage in God's eyes. The ring provided to us, the sons and daughters of liberty, is nothing less than the Bill of Rights. They are the sacred vows made to you, to me, and to every generation of Americans. These vows were made before Almighty God, the citizens and their nation, and to all the world. They were intentionally and specifically made public and transparent, for a vow made with such visibility is much more difficult to break, and, if broken, much easier to recognize the culprit. So, America, our vow as the people is to care for this nation, but our nation's vow to us is provided here, never to be broken. When America breaks these vows, the union is trampled, and there will be consequences. On the other side of the table, when a citizen breaks their commitments, they too risk their inheritance.

The vows of our nation were made with the highest of ideals in mind. Our founders were inspired to create a nation that radically altered the relationship between the people and their government. This was a watershed moment in the world's history, and a moment unlike any before its time. Each year, on Christmas, we celebrate the birth of Jesus Christ, who did not come to the earth to be a king. He came to earth to serve, and serve He did. It was through His service and ultimate death on the cross where the veil between man and his god was torn away. For the rest of time, man had direct access to God's power, kingdom, and throne. The individual reckoned with God's just character, but also was invited into a relationship between the *Creator* and the *created*. Similarly, as the death of Jesus Christ redefined the relationship between man and God, the birth of America redefined the relationship between man and his government. America, these rights provide you your direct access to the power and the throne of America. There were no special access privileges to select citizens. All Americans were invited into a relationship between man and the state. The permanent change to this relationship and the profoundness of this moment were difficult to comprehend, for a child who comes from a wealthy family rarely sits back and understands the tremendous blessings that have been bestowed upon him. So, for the first ten rights, can we sit back, America, and begin to comprehend how rich we are? Can we appreciate the grace shed unto thee as we unpack the relationship between you, me, and our state?

Amendment I—Freedom of Religion, Speech, and Press

❧⦿❧

"Congress shall make no law respecting an establishment of religion, or prohibiting the free exercise thereof; or abridging the freedom of speech, or of the press; or the right of the people peaceably to assemble, and to petition the Government for a redress of grievances."

- The Bill of Rights (March 4, 1789)

Should it be considered ironic that the first vow made to this young nation and her people was none other than that of freedom of religion? We know from our Christian heritage that the Bible says: "But seek first his kingdom and his righteousness, and all these things will be given to you as well. Therefore do no worry about tomorrow, for tomorrow will worry about itself. Each day has enough trouble of its own," (Matthew 6:33). Perhaps those wise men of old knew the importance of placing the right of religion first, for we all know when we take care of God, the rest takes care of itself. This is a principle true throughout the Christian heritage, where God asks his people to bring the best of the first fruits to Him (Exodus 23:1).[96] Here you have a nation who decided to acknowledge the need for God so early in the morning of this text. Some suggest we were a nation based in neutrality, secularism, or benign ideals on things of faith. Contrary to their thoughts, what our founders so creatively did was restrict the state from mandating a faith, for our fathers knew a faith compelled by the state was really no faith at all. The tenet of

---

96   Scripture taken from the Holy Bible, New International Version®. Copyright © 1973, 1978, 1984 by International Bible Society. Used by permission of Zondervan. All rights reserved.

this belief resides in the Bill of Rights, but if I were a betting man, it really finds its roots in Scripture itself. For God, who created the heavens and the earth, made the Old Testament and the New, believed in a relationship between Himself and His creation, man. Recall Adam and Eve's tragedy in the garden. God provided them but one restriction, and blessed them with such an inheritance, including the right of choice. They were able to choose to rebel against God's own desire and bring sin into the world and fill themselves with shame. It would have been easy for God to force their obedience. After all, He designed their inmost being (Psalm 139:13), but God knew a compulsory relationship was really not a relationship at all. Our Creator risked the downside of their choices, but God was after something more profound—a relationship rooted in faith, hope, and love. Therefore, it isn't much of a jump to believe our founders held tight to this truth and attempted to instill into America the same foundation of this relationship. So, Americans can choose to pursue God or to run for the forbidden apple. Our God and our founders have made their choice to provide the avenue and access for a uniquely different way of relating. They instilled this by putting God first and providing us with the choice!

Our forefathers provided to us this choice, oftentimes referred to as *freedom of conscience*. The original intent of the first amendment was in no way a maneuver to deny the existence of religion or its influence upon America. Contrary to present-day cultural trends, the intent behind the first amendment was to ensure the influence of religion and morality remained vibrant. Religion and morality were considered essential to the functioning of the American democracy. Look at the words of the first and second presidents of the United States of America.

During President George Washington's Farewell Address, he spoke the following words regarding religion and morality:

> Of all the dispositions and habits which lead to political prosperity, religion and morality are indispensable supports. In vain would that man claim the tribute or patriotism, who should labor to subvert these great pillars of human happiness, these firmest props of duties of men and citizens. The mere politician, equally with the pious man, ought to respect and to cherish them. A volume could not trace all their connections with private and public felicity. Let it simply be asked, Where is the security for property, for reputation, for life if the sense of religious obligation desert the oaths which are the instruments of investigation in courts of justice? And let us with caution

indulge the supposition that morality can be maintained without religion. Whatever may be conceded to the influence of refined education on minds of peculiar structure, reason and experience both forbid us to expect that national morality can prevail in exclusion of religious principle.

Tis substantially true, that virtue or morality is a necessary spring of popular government. The rule, indeed, extends with more or less force to every species of free government.

On October 11, 1798, the second president of the United States, John Adams, declared the following in his address to the military:

We have no government armed with power capable of contending with human passions unbridled by morality and religion. Avarice, ambition, revenge, or gallantry, would break the strongest cords of our Constitution as a whale goes through a net. Our Constitution was made only for a moral and religious people. It is wholly inadequate to the government of any other.

On August 28, 1811, President John Adams wrote this:

Religion and virtue are the only foundations, not only of replublicanism and of all free government, but of social felicity under all governments and in all the combinations of human society.

There is much controversy in our nation over the separation of church and state and even more confusion. The First Amendment of the Constitution restricts the state from mandating a religion, but throughout our history our institutions, our traditions, and the words of our forefathers, it is clear religion and morality were viewed as essential and interwoven ingredients to the functioning of our nation. Even more recently, President Ronald Reagan was requested by a joint resolution of the Ninety-Seventh United States Congress to declare 1983 the "Year of the Bible." Resolution Public Law 97-280 states the following:

WHEREAS the Bible, the Word of God, has made a unique contribution in shaping the United States as a distinctive and blessed nation and people:

WHEREAS deeply held religious convictions springing from the Holy Scriptures led to the early settlement of our Nation;

WHEREAS Biblical teachings inspired concepts of civil government that are contained in our Declaration of Independence and Constitution of the United States;

WHEREAS many of our great national leaders—among them Presidents Washington, Jackson, Lincoln, and Wilson—paid tribute to the surpassing influence of the Bible in our country's development, as in the words of President Jackson that the Bible is "the Rock which our Republic rests";

WHEREAS the history of our Nation clearly illustrates the value of voluntarily applying the teachings of Scriptures in the lives of individuals, families, and societies;

WHEREAS this Nation now faces great challenges that will test the Nation as it has never been tested before; and

WHEREAS that renewing our knowledge of and faith in God through Holy Scripture can strengthen us as a nation and a people:

NOW, THEREFORE, be it

Resolved by the Senate and House of Representatives of the United States of America in Congress assembled, That the president is authorized and requested to designate 1983 as a national "Year of the Bible" in recognition of both the formative influence the Bible has been for our Nation, and our National need to study and apply the teachings of the Holy Scriptures.

Thomas P. O'Neill   Strom Thurmond
Speaker of the House   President of the Senate – Pro Tempore

Approved October 4, 1982
Ronald Reagan

It is historically and logically difficult to conclude that the intent of the First Amendment was a strict wall of separation between the church and state. It is more accurate to conclude our founders recognized the vital importance of religion (primarily Christianity) and intended for religion and morality to permeate our nation. This has been reaffirmed throughout America's history, recorded repeatedly into our national archives, and expressed with moral clarity by the joint resolution signed by Ronald Reagan in 1982.

Freedom of Speech

Was it by random chance or by design that freedom of religion was mentioned first? This put God on high, and then came the second part to this relationship, where the people found freedom in their voices and access to the state. For most of the world's history, both in matter of things of the government and matters of faith, man needed an intermediary between himself and the institutions. The king wielded such great power that no man or woman dared to speak freely, frankly, and clearly, or else they risked most certain punishment. Look at the story of Esther, who was created for such a time as this. She risked death when she appeared uninvited before the king to voice her opinion. Esther risked it all, and began to show us the need for this freedom, access, and choice (Esther).[97] This has been seen throughout the history of the world, from Herod to Hitler to Hussein. They hated dissent and discord of any kind. It threatened the relationship between the state and the people. Not in America. People were set free to speak against the government, for in our young democracy this was considered a source of strength. Freedom of speech occurred after great divide had been bridged. Now a citizen could appeal, gripe, and take up their cause toward the state. They didn't need to await the invitation of a king. They had freedom of access. As Christians, we often overlook the great gift we were given when we no longer needed a priest, a method, or a temple to talk to our God. Since the death of Jesus, we were able to speak to God directly. How warm, personal, and loving. This was achieved through something we have come to know as *prayer,* where God's children can speak to their *Creator* or just bask in His sunset. As with our Father in heaven, He desires to hear our voice and let us know He cares. There lies within the human experience a peace we experience when we know we have spoken and have truly been heard. Perhaps our founders knew the individual needed an avenue to speak and to be heard. This shouldn't be confused with worshipping of the state. Rather, this approach facilitated both the

---

97 Scripture taken from the Holy Bible, New International Version®. Copyright © 1973, 1978, 1984 by International Bible Society. Used by permission of Zondervan. All rights reserved.

people and their state with the ability to hear grievances before they grew too great, thus creating a condition where both parties felt represented and understood, the precursors to resolving any misgivings. At the root of this right lies the difference between tyranny and liberty. The first governs with fear while the other governs with care. Therefore, sons and daughters of liberty, please find your voice. You've been dormant for so many years. Demand to be heard and understood by your state. Place them on notices for the grievances on your heart!

Freedom of the Press

The third vow of our nation was to establish a relationship based in transparency, accountability, and truth, for the battle for a nation's heart begins with its head. A press controlled by the powers of the state sets up an environment of deception, secrecy, and sin. Those dictators throughout history always made their move to seize the flow of information with the goal of manipulating it. Freedom of the press is a guardian for sure, as it seeks to hold the state accountable. We are reminded by the Apostle Paul that the battle for our hearts occurs in our heads. Perhaps this is why Paul instructed us to "... *stand firm then, with the belt of truth buckled around our waist ..." (Ephesians 6:14).*[98] We are reminded of another characteristic of *love,* mainly "... *Love does not delight in evil, but rejoices with the truth" (1 Corinthians 13:6).*[99] Can you see it, America? Can you see how deeply cared for you are by those fathers of this nation's birth? They, like Paul, understood how subtle, how deceptive, and how crafty the character was of this enemy of the faith. The enemy of freedom, the tyrant, thrives to erect a stronghold of deception over the collective national mind. He too understands the battle for the mind. More profoundly, freedom of the press provides a mechanism where the sins and evil warts of the state can be brought forth in the light. The founders of this text knew from their conscience "... *if they confessed their sins, He is faithful and just and will forgive us our sins and purify us from all unrighteousness" (1 John 1:9).*[100] Right here in this text an avenue was afforded for America to confess her sins and to place her wrongs upon display, but not to be mocked or to tear her down. Rather, the idea was to transform the heart of the state

---

98   Scripture taken from the Holy Bible, New International Version®. Copyright © 1973, 1978, 1984 by International Bible Society. Used by permission of Zondervan. All rights reserved.
99   Ibid.
100 Ibid.

and restore the relationship with her people. This in turn allowed the citizens to receive the confessions of a haughty state, to determine and then decide if this wayward state should be granted forgiveness. Think for a moment when the weight of sin, performed in secret, goes unconfessed for a period of time. The longer the sin hides, the heavier it grows, the more it destroys, and the harder it is to hide. A sin confessed early and often tears down the tyrant's hold. Perhaps this is why we are told by God to "... *confess our sins to each other and pray for each other so that you may be healed" (James 5:16)*. It is in this vein that the responsibility of the press is to keep the state's account current with the people. An effective press, unencumbered by the state's hand, grounded in truth, has the ability to expose the wrongs, the mistakes, and the inevitable stains which occur when men seek power without the light. So, all of you media friends: stand up and stand for restoring the truth. We call our press to return to your lane, to shove off all attempts to be controlled or entangled, and bring those things done by the state in the cover of darkness right out into the light!

Freedom to Peaceably Assemble & Petition for Redress

Labeled as rebels, the band of colonists endured year after year during which their voices were not heard and they were denied the mechanisms to bring redresses to the state. Our founders knew from the way they fought the battle that alone they were weak, but united they had great strength. So right here, tucked at the end of this first amendment, we are granted the right to gather, to put legs to our speech, and to confront the state. We were told from our Christian heritage that "*If your brother sins against you, go and show him his fault (freedom of speech), just between the two of you. If he listens to you, you have won your brother over. But if he will not listen, take one or two others along, so that 'every matter may be established by the testimony of two or three witnesses. If he refuses to listen to them, tell it to the church; and if he refuses to listen even to the church, treat him as you would a pagan or a tax collector" (Matthew 18:15–17).*[101] We begin with the feeble voice of a single person's speech, then it grows from one to two, and before long, if the grievance is true and shared by others, we are instructed to go before the entire community and to never stop confronting our brother until he recognizes his fault. The process is slow and often times methodical, but

---

101 Scripture taken from the Holy Bible, New International Version®. Copyright © 1973, 1978, 1984 by International Bible Society. Used by permission of Zondervan. All rights reserved.

this gift given to us as a people of this land provides a path to open the eyes of the state. With each step of confrontation, the pressure grows until the tipping point is reached and the state decides to resolve the matter. Our founders knew a state left unchecked would run amuck, so with this tenet of faith and heritage, Americans everywhere must begin the process of assembling with the goal of change.

Amendment II—Right
to Bear Arms

❦❧❦

"A well-regulated Militia, being necessary to the security of a free State,
the right of the People to keep and bear Arms, shall not be infringed."

- *The Bill of Rights (March 4, 1789)*

The Second Amendment to the Constitution of the United States outlines two rights and identifies two enemies of liberty. The first right is the right to have a secure and free State, and to protect us from the threats abroad. The defenders of liberty must be prepared during the convenient and inconvenient moments of history to defeat her foes across the globe. The young revolutionaries in America could still smell the gunpowder from a long, hard fight with an enemy who desired to defeat the experiment in democracy. They knew the strength of the American military was essential to America's destiny. Throughout the throes of time and the vestiges of youth, the might of our military has brought freedom and security to the globe. It is incumbent upon our elect to simultaneously look across the sunset of history and the horizon of destiny to ensure our government, above all else, takes this most solemn duty to heart. Our founders understood a democracy is fragile, and the jealous desires of evil seek the complete annihilation of our freedom-loving society. We've seen it in wars of old and we see it in the wars of new. Whether in the redcoats of the English or the suicide bombers of today, the desire remains the same: to stop liberty and remove America as a force for good. To our elected officials, there is no greater responsibility than the right to a secure society. We witnessed what happened in Iraq when a young democracy attempted to take root, but lacked the firm rock of security. Remove those who support political whims to dismantle, defund, and diminish American military and intelligence organizations. It is our might that breeds such peace, prosperity, and human awakening. Ironically, undermining our security creates the conditions for conflict. Across the globe and here at home, there is an epic struggle between good and evil. When American might is dampened, the enemies of light creep in, and where darkness reigns, all sorts of evil will prosper. Restore to America and to her patriots the rewards of laying down one's life for the sake of your countrymen. To do anything less brings us to the enemy within.

What if we could sit around during the times of old, when the framers stood and studied the history of civilizations like Rome, where the enemy grew not from outside, but from within, where the republic was replaced by dictates of tyranny? Perhaps our founders intentionally put fear into the arsenal of the governed to give teeth to the words engraved into the Declaration of Independence, which instructs Americans:

> *"... that whenever any Form of Government becomes destructive of these ends, it is the Right of the People to alter or to abolish it, and to institute new Government ..."*[102]

It would appear the intention of the Second Amendment is congruent with our birth. The governed always have and always should maintain the right to bear arms, if nothing else, to snap back when the lustful government attempts to stretch beyond its bounds. Here, we see love's heart proclaimed to the citizens across this land. We are told by the Apostle Paul that love *".... always protects, always trusts, always hopes, always perseveres" (1 Corinthians 13:7).*[103] Our founders placed into this tapestry their plan to preserve individual liberty for each of the sons and daughters of liberty for every generation. They didn't leave us naked and unclothed, oh no, not our forefathers. They provided from heaven's edge America's right to protect.

Oh, America, you sleeping giant. Awaken, and lift the veil which has covered our eyes far too long. We are Americans. The right to bear arms is our duty, and to be derelict means we forsake our countrymen and restore the bondage of tyranny to our shores. Our dulled sense of responsibility has been categorized as outdated, outmoded, barbaric, and uncivilized.

---

102 See Appendix A - The Declaration of Independence.
103 Scripture taken from the Holy Bible, New International Version®. Copyright © 1973, 1978, 1984 by International Bible Society. Used by permission of Zondervan. All rights reserved.

Contend to the contrary, America, because liberty calls us to defend her honor, and defend it we must as we take up our right to bear arms and restore to our conscience the fullness of each right enumerated in the Constitution of the United States. Many will use the argument that the Second Amendment is out of date. It was most useful during a time when America lacked an organized military and police force. Others will say we need to restrict this right by citing the examples of violence on university campuses, military bases, and communities across our nation. At their root, both arguments attempt to substitute the power of the government for the rights of the people, and attempt to place government into a role reserved for God. The reflex to thrust government into the role of solving America's ailments with violence is a fleeting attempt to treat the symptom of the matter. Those who attempt to legislate morality and ethics from Washington soon learn government is fallible, and in time causes its own demise. This isn't to say our lawmakers should not establish laws governing America, but laws cannot change the condition of man's heart. What is wrong and missing with this triumphant land is not greater gun control or greater denunciation of those whose hold dear to this right. Rather, it is the cracking of the American moral fabric found in our Creator. The signs of violence and the desperation of those who make mass casualties their voice will never be stopped by better laws or stricter enforcement. Rather, the hearts of rage must come to find the calm from the storm in a society that embraces the solace of Christianity. There is something awry when our young become so full of rage and see no hope in sight. The elders of this land must reach across generational lines with deep convictions and hearts of compassion to build a bridge from the hearts of the youth to the heritage of old. The entirety of our democracy and the full expression of our freedom work in conjunction with the invisible hand of faith, which governs the affairs of men without the intrusion of bureaucrats.

Stand strong, America, and receive your right to bear arms with fervency, as if your next breath depends upon it. The spirit of our framers was not concerned for the momentary lapses of a few violent episodes. Rather, the framers were more fearful of a government that knew no boundaries. The path of tyranny begins with subtlety, but its branches grow until tyranny has complete control of the governed. When this moment occurs, the governed no longer fear a few episodes of violence when staring down the establishment of tyranny, the dominance of the state, and the corruption of power. The world has known the dark horse of tyranny where men come in the night to steal from, destroy, and kill the innocent. Look across the sunsets of history into the eyes of Hitler, Hussein, Chavez, and Stalin for the shadows these men cast across this globe cost the lives of millions. There is something more noble, much more grand, at stake in the second amendment. We seem to enjoy the scratching of the surface for the hope of political gain. America, we may be young in years, but the rights of liberty are deeply ingrained! Exercise your rights and discharge the duties of a citizen of the United States of America by upholding the Second Amendment.

Amendment III—Property Rights

―――――――――― ✑ ――――――――――

"No soldier shall, in time of peace be quartered in any house, without the consent of the Owner, nor in time of war, but in a manner to be prescribed by law."

- The Bill of Rights (March 4, 1789)

Look at amendment three, which places the rights of home ownership right smack into the hands of the people and not into the hands of the state, to the point where soldiers have to ask the permission of the owner to be quartered in someone's home. What a unique concept. The state and the military could not unilaterally confiscate someone's home without the express permission of the homeowner. It does, however, if prescribed by law, provide a method for soldiers to quarter in someone's home without the landowners permission. How does a democracy create laws? By its legislature. How is a legislature created as prescribed under Article I of the Constitution of the United States? By the will of the people through an elections process. So in essence, the people hold the power, whether through their own decisions or expressly through the representative system created in the Constitution. The military has to ask permission of little old me to stay in the spare bedroom. That's America, where the little guy has as much strength as the big guy. Never before had the world witnessed a system of equality designed to protect the rights of the individual over the rights of the state. Again, this principle of individual ownership finds its roots in none other than Scripture itself. God informs us love *"... is not rude ..." (1 Corinthians 13:5)*[104] and further demonstrated when John records *"Here I am! I stand at the door and knock. If anyone hears my voice and opens the door, I will come in and eat with him, and he with me" (Revelation 3:20).*[105] You see, the God of our Christian heritage never forced His will upon us or thrust Himself in. He is held by the boundaries of His Word, a God who desires a relationship based in love and respect, not fear and control. Look at the communist Soviet Union, who with fear on their side, owned all property and essentially could evict anyone at anytime for any reason. Look at other dictatorships of the world, where the government maintains the primary right to property. It eventually leads to corruption and abuse. This is yet another check brilliantly placed into our foundational blocks to protect America from tyrannical rule. Therefore, America, stand up for home ownership. Stand up for your right to property, and stand up to the attempts to evade this right.

---

104 Scripture taken from the Holy Bible, New International Version®. Copyright © 1973, 1978, 1984 by International Bible Society. Used by permission of Zondervan. All rights reserved.

105 Ibid.

AMENDMENT IV—
SEARCHES & SEIZURES

⟡

"The right of the people to be secure in their persons, houses, papers, and effects, against unreasonable searches and seizures, shall not be violated, and no Warrants shall issue, but upon probable cause, supported by Oath or affirmation, and particularly describing the place to be searched, and the persons or things to be seized."

- *The Bill of Rights (March 4, 1789)*

Amendment IV is brilliant. It expressively defines the proper role of the executive branch (Article II) and the judicial branch (Article III). The executive branch, those responsible for enforcing the laws, must demonstrate to the judicial branch, those responsible for interpreting the law, that they possess probable cause to violate a person's rights. The executive branch cannot just go off and do as it chooses against the citizenry without seeking the permission of the judicial branch. This is nothing short of pure brilliance. The executive branch has to meet the standard of the law, probable cause, or else it is powerless to do anything. Here we can see the hand of our protective father as another strand to our relationship was put into place. We are told love *"... is not self-seeking ... always protects, always trusts, always hopes, always perseveres" (1 Corinthians 13:5, 7).*[106] The source of tyranny was restrained so the state itself could not seek its will without due cause. Our founders knew this uniquely different relationship was based on restraint, where the security of the people was guarded from

---

106 Scripture taken from the Holy Bible, New International Version®. Copyright © 1973, 1978, 1984 by International Bible Society. Used by permission of Zondervan. All rights reserved.

the state. This right given to the people illuminates the characteristic to *always trust,* not in the government itself, but in the rights of the free. The invisible hand of our forefathers placed in this right for all to witness. We see how our government finds the source of authority directly in the people of this great land, not in the state or the judiciary. Protect the people with the laws the people created by ensuring the government is meeting the standard, *probable cause,* established by the people, to ensure our society operates the way the people will for America to operate. The wisdom placed into this right lays the foundation where trust and security may be built.

AMENDMENT V—DUE PROCESS

—————————— ◈ ——————————

"No person shall be held to answer for any capital, or otherwise infamous crime, unless on a presentment or indictment of a Grand Jury, except in cases arising in the land or naval forces, or in the Militia, when in actual service in time of War or public danger; nor shall any person be subject for the same offence twice put in jeopardy of life or limb; nor shall be compelled in any criminal case to be a witness against himself, nor be deprived of life, liberty, or property, without due process of law; nor shall private property be taken for public use, without just compensation."

- The Bill of Rights (March 4, 1789)

mong the right to a grand jury is the protection against double jeopardy, the right to withhold from self-incrimination, and the right to due process of law. The lengths which were afforded to every citizen who commits a criminal act in the United States of America are amazing. In some ways, after reading this amendment, it almost seems unfair to the government for the hurdle it must meet to charge and successfully prosecute a person for a crime. How many nations in the history of civilization put such extraordinary rights into the hands of the citizen? Clearly, the wisdom of the ages was crafted into amendment number five. As Americans, we should stand proud to be a part of a nation who affords its citizenry such fair and transparent interaction with the criminal justice system. It isn't much of a stretch to say the protection was clearly on the side of the citizen, and the fear was most definitely the abuse of governmental power and the judicial system.

Even more amazing than the abundance of rights afforded to the accused was a timeless gem of an exception to those rights, written some two hundred plus years ago, which applies during times of war or intense public danger. Wow! Did we read this correctly? You heard it, and you have read it straight from the horse's mouth. I quote *"... except in cases arising in the land or naval forces, or in the Militia, when in actual service in time of War or public danger."* This exception clause to the Fifth Amendment leads to two critical points concerning the Constitution of the United States of America. First, the principles and the rights written into the Constitution are enduring, relevant, and have stood the test of time. It is not our place to play doctor with the Constitution as if the authors lacked wisdom or foresight. The document wasn't created overnight. It was forged through centuries which culminated with its creation and the birth of a young nation. The masterminds behind the document understood the lessons of history and benefited from the suffrage of tyranny. You see, the greatest creations of history arrive on the heels of the most intense periods of trials and tribulation. It is just the way it works. Take the death of Jesus Christ, who some two thousand years ago was persecuted and crucified for his countercultural belief system. His death on a cross was horrid then and horrid now, but the conclusion of his death brought the birth of Christianity and literally separated our calendars from BC (Before Christ) to AD (After Christ), all on the shoulders of this one man who hung on a Roman cross, forever altering the course of history and the course of the world. In a more modern day example, look at the second Gulf War and the establishment of an Iraqi democracy. For the better part of the last decade, American and Iraqi blood and treasure were put to the test as we removed a heinous dictator and provided the Iraqi people with the opportunity for freedom and democracy. I recall during the early years of the war both Americans and the Iraqis were taking casualties. It seemed as though failure and more bloodshed were the only constants, and the ability to establish a democracy was slipping out of our hands. With much pain, death, and sacrifice (not to mention a new strategy) the tide began to turn in Iraq and hope arrived on the scene. In late 2009, Americans were beginning to believe Iraq was a success. The point is, it took the mutual sacrifice of both our nations to produce what appears to be the beginning of democracy in the gut of the Middle East. The point of all of this is the Constitution was forged out of suffering. It was the results of years of birth pains, the gift of sacrifice provided to all the world, and for mere men of our time to take the document lightly is historically inaccurate and flagrantly dangerous. It is enduring and should be handled as such.

Amazing how the Constitution is as relevant today as it was at its inception. This exception clause to the Fifth Amendment during times of war demonstrates the wisdom of the architects, and settles a central issue of our generation. Can terrorists who have declared war on the United States of America be interrogated by intelligence officials, or should they be afforded rights under the Constitution? It says in times of war and public danger the rights of the Constitution of the United States do not apply. It is as clear as day in the Fifth Amendment. What is amazing is that something so clear can create such widespread debate and dissension. There is no greater responsibility afforded to the United States government under the Constitution than the security of the citizenry. They recognized that without security, a democracy will not stand. It would seem the terrorists understand this strategic vulnerability toward America's existence and ultimate prosperity. On September 11, 2001, the terrorists didn't just attack New York City, and the seat of our government. They struck a direct blow to the security of this nation. Recall the feeling when we all thought our nation was under siege. Something deep within us was shaken. This is exactly what our founders and the writers of the Fifth Amendment understood. Remember, this document was developed with the memories of war close at hand. Most of the men who partook in writing the Constitution understood the harsh realities of war, when thousands of lives were at stake and time was crucial to battlefield decisions. Could you imagine being George Washington, having to wait for months or perhaps years for battlefield intelligence after a prosecutor was selected, a defense attorney assigned, motions filed, a venue selected, and a jury determined? Prompt and timely intelligence was central then as it is now, and consistent with the Constitution of the United States.

AMENDMENT VI—RIGHT TO GRAND JURY

⌘

"In all criminal prosecutions, the accused shall enjoy the right to a speedy and public trial, by an impartial jury of the State and district where in the crime shall have been committed, which district shall have been previously ascertained by law, and to be informed of the nature and cause of the accusation; to be confronted with the witness against him; to have compulsory process for obtaining witnesses in his favor, and to have the Assistance of Counsel for his defense."

- The Bill of Rights (March 4, 1789)

The Sixth Amendment affords the people such transparency and impartiality to ensure a fair and just outcome to any judicial preceding. The spirit of this amendment is to ensure justice is performed in the open, with independent representation, and in a timely manner. It protects citizens from allowing the state to abuse its rights and privileges, and to minimize the amount of time a person's rights are infringed upon. This amendment yet again reiterates the imperative nature the authors placed upon preserving the right to life, liberty, and the pursuit of happiness. They provided the state a method to ensure justice and tranquility, but removed, impartiality and the prolonged removal of a citizen's liberty. You might know from watching television or a brief study of law that the burden is upon the state to prove guilt, not the defense to prove innocence (you are innocent until proven guilty). Therefore, the state must have compelling evidence for the removal of a person's freedoms. For law enforcement, an intensive effort is exerted to protect the rights of the individual, to adhere to the rules governing the handling of evidence, and to follow the maze of judicial rules involved in any prosecution. America is different in that we desire impartial justice to ensure the government and its citizenry maintain the sacred bond of trust between the people and the state, which is so critical to the functioning of a free and open democracy. The founders recognized secrecy and anything done behind closed doors would lead to corruption and abuse. Openness and transparency provided a sense of accountability between the governmental power and the rights of the citizens. As previously mentioned under the discussion on the First Amendment, this is immensely consistent with our Christian heritage where we are told "... *If your brother sins against you, go and show him his fault (freedom of speech), just between the two of you. If he listens to you, you have won your brother over. But if he will not listen, take one or two others along, so that 'every matter may be established by the testimony of two or three witnesses. If he refuses to listen to them, tell it to the church; and if he refuses to listen even to the church, treat him as you would a pagan or a tax collector" (Matthew 18:15–17).*[107] Brilliant, as the arm of those protective fathers further place security and trust at the base of America by making our peers our jury!

---

107 Scripture taken from the Holy Bible, New International Version®. Copyright © 1973, 1978, 1984 by International Bible Society. Used by permission of Zondervan. All rights reserved.

Amendment VII—Right to Trial by Jury

"In suits at common law, where the value in controversy shall exceed twenty dollars, the right of trial by jury shall be preserved, and no fact tried by a jury, shall be otherwise re-examined in any court of the United States, than according to the rules of the common law."

- *The Bill of Rights (March 4, 1789)*

Trial by jury, or a trial by peers, focuses our attention upon the right of the people to be tried by the people. Not surprisingly, our founders placed great trust and respect in the integrity of the people and their ability to effect justice. It is clear they never intended for justice to be conducted at the hands of one man or one woman, and placed little to no value on intellect versus a trial by peers. Perhaps our founders recognized that when we are tried by our peers, our peers will have the most exacting perspective. They must have recognized the need to keep the power out of the state and in the hands of the people. The justices become mere referees, ensuring the rules of law and court are maintained. In the end, the ultimate power resides with the people, the jury. It's amazing how twelve jurors with varying experiences can be trusted to bring the right judgment to bear over a single authority. Again, the Constitution consistently places the power into the hands of the people, another check and balance upon the federal government. Our founders placed emphasis on how ordinary, commonsense Americans can do the right thing. This is one of my frustrations with today's political climate and over-emphasized educational culture. We have developed into a nation that values education and intellect over common sense. This isn't to say education isn't valuable or should be avoided, but there is another kind of smarts and it is called the smarts of real life. Some of you reading this never received a college education or a master's degree from an Ivy League school. I'm here to tell you that your forefathers, of which many were educated men themselves, saw straight through the prism of the educated echelon to place emphasis on the decision making ability of commonsense Americans. So, America, level of education aside, you have a vital role to play in the functioning of this nation. Spend no time looking at your degrees, diplomas, or your financial status. If you can be considered part of the people, then you have been admitted into the elite status of a commonsense American, and should take great pride and ownership in this responsibility. I compel each American to throw off the cultural barriers that say you aren't smart enough, rich enough, or good enough. You are an American, and for that you bring ample wealth to the table to participate in our democracy. After all, it is your democracy too. Not to digress too far, but in amendments IV, V, VI, and VII the concept of innocent until proven guilty is heavily present. Even deeper than the presumption of innocence is the foundation of love, which "... *always hopes* ..." *(1 Corinthians 13:7),*[108] where a nation would rather see her people free and full of rights than have liberty removed. We are a land which hopes for the best and clings to optimism, and perhaps, this fabric of America finds inspiration in the tapestry of this scripture. Rise up, nation of peers, and make your voice count!

---

108 Scripture taken from the Holy Bible, New International Version®. Copyright © 1973, 1978, 1984 by International Bible Society. Used by permission of Zondervan. All rights reserved.

Amendment VIII—
Excessive Bail nor Cruel
and Unusual Punishment

⊶⊙⊙⊷

*"Excessive bail shall not be required, nor excessive fines
imposed, nor cruel and unusual punishments inflicted."*
- The Bill of Rights (March 4, 1789)

The Eighth Amendment says excessive bail shall not be required, nor excessive fines imposed, nor cruel and unusual punishment inflicted. In layman's terms, the punishment should be fitting to the crime. The more heinous the act, the more excessive the bail, fines, and punishment. Our Christian heritage instructs us *"... to take life for life, eye for eye, tooth for tooth, hand for hand, foot for foot, burn for burn, wound for wound, bruise for bruise" (Exodus 21:24).*[109] This principle was handed down by Moses to the Israelites right on the heels of the Ten Commandments. As a newly free nation, Israel was establishing the bedrock of its society. From within the origins of this new free nation, we find one of God's great characteristics, for *"...He is the Rock, his works are perfect, and all his ways are just. A faithful God who does not wrong, upright and just is He" (Deuteronomy 32:4).*[110] Just, or justice, as we have learned, is impartial, equal, or considered fair. This principle upon which God built the nation of Israel, a righteous foundation, is the same building block our forefathers instilled into the very core of America. America, we are fair and our cause

---

109 Scripture taken from the Holy Bible, New International Version®. Copyright © 1973, 1978, 1984 by International Bible Society. Used by permission of Zondervan. All rights reserved.

110 Ibid.

is just. Don't lose faith, you patriots out there, for at the core of this nation we will find hope. Not hope within ourselves, but the hope which has been handed down through the ages. You guessed it, this first originated with God, and then our forefathers had the inspiration to grab hold of God's great character so the world would know that America is just. Our responsibility—more acutely, our duty—is to receive the inheritance by unwrapping this gift, accepting our origins, and living up to the demands of its high calling.

Amendment IX—Rights Reserved to the People

⠀⠀⠀⠀⠀⠀⠀⠀⠀⠀⠀⠀⠀⠀⠀⠀⠀⠀⠀⠀⠀⠀⠀⠀—⠀ᥫᩣ⠀—

"The enumeration of the Constitution, of certain rights, shall not be construed to deny or disparage others retained by the people."
- The Bill of Rights (March 4, 1789)

If in doubt, the rights belong to the people, not to the government. It is unique how consistent this principle is with the major themes of the Declaration of Independence. In the rest of the Constitution of the United States, the rights begin with the people, and only those rights given by the people to the government, as outlined in the Constitution, remain with the government. Anything else belongs to the people. Sounds almost like a loan, and the banker isn't the government, it is the people. Awesome stuff if you ask me. The people can call the loan due at their will, not the will of the government. This is an irrevocable aspect to our American inheritance. The American heart bleeds for the people, not for the government. It is the essence of our heritage, and to change this aspect of our heritage is to deny ourselves the dream of liberty. This was the last will and testament of our forefathers to every generation of Americans. They memorialized their will so the whims of history could not revoke the wishes of their hearts. When someone leaves us an inheritance and records it into their will, once that person has left this life for the next, there isn't anything anyone can do to change what is written in their will. It is through their last will and testament where their wishes are fulfilled. This is like the great blessing that was bestowed upon the eldest son when the patriarch was about to pass away. This blessing we witnessed was administered by Isaac, which was meant for Esau, but through trickery it was given to Jacob. When Isaac began to realize what had occurred, Esau asked if Isaac could provide him a second blessing. Unfortunately for Esau, once the blessing was given, it could not be revoked. America, no matter what they say, no matter what they do, these rights are the blessing handed down from the fathers of this land. When these rights were ratified, our inheritance was secured.

Amendment X—Rights Reserved to the States

⌒⌒⌒

"The powers delegated to the United States by the Constitution, nor prohibited by it to the States, are reserved to the States respectively, or to the people."

- The Bill of Rights (March 4, 1789)

If right or power is not enumerated in the Constitution, then it is reserved for either the States or the people. This Tenth Amendment doesn't sound like it envisioned a large central government with control over virtually every aspect of American life. Rather, this right seems to operate out of the principle of decentralized power. Today's political theatre has created the stage for a large bloated central government attempting to control and regulate virtually every area of American life. We need look no further than the 2010 passage of universal healthcare reform, which in its entirety dismantles a large segment of the private sector, establishes the federal government as the decider and provider of medical care, and will most certainly lead to massive cost overruns and the debilitation of a generation that substitutes government for God. This is dangerous and dangerously crosses the line of our Tenth Amendment. When put in context, our nation was birthed out of the tyranny of the king of England. The king of England had sole power, authority, and control over English life. Sound familiar, America? Does something not sit well in your soul as the size, scope, and span of government dramatically increases? Does something inside feel like it is about to die and give cause for concern? The free America birthed on the heels of tyrannical England must heed the warnings of history, herald the call of liberty, and root out all those who desire to deny the rights granted to us in the ultimate guardian of liberty, the Constitution of the United States. Next to the Civil War, I could never recall a time of such great division in our union, where the states felt the need to bond together in defense of the decrees of the federal government itself. Unlike the days of the Civil War, whose cause was just and the sanctity of the union was best kept by heeding the call of freedom, it would appear the civil war of today will be drawn when states must unite to combat the forces of tyranny growing from the seat where Lincoln defeated it. History possesses both humor, humility, and such irony it would seem our nation must remain on bended knee, for the wisdom of our rights operate by lowering the proud to the hearts of the humble. This is why our democracy transformed the world. Our nation operated from humility, where tyranny operates from pride. The federal government is now on notice. It has begun to tread beyond the bounds of this amendment, and when a government treads beyond the limits of the Constitution, the still small voice of freedom heralds the defenders to her call. You watch, George Washington, while the lovers of freedom leave the comforts of life, the security of their jobs, and the tenderness of their families to combat the decreed forces of tyranny. Our cause is just, our calling is without doubt, and the time is now, for tyranny has gained traction. As history cycles through, we must take up the yoke of our heritage and revolt we must!

The Bill of Rights represents the first ten amendments of the Constitution of the United States. Even a novice reading of the amendments speaks volumes of what was near and dear to the authors. Every right regards the protection of the individual from the central government, from freedom of speech, press, and religion to the right to bear arms, property ownership, the right to due process and a speedy trial. Our founders understood the dangers of an all too powerful state. Throughout the document, the benefit of power is consistently placed into the hands of the people, not into the hands of a conglomerate of bureaucrats. These protections are essential checks and balances to maintaining a fully functional democracy. They place firm limits on the powers enumerated to the government and the rights protected by the people. There was purpose and passion behind each. The events, the persons, and the hand of reckoning which orchestrated the circumstances to produce the Bill of Rights understood the pitfalls of governmental power. We are instructed all too well from the lessons of history that when power is centralized, corruption and evil reign. Look at the governments of Stalin, Hitler, Hussein, Castro, and Ahmadinejad. These are just a few governments whose terrors have their origins in tightly controlled societies where freedom is drowned. Our founders went to great lengths to protect the rights of rugged individualism, and we should go to great lengths to honor their efforts and preserve them for generations to come. America, stand tall. Stand proud, and arise, you sleeping soldiers, for your rights and your liberties were won with great peril during that moment in history when liberty was declared!

The Promise

~⚬⚬⚬~

"Just as no one can set aside or add to a human covenant that has been duly established, so it is in this case. The promises spoken to Abraham and to his seed. The Scripture does not say "and to seeds," meaning many people, but "and to your seed," meaning one person, who is Christ. What I mean by this: The law, introduced 430 years later, does not set aside the covenant previously established by God and thus do away with the promise. For if the inheritance depends on the law, then it no longer depends on a promise; but God in his grace gave it to Abraham through a promise."

Galatians 3:15–18[111]

America, lay hold of your inheritance passed down through the ages. These promises were created from our forefathers and renewed with each American. The times have changed, and two centuries have clicked by, but the promises handed down to each American still stand. We are Americans, and with that title comes the entirety of those blessings. Our culture may shift, the political winds may change, but the anchors found in these rights are unchangeable. When a person unites their life in the family of Jesus Christ, they connect their life unto the entire heritage of God whom we have come to know and love in the Holy Bible. We are told from Scripture *"... remember your leaders, who spoke the word of God to you. Consider the outcome of their way of life and*

---

111 Scripture taken from the Holy Bible, New International Version®. Copyright © 1973, 1978, 1984 by International Bible Society. Used by permission of Zondervan. All rights reserved.

imitate their faith. Jesus Christ is the same yesterday and today and forever" (*Hebrews 13:8*).[112] If God is the same, unchanging, and He is a just God, then it would stand to reason His promises of all times are still in effect over every Christian's life of all times, or God isn't God. The blessing is the same blessing the Lord cast upon Abraham when He told Abraham *"… I will make you into a great nation and I will bless you; I will make your name great, and you will be a blessing. I will bless those who bless you, and whoever curses you I will curse; and all the peoples of the earth will be blessed through you" (Genesis 12:2–3.)*[113] With the perspective of several thousand years of history, from the moment of that promise we now know the promise made to Abraham stood true. America, can't you see? Can you hear? These rights passed down from our leaders of old are the permanent hand of those great men who gave us America. For the first two hundred years of our history, the name *the United States of America* has been made great. We have blessed many, and many of us have been blessed. This isn't a coincidence. It was the result of the promise handed to us through the Constitution and the Bill of Rights. Accept your blessings, receive your inheritance, and trust the promises contained in these ten amendments. There are times when even great Abraham needed to be reminded of God's great promise. There were moments when he lost faith in God and turned to himself, only to rediscover God is faithful and is to be trusted. Ultimately, Abraham received the beginning of his promise, a son named Isaac. America, we are part of our forefathers' promise. We are the sons and daughters of liberty. Lay hold of your promise by allowing your hearts to be reconnected with the first ten amendments of the Bill of Rights.

Thus far, we have traveled through the muck of our culture, traversed through the heart of this nation, known as the Constitution, where with love our forefathers outlined a nation that would have a uniquely different relationship with its people. A relationship based in faith, hope, and love. Then, we discovered the greatest of these gifts, where love found its expression in the Bill of Rights, where Americans of all generations receive their promised inheritance of old. We traveled, we've stopped, we have even taken a few detours along the way, but may I present to you the greatest document this nation gave to us. The document where *liberty* was declared.

---

112 Ibid.
113 Ibid.

Prayer

Lord,

Thank you for leading us by the hand through the Constitution and the Bill of Rights. We are a proud nation with a deeply rich heritage for sure. We thank you for the inheritance you have given to each American of all times. We ask You, the great I Am, to stir into the collective conscience of each American the burning desire to reconnect with the founding faith and these documents, where Providence birthed America into existence. Now Lord, we ask You to open the eyes to our hearts, as we take the last leg of journey, unearthing and rediscovering the strands of truth placed into the core of America, known as the Declaration of Independence. Grant our supplication, we beseech Thee, through Jesus Christ our Lord, Amen.[114]

---

114 United States of America, Congressional Record, Proceedings and Debates of the 108th Congress First Session Volume 149-Part 3, Senate-Monday, February 24, 2003, Prayer by Chaplain Dr. Lloyd John Ogilvie who recognizes the day as George Washington's Farewell Address and says it is appropriate to recite the "Prayer for the United States of America as it is preserved in the chapel at Valley Forge," page 4198. The last sentence from the prayer has been quoted above.

Section V—Liberty Declared
(The Declaration of Independence)

THOSE ARE FIGHTIN' WORDS

—————————— ⚬◦◉◦⚬ ——————————

""I have sworn upon the altar of god, eternal hostility against every form of tyranny over the mind of man."
Thomas Jefferson[115]

"Is life so dear, or peace so sweet, as to be purchased at the price of chains and slavery? Forbid it, Almighty God! I know not what course others may take; but as for me, give me liberty or give me death!"
Patrick Henry (March 23, 1775)[116]

Our nation, America the Beautiful, was birthed through the years of struggle with the tyrannical rule of the king of England, culminating in the Revolutionary War of 1776. You may recall from elementary school the heroic stories of the men of those times who gave up wealth, status, and power for the hope of a free nation. At the Virginia constitutional convention, Patrick Henry famously said, "Give me liberty, or give me death!" Those famous words still ring true. In America today, this kind of passion would be considered extreme, or maybe a fringe element of society that needs to be controlled. Consider Paul Revere's

---

115 Jefferson discussing the fight over the establishment of one form of Christianity in the U.S. to Dr. Benjamin Rush, September 23, 1800. Peterson, Merrill, ed. *Jefferson: Writings*. New York: Literary Classics of the U.S.: Distributed to the trade in the U.S. and Canada by the Viking Press, c1984, p. 1082.

116 This speech was given at Saint John's Church in Richmond, Virginia on March 23, 1775 to the Virginia House of Burgesses. It first appeared in print in 1817 in Life and Character of Patrick Henry by William Wirt.

famous ride, which is best captured by Henry Wadsworth Longfellow's poem "Paul Revere's Ride"[117]:

> *Listen, my children, and you shall hear*
> *Of the midnight ride of Paul Revere,*
> *On the eighteenth of April, in Seventy-Five:*
> *Hardly a man is now alive*
> *Who remembers that famous day and year!*

Hardly a man is now alive who remembers that famous day and year. How true are those words. What would motivate men like Patrick Henry, Paul Revere, George Washington, Thomas Jefferson, and the like to give up the comforts of English life, to risk life and limb, for the possibility of a nation promoting liberty for all? Will the Reveres and Henrys of the twenty-first century rise to the occasion, or will comfort, civility, political correctness, and passivity contain man's yearning for freedom?

You see, some have tried to imitate freedom, others have attempted to dominate man's inner yearnings, and even more ambitious are those who have tried to redefine the meaning of liberty. The cause of liberty is the heart and soul of this land, and for those of us who find ourselves at the crossroads of life, we need look no further than the heartbeat of freedom. Those young revolutionaries arrived at their moment with destiny. Their moment was gripped with fear, but they chose courage, the courage to attach their lives to something more grand, a purpose more worthy than life itself. The shot heard around the world ignited the hearts of young Americans. It compelled them to bloody warfare. One could hardly imagine our lawns, neighborhoods, and churches being the frontlines of the nation's first war. What cause could motivate men to witness the ravages of war, yet remain steadfast in their convictions and sure of their spirit? What would motivate the colonies to face the barrels of the most powerful military on the globe? It is incomprehensible to the mind of man, because the call of freedom possesses a divinity that captivates our attentions and grabs our hearts. Look, America. Look now at the document that began it all, the Declaration of Independence.

---

117 A Maine Historical Society website which describes Henry Wadsworth Longfellow's poem, the historical context, and provides sourcing information. http://www.hwlongfellow.org/works_paul_reveres_ride.shtml

WHEN IN THE COURSE
OF HUMAN EVENTS

⟨⟨◦⟩⟩

*"**When in the Course of human events,** it becomes necessary for one
people to dissolve the political bands which have connected them with
another, and to assume among the powers of the earth, the separate
and equal station to which the Laws of Nature and of Nature's God
entitle them, a decent respect to the opinions of mankind requires that
they should declare the causes which impel them to the separation."*

- The Declaration of Independence (July 4, 1776)

The Declaration of Independence[118], the so-called bible of liberty,
created the dividing line between friend and foe. The majestic words
so eloquently woven in this document thrust this young nation into
a reckoning with liberty. As the toll of our plight began to mount up, the
Declaration of Independence became our guiding light. The words of this
fine manuscript breathed life into the hearts of men who found themselves
motivated and captivated by their moment in history. Oh, the innocence of
youth, where we receive life with such purity of conviction. It was by faith
those signatures were certain of what they did not see (Hebrews 11:1).[119] It was
by faith young America refused to bow as sons of England, and it was by faith
the words of independence brought life to liberty. As the dusk of youth fades,
we need look no further to discover the freshness of our identity than the text
of the Declaration of Independence. The document bonds us with generations
of old and generations of new, continuing in the epic cause of liberty. In this

---

118 See Appendix A – The Declaration of Independence.
119 Scripture taken from the Holy Bible, New International Version®. Copyright © 1973, 1978,
    1984 by International Bible Society. Used by permission of Zondervan. All rights reserved.

text were the words that took this nation from a formless and empty void, covered by the darkness of tyranny, and created the greatness known as the United States of America. In the dawn of the twenty-first century, it would seem America is torn and grows restless. We have known the pleasures of wealth and the power of influence, yet our hearts know something is missing. You see, we were birthed with the high call of freedom. It was our life's work during 1776, and remains entrusted to America until each of our seasons are complete. Nothing has changed in the document of our birth or the nobility of our calling except the drifting of our hearts. To live for the pleasures of this earth is wholly unsatisfactory. Many were born in America. Others chose to call this their home. Your arrival aside, we must accept the banner of freedom and make it our own. So pause, America. Take note of the lessons of old, and follow the voice of liberty, for it is sure to lead your heart back home. Come, America. Come now. Here are the words which brought such life and ignited such passion:

> *When in the Course of human events, it becomes necessary for one people to dissolve the political bands which have connected them with another, and to assume among the powers of the earth, the separate and equal station to which the Laws of Nature and of Nature's God entitle them, a decent respect to the opinions of mankind requires that they should declare the causes which impel them to the separation.[120]*

America was birthed, the lines were drawn, conflict was over the horizon, and no longer was America able to go back to the colonial comforts. It was now or never to stand up. *"When in the course of human events ..."* conveys an image of something more grand than the men and women themselves. Perhaps the writers believed the collision of history with destiny was upon them, and with the surety of their faith in this cause, decided to sever the political bands that connected them to England. You see, this wasn't just severing ties with a known enemy. It was man against father, daughter against mother (Luke 12:53).[121] It was war within each household. One moment we were all part of one nation, and in the next moment we cut ties with the heritage of old. Like a young man who leaves home to establish his own, young America knew they must break the bonds of paternal control, for

---

120 See Appendix A - The Declaration of Independence.
121 Scripture taken from the Holy Bible, New International Version®. Copyright © 1973, 1978, 1984 by International Bible Society. Used by permission of Zondervan. All rights reserved.

liberty would not grow if America remained tied to English rule. Those brave of old did not deny liberty its voice as they chose its call over their own.

The word *course* conveys an image of inevitable progression with a beginning and an end. *Course* is defined as the continuous passage or progress through time or succession of stages, or the path, route, or channel along which anything moves.[122] Put in simpler terms, when a family goes on a road trip, it has a starting point, an ending point, and a purpose. The starting point to America's road trip was a world dominated by the forces of tyranny. The end point of America's road trip was the birth of liberty. The purpose of America was to shine liberty across the globe. In the words of Ronald Reagan in a 1961 speech on socialized medicine:

> *In this country of ours, took place the greatest revolution that has ever taken place in the world's history. The only true revolution. Every other revolution simply exchanged one set of rulers for another. But here for the first time in thousands of years of man's relation to man, a little group of men, the founding fathers—for the first time—established the idea that you and I had within ourselves the God given right and ability to determine our own destiny.*

The concept of servant-based leadership, reflected in Ronald Reagan's words, is also found in Scripture. Two of the disciples' mother requested whether one of her sons could sit at the right hand and the other one at the left hand of Christ. Christ's response is simple. Jesus compares how the rulers of the world lord it over the people and act like tyrants over them. Jesus goes to the root motivation of the disciples' mother, which is tyranny. From this example, Jesus sets a new standard for leadership by defining servant-based leadership. In His words:

> *When the ten heard about this, they became indignant at James and John. Jesus called them together and said, "You know that those who are regarded as rulers over the Gentiles lord it over them. Not so with you. Instead, whoever wants to become great among you must be your servant, and whoever wants to be first, must be slave to all. For even the Son of Man did not come to be served, but to serve, and to give his life as a ransom for many.*

---

122 Dictionary.com Unabridged. Based on the Random House Dictionary, Random House Inc. 2010.

Mark 10:41–45 (NIV)[123]

This is exactly what America did in this transformational moment of history. America birthed a government where the founders did not come to grab hold of power. Rather, the founders came to give power to the people. Game changer!

More specifically, the definition of the word *course* impresses upon the reader of an ordered set of events or plan of sorts that culminated in the Revolutionary War. If there was a plan, it begs the question of who created the plan. Was it randomness or Divine Providence? As we will see later in the text of the Declaration of Independence, our forefathers acknowledged Divine Providence. Look at the back of a one-dollar bill. On it, you will see a pyramid with an eye at the top. The pyramid is an unfinished pyramid known as the Eye of Providence. There were two Latin phrases surrounding the pyramid, *Novus Ordo Seclorum,* meaning a new order of the ages, and *Annuit Coeptis,* meaning Providence has Favored Our Undertakings.[124]

This nation, motivated by "...the Laws of Nature and Nature's God..."[125] put America on a map as separate from all. It was not by mistake the framers of this masterpiece understood the vast odds against the desire for independence, and that to secure liberty for all it must be sanctioned from above. Our nation, born anew, recognized that its submission to its Creator made possible her standing amongst the globe. You see, it wasn't logical nor probably wise to stand against the war machine of England. Somewhere in the collective heart of this new nation, the confidence of standing in agreement with nature's God forged the courage to say no to tyranny and yes to liberty. Our land began with recognition of Nature's God and without shame or reserve. We should not deny the existence of Him, nor the divine hand that produced the land we call home. Many would argue that we need to sever our ties to nature's God. I say give me God, or give me death! How can you separate God when God is the source that produced the call to this young nation?

Today, each American must come face to face with destiny, and collectively we must yoke ourselves to the epic cause of liberty. We too must be willing to sever our ties with the dictates of old. In this modern day, the appearance of tyranny may take different forms, but the enemy

---

123 Scripture taken from the Holy Bible, New International Version®. Copyright © 1973, 1978, 1984 by International Bible Society. Used by permission of Zondervan. All rights reserved.

124 www.greatseal.com/committees/finaldesign/index.html

125 See Appendix A – The Declaration of Independence.

is the same as the one of old. Once we place our hand over the heart of this great land and discover the rhythm of liberty, we will witness the wild flames of freedom ignite. Will you join me, America? Will you link your calling to that of Thomas Jefferson, John Adams, Benjamin Franklin, and George Washington? Will you unearth yourselves from the comforts of modern life and stand up for your brethren of old? Will you remove your self-interest and allow liberty to take hold, to transform your heart and redeem a nation back to her roots? The cry of our hearts aches for us to meet our call and restore our land. Let's stake our claim and live up to our national emblem, the bald eagle that soars so high, lives so free, and carries the Latin phrase: *E Pluribus Unum*—out of many, one![126]

We are many people united into the singular cause of liberty.[127] The stage is set, the choice is clear. Will the Americans of the twenty-first century take up the call of freedom? It is our choice, it is our land, and it is our gift, endowed to us from our Creator.

---

126 *The New Oxford American Dictionary, Second Edition*, Erin McKean (editor), 2051 pages, May 2005, Oxford University Press, ISBN 0-19-517077-6.

127 Source: http://www.treas.gov/education/faq/coins/portraits.shtml#q7

WE HOLD THESE TRUTHS

⸻ ⚬⚬⚬ ⸻

*"**We hold these truths** to be self-evident, that all men are created equal,
that they are endowed by their Creator with certain unalienable Rights,
that among these are Life, Liberty and the pursuit of Happiness."*
- The Declaration of Independence (July 4, 1776)

Bold, fresh, and inspiring are adjectives conjured up by the words *"We hold these truths to be self-evident, that all men are created equal, that they are endowed by their Creator with certain unalienable Rights, that among these are Life, Liberty and the pursuit of Happiness."* The second sentence, so perfectly placed on the heels of severing ties with the king of England, wastes but one breath before America develops roots of her own. In the moment between the two sentences, a historical transformation occurs. America had rejected the heritage of old and laid claims to the promises ahead. No longer were our citizens held captive by the bondage of tyranny, for in her next breath America received the promised destiny. The grip of centuries lost hold as the roots of unity, truth, and equality paved the way and we recognized man's rightful place as the created. England was shocked as our story unfolded from a position of many, not the glory of one. Our founders rocked the globe as they erected unity into the core of this young nation. They drew strength into our foundation through unity of spirit, unity of mind, and unity of purpose. America would move forward with one mind and with precise accuracy. This isn't to imply our young democracy did not witness division or heated debate. In fact, unity places preeminence upon diversity of thought. It welcomes distinctions of others. It is tyranny that thrives on factions and desires to divide. This is not so with our nation. We placed unity at our core as we shoved off to war and as we began the process of governing a sovereign nation. The wisdom of the ages declares though one may be overpowered, two can defend themselves, and a cord of three strands are not easily broken (Ecc 4:12).[128] So it was established from the beginning that by unity we, America, would soon discover the bonds of peace and the security thereof.

Unity alone was not enough to create a nation whose fate would endure the test of time. Our faithful founders decided to remove the gray and to declare to the world that truth mattered. There is no doubt our founders possessed a perspective on life that security was found when truth remained unchanged. They declared in the text that it wasn't their truth that mattered, it was the truth of the *Creator*. While living in the throes of such uncertainty and with bloodshed ahead, America planted this root, and as the story goes, truth precedes freedom and has served her well. We live in an era where black and white have been blended into gray, where right is confused with wrong, and the Creator is replaced by the created. Oh, America. How the fathers of America sit at heaven's edge with moods of despair and eyes full of tears, for our land was built for truth, the kind of truth that endures. Our society has come to a crossroads where we must choose to either return to truth or thrust beyond its borders. The former produces the fruit of peace and security, and the latter ushers in an era where chaos will reign supreme. So, America, our founders cast their lots on truth some two hundred years ago. As history cycles by, it is our moment to decide. There is a way that seems right to man, but in the end leads to death (Prov 14:12).[129] For so long we have denied the truth, but now the time has come to return to our roots. There may be suffering and tolls along this road, but do not despair. Life, liberty, and happiness are the ultimate goal.

The belief that all men are created equal changed the world. It altered the relationship between man and his government, for the dream of our

---

128 Scripture taken from the Holy Bible, New International Version®. Copyright © 1973, 1978, 1984 by International Bible Society. Used by permission of Zondervan. All rights reserved.

129 Ibid.

land was equality for all. The bar was set high, and the expectations soared. No longer were the riches of this world, or the family of our births, or the adornment of clothes justification for receiving the finest seat in the house. You see, our nation broke down aristocracy and established freedom for all. With this new land we established a new government, one that desired the destruction of favoritism by opting for justice for all. The playing field was leveled, the proud were brought low, and men began to believe in equality for all. The Declaration of Independence opened the door that rewarded the size of our dreams and ingenuity of our work. By firmly placing happiness within everyone's grasp, the nobility were no longer the only ones to succeed. With this moment came the realization that, as individuals, it was up to us to shape our future. Our government did its job. Now, it was time for us to do ours. Somewhere between the creation of this text and today, Americans have fallen prey to the belief that without the government there is no way to succeed. In the moment when America made history, there was but a frail government held up by band-aids and bubble gum, yet it never held back the fury of America to achieve her dreams. To the contrary, these young colonials endured trials and tribulations that would make any man weary. They knew not the comforts of Social Security, Medicare, welfare, and the 2010 universal healthcare reform. The source of their strength was found in their faith in the Creator and the gift of freedom. It was from this gift that they brought forth the greatest achievement the world has known. They never stood by waiting for a handout, for they learned early on it was up to them to surpass the expectations of the world audience. Through grit and grind and rock-solid determination, these men and women stood tall.

They stood tall to their foes, but remained low to their Creator. Not for a moment did they believe it was chance or pretend that it began with man. The belief that liberty would flow when man was in his proper role pervades this sentence of the Declaration of Independence. The spirit of humility, so subtle, yet so strong, places the Creator on high and man so low. With our position of humility, we can see the warmth of our Creator, a Creator so kind who desires man to have within his grasp the rights of life, liberty, and the pursuit of happiness. The word *endow* is defined as to give or bequeath an income or property to a person.[130] As the text so states, we were endowed by our Creator, or in simplistic terms, we were given the unalienable rights of life, liberty, and the pursuit of happiness. It

---

130 *The New Oxford American Dictionary, Second Edition*, Erin McKean (editor), 2051 pages, May 2005, Oxford University Press, ISBN 0-19-517077-6.

would seem the craftsmen of this text found a common design imprinted into the dignity of each man. Did you hear that America? These rights were given to us freely, not based upon our ability to earn it, but based upon the unmerited favor of God and His bestowal of these blessings upon mankind—otherwise known by the Christian as God's *grace*.[131] To probe further would only lessen our doubt. *Unalienable,* a word that stands-out, denotes something which we are unable to give away or that is unable to be taken away from the possessor—a moral absolute.[132] Christianity, the dominant religion is based in the belief that God has revealed absolute and unchanging standards of right and wrong, based ultimately on His own holy character.[133] By contrast, the moral relativist views nature as all there is and there is no transcendent source of moral truth, and we are left to construct morality on our own.[134] Every principle is reduced to a personal preference.[135] There is a great debate raging in America whether morality should be defined in absolute terms or relative to the person and situation. By taking into consideration the words *truths, self-evident, endowed* and *unalienable* the only logical conclusion is America was founded upon moral absolutes. Now, we have found the heart of the matter and the core of the struggle between good and evil. Tyranny attempts to rob us of truth and moral absolutes. We see this occurring throughout twenty-first century America where a war rages on between moral absolutes and moral relativism. Tyranny can deceive and produce despair, but no matter how frail we become, tyranny cannot take away or give to man what its Creator gave, those unalienable rights. Tyranny may attempt the re-writing of history, but the memory of history and the dried ink on the Declaration of Independence are proof of a nation who built its foundation upon moral absolutes. Tyranny may prevail for a season of history, but in the end, despite all of its lustful and destructive attempts, our rights from above are as secure as the Creator Himself. Neither the tyrant nor the created can deny this truth, which bears contempt in the heart of the tyrant. This belief frustrates the tyrant's lust for power and challenges the belief that they themselves are greater than Thee. Be wary, America, when we deny the existence of our Creator or attempt to remove moral absolutes by falling prey to the spell of the tyrant. Find comfort, America, in the shelter that

---

131 Ibid.

132 Ibid.

133 Colson, Charles, and Nancy Pearcey. *How Now Shall We Live?* Tyndale House Publishing, Inc., 1999.

134 Ibid.

135 Ibid.

the rights of life, liberty, and the pursuit of happiness may be insecure in the eyes of man, but remain within the firm grasp of the Divine.

Even beyond the words *truths, self-evident, endowed,* and *unalienable,* our forefathers went further by providing us a linkage between the core of our nation and the Creator Himself. Look, America, at the context from the document in which "Life, Liberty and the pursuit of Happiness" are defined—they are defined in relationship to the Creator. The text states "they are endowed by their Creator with certain unalienable Rights ..." The rights were the property of the Creator, which He gave to mankind. Logically, if the Creator freely bestowed upon man the right to "Life, Liberty and the pursuit of Happiness," then intuitively those rights must be defined from the enduring perspective of the Creator and not from the temporal perspective of man. At the time of the founding of America, our nation was largely comprised of men and women who had fled Europe with the hope of discovering a better life and the desire to escape religious persecution. With historical precision, we know Europe was the center of Christendom, making Christianity the dominant worldview of Europe. Therefore our forefathers' presuppositions about the Creator and the right to "Life, Liberty and pursuit of Happiness" would have been heavily biased toward Christianity.

Interestingly enough, when the authors of the Declaration of Independence defined those rights in terms of the Creator, they declared their recognition of the sovereignty of God over man, over the state (the government), and over the church. The definition of *inalienable*—something that can neither be given nor taken away—implies there are limits to the church and to the state in relation to the Creator. Said another way, neither the church nor the state have the authority to remove our unalienable rights; both are subordinate to the sovereignty of God. With brilliance and much foresight, our forefathers simultaneously instilled a check and balance to the church and to the state and defined an intersection point of the church with the state—through mutual recognition of God's sovereignty. Therefore the church and the state find unity when each recognizes the sovereignty of God within its respective sphere of influence. United States Supreme Court Justice William O. Douglas's remarks summarize it best when he said, "We are a religious people whose institutions presuppose a Supreme Being."

From a historical perspective, we know our forefathers were trying to flee the religious tyranny exerted from the Church of England. In recent days, we witnessed this from the former Soviet Union, where the state, through its control of the church, virtually stamped out the influence of religion for over half a century. Our founders brought a new doctrine to the relationship among the church, the state, and man. This America is where the richness, the revival, and the renewal to our land will take root when the church, the state, and the citizens awaken to the reality that God is sovereign over all. After all, our pledge of allegiance says "one nation under God" and not "one nation above God." There is wisdom in the ordained order of America and undeniable foresight woven into the fabric of our great nation.

The mosaic is clear as we see the roots of unity, truth, and equality grow strong and take their intentional place beneath the wings of the Creator, who in His great love gave us those rights we hold dear, the rights to life, liberty, and the pursuit of happiness. Life itself was given to us from above. This is beyond what we are owed, but in the generosity of the Creator's heart, He desired much more. You see, the Creator must have known a life devoid of liberty was no life at all. As liberty takes shape, we are free to come and free to go in our pursuit of happiness. We were granted the desires of our hearts for so long, we remained within the bounds of unity, truth, and equality for all. We have been given a unique place in history for sure. Our blessings are great, and where much is given, much more will be asked. As our journey continues, let's look more acutely at the right to life, liberty, and the pursuit of happiness!

THE RIGHT TO LIFE

⟜⊙⟊

*"**We hold these truths** to be self-evident, that all men are created equal, that they are endowed by their Creator with certain unalienable Rights, that among these are **Life**, Liberty and the pursuit of Happiness."*

- The Declaration of Independence (July 4, 1776)

The right to life was given with permanence from our Creator, and etched into the tablet of the American beginning for all the world to see. In the few strokes of a pen, the birth of America was united with the beginning of time. Our Creator formed man out of the dust, and through the breath of life established man as a living, breathing being. America was yet a dream until the words soaked with potency found in the Declaration of Independence took root and brought life to a nation. In the establishment of this young state, moments before it was declared, these men of old understood the gift of life and the need to preserve and protect this right. Our declaration stated that the right to life could neither be given nor taken away. It was now endowed to the United States of America to guard this right and shepherd its cause. From this day forth, life would be valued, cherished, and upheld. No longer could a tyrant remove a life without due cause. Our right to life set America apart. Our nation was brought forth to provide, protect, and project this right. It is in the depths of this right that the stage is set for liberty and happiness. When the right to life is viewed with disregard, the forces of tyranny have already begun. The light of liberty will grow dim, and our hope-filled attitude toward what lies ahead will be withdrawn. History recounts how countless nations, both young and old, would come in the middle of the night without cause to remove the right to life. We need look no further than Hussein or Hitler, where the whims of the states could take a life without account. Our founders were firm in their resolve that without this right to life, liberty would fall.

We were surely endowed with this right as individuals and as God's created. History has shown the dangerous path that unfolds when untold millions are annihilated for the glory of the state. The world has known genocide and wholesale slaughter of a race at the hands of a tyrant, but not in America, for our nation was established for something more grand. Our purpose was clear: to demonstrate to the world what could occur when the right to life was allowed to thrive. The belief in this right to life laid the foundation to take a group of rag-tag colonists to the status of global superpower in two short centuries. The pace of our success and the size of our accomplishments are no accident. They are forever linked with our vow to protect the right to life. Somewhere in our history, we initiated a way to challenge this right. We began to test the boundaries of our liberty, to choose when we allowed life to exist and when to deny life's entry into this world. It was not by mistake our framers placed life before liberty, for they knew the day would come when liberty would challenge the right to life. Furthermore, the Creator endowed us with certain unalienable rights, which even by modern definitions denotes something we are unable to take or give away. The fears of the framers' conscience have come to bear as we witness the tragedy of untold millions of children denied this right. Each time an abortion occurs within America men replace the Creator with the created. Despite the ruling of the Supreme Court on abortion, it stands to reason, if a judgment conflicts with the Declaration of Independence then the Declaration of Independence should be relied upon as precedent—the document where all precedent should be rooted. I am not a legal scholar, but commonsense would incline me to believe the Constitution cannot be interpreted outside of the overarching framework of the Declaration of Independence. The Declaration of Independence provides the foundation from which the Constitution sits atop and the lens from which it must be interpreted. Sadly, this is not the case as we drift further away from the original intent of America.

If we could sit down with these men of old, shouts of revolution would be heard as they would stand in disbelief at the contempt for life. Liberty was never intended to operate in isolation. It was meant to be placed in the order of the text. When liberty operates beyond the bounds of life and the order ordained from above, it can morph into all sorts of evils. Freedom was not given to us for our selfish ambitions. Freedom was given to us so others may be free. Be cautious, America, for one day we will account for the faithful stewardship of this right to life. Is it true, the enemy is within?

As a nation, the right to life has been seriously compromised, but we are not without hope. Remaining within the character of America are a remnant of citizens and societal institutions that take extreme measures to uphold the foundational "right to life" afforded to us under the Declaration of Independence. Specifically, with duty, honor, and service to country, the men and women who serve in the United States military exemplify the right to life by the "no man left behind" mentality. Our military is one of the few combat forces in the world where extraordinary measures are taken to rescue a wounded warrior—even if it means incurring additional casualties. The value system, mainly to place the life of another over personal safety, instilled into our fighting heroes is magnificent. The value system creates a sense of unity, cohesion, and trust across our combat forces. This phenomenon in American military continues to be played out time and time again in Afghanistan and Iraq. Through the media, we frequently hear how an improvised explosive device (IED) wounded American forces and on the heels of being wounded were other military members who placed their own lives on the line to give the wounded soldier the best possible chance to survive. Our forces spend considerable time preparing for the rescue of a wounded soldier, marine, or sailor. Watching these fine men and women rush into a stream of incoming bullets, mortars, and explosives to rescue one of their own is counter to a person's survival instincts. What would drive a person to place a soldier's life over his own? The answer: a deeply held value system in which preeminence is placed upon life at all possible costs. What would happen in America if we instilled a similar value system into our society when dealing with the most innocent, naïve, and defenseless humans: the unborn and the elderly? The answer: a restoration of trust, cohesion, unity, and common dignity across our nation. Our Declaration of Independence began with the "right to life" and if we are going to begin the arduous journey toward restoring our national character then we must begin with the most foundational right of all: *the right to life.*

Our value for life is not something to deny or be ashamed of. It is this enduring right which sets our democracy apart from tyrants of old and the terrorists of new. Yesterday's challenge to the right to life found form in Hitler and the Nazi's attempt to remove the Jewish race. Today, we bear witness to a generation of Islamic fundamentalists who utilize death as the primary method to propel their goals. Recall the vivid memories of September 11, 2001 when thousands of Americans faced a tragic death. We stood amazed as the towers collapsed, as we witnessed the destruction imposed when men know nothing of the right to life. Look across the sea to the continent of Africa, where genocide has taken root. Africa has become all too familiar with death, destruction, and civil unrest. As the stench of death makes its way around the globe, the lesson is clear and the call is direct. The world needs America to stand up for the right to life. We must heed history's call, but first let's restore the purity of old. Without America, life will flicker and fade. So stand strong, America! Bring back to the world the right to life!

THE RIGHT TO LIBERTY

⎯⎯⎯⎯⎯⎯⎯⎯⎯⎯ ⏡ ⎯⎯⎯⎯⎯⎯⎯⎯⎯⎯

*"**We hold these truths** to be self-evident, that all men are created equal,
that they are endowed by their Creator with certain unalienable Rights,
that among these are Life, **Liberty** and the pursuit of Happiness."*

- *The Declaration of Independence (July 4, 1776)*

Upon the bedrock of life, the right to liberty finds its place. It is within the security and comforts of a land who secures life where liberty begins her work. This right to liberty, this gift from above, is a friend to most, but a foe to the tyrant. Since the beginning of mankind, man has had a love affair with liberty. We see it over and over in the history books and in the Bible for sure. One group of people enslave another until the day liberty calls her people home. What is certain about liberty is that you either stand with it or against it. When the children of Israel were held captive to the Egyptians, Moses was given the task to pry these people from a tyrant and lead them to freedom. It wasn't easy for Moses back then, and it wasn't easy for the colonists of this great land, but through Divine Providence and a firm faith, freedom was found. Our own history tells it best. Here was a group of people who left the English shores in search of a better life where liberty would bloom. Year after year and grievance after grievance, it became clear that they would either have liberty or death. You see, what gripped those brave hearts and solidified their convictions was the sweet taste of liberty. For some strange reason, they were chosen, for this moment in history, to show the rest of the world that freedom isn't free. They fought for this right in their backyards, where their homes and communities were toppled. They were displaced from their native land. They became no strangers to death, but something drove this band of brothers on. I say it was the ache from deep within, when the awareness of living without liberty became greater than life itself. This courageous group stood tall and stood strong. There were no guarantees, but for a life to live, it must be lived freely. They developed close friendships with sacrifice, service, and self-denial, for to win this struggle there had to be a cost. When the dust settled and the British acknowledged surrender, America knew something grand had occurred. They stood in awe as the bells of liberty rang from the steeple of Independence Hall, and they heard the hearts cry out, "Liberty for all!" Yes, liberty was born anew to this fresh land, but it is certain the pains and scars of war live long after the war is forgotten.

So, America faced the ups and downs as it wrestled with liberty and the question of what it meant. You would think a nation united to be free would live with such ease. It wasn't long before another cry was heard from a group of people who wanted to be free. Yes, it occurred again on our shores, where liberty was after the hearts of all. The call came during the war between the North and the South, at a time when one race presumed a position over another. This nation could not stand for this, because we were born to bring freedom to all. The nation was torn as death amounted, but in the end, we saw fulfillment of the Emancipation Proclamation. Lincoln's convictions stood strong as he used our growing might not for selfish gain or political advantage, but to ensure our land was free. This wasn't Lincoln's victory, it was liberty's moment to rise above the ailments of a nation and call us to greater heights. Where liberty reigns, people soar. It is hard to describe, but we know it when we see it deep in our souls. America, we could go on about our call in World War I and World War II, where the world's last hope was the red, white, and blue. Our story is majestic to say the least. We should be humbled and honored to receive divine providence's calling. The road wasn't meant to be easy, for something so precious must come at great cost.

As we arrive into the twenty-first century, something has been lost. The beacon of liberty is growing dim as our freedoms are sucked away. We brought liberty to Iraq, and twenty-five million people are now free, but the spotlight has turned. *Liberty* is defined as the state of being free within society from oppressive restrictions imposed by authority on one's way of life, behavior, or political views.[136] We live in an era where the reach of government is expanding into every aspect of society in America. Look at the control the government exerts over private enterprise compensation, the demonization of the auto industry, the financial industry, and the healthcare industry. Is anything not up for grabs these days? With the passage of the recent healthcare reform, the government will be hiring an additional sixteen thousand Internal Revenue Service (IRS) agents, not to protect our security, but to force us to buy healthcare the majority of Americans never desired in the first place. If there was ever a time when liberty was under assault, it is now. Step back, America. We used to condemn Iraq, Iran, Cuba, the Soviet Union, and Venezuela for their secret police force that they used to carry out the will of the state instead of the will of the people. The subversion of our liberty isn't even subtle. It is bold and it is brazen. We are a free people, so why aren't we free?

Have we forgotten, America, our roots of old? Have we grown tired, or has the deceitfulness of wealth and personal power choked the voice of freedom? Look around, America. We live as if the problems in life are someone else's to deal with. This isn't America. We told the world in Emma Lazarus' poem, engraved on the Statute of Liberty:

> *Give me your tired, your poor,*
> *Your huddled masses yearning to breathe free,*
> *The wretched refuse of your teeming shore.*
> *Send these, the homeless, tempest-tossed to me,*
> *I lift my lamp beside the golden door!*[137]

We knew the land of freedom and opportunity was full of hope, and it wasn't based upon status or intellectual capacity. Rather, we placed our faith in liberty. Look back a few generations ago when we sent what Tom Brokaw coined the "greatest generation" off to war. When they returned, they didn't complain. They didn't wallow in pity or sulk in sadness. Something happened to these men and women in Europe. They learned the lesson that freedom isn't free. They arrived back to our shores with grateful hearts that they lived in a land full of liberty and raised on hope. They built homes and business and raised up our communities. They didn't wait for the government or blame others for any shortcomings, for they knew liberty alone was enough. September 11, 2001 foreshadowed

---

136 *The New Oxford American Dictionary, Second Edition*, Erin McKean (editor), 2051 pages, May 2005, Oxford University Press, ISBN 0-19-517077-6.

137 Source: http://www.loc.gov/exhibits/haventohome/images/hh0041s.jpg

what occurs when we turn a blind eye toward the enemies of liberty. It was no one person's fault, nor did we do anything to warrant those tragedies, but it is a vivid reminder of the struggle to be free. In a few blinks of an eye, liberty can be taken away.

There are no easy answers and no panacea. Our culture has grown hostile toward the idea of providing liberty for all. Our culture will hide behind social programs of all sorts, and with craftiness and cunning make the programs appear righteous when in fact they cripple. As our grandparents used to say, when something seems too good to be true, it usually is. One thing is for sure, when liberty is taken, it leads down the treacherous path of tyranny. Do you think Hitler, Stalin, or Hussein began all at once? America, we find ourselves at the crossroads again, between liberty and tyranny. Liberty is calling us upward toward love, toward truth, and toward justice for all. Tyranny, in its finest deceit, will even label bondage and slavery as freedom. America, rise up! Rise now, hear the cry of liberty, the beacon that has been faithful and true, and heed her call. This is our meeting between history and destiny, and may it be said the flames of liberty were ignited again!

THE RIGHT TO THE PURSUIT OF HAPPINESS

---- ∾⊙⊚⊙∾ ----

*"**We hold these truths** to be self-evident, that all men are created equal, that they are endowed by their Creator with certain unalienable Rights, that among these are Life, Liberty and **the pursuit of Happiness.**"*
- *The Declaration of Independence (July 4, 1776)*

The right to the pursuit of happiness is the right for each individual to discover their God-given talents, gifts, and capabilities. No other right or aspect of the Declaration of Independence more centrally communicates the American dream than this right. This right is the promise of a nation to her people. It is for this right that immigrants flocked to the United States in hopes of finding a better life. Recall President Ronald Reagan's reference to America as that shining city on a hill. America, the shining city on a hill provides hope for the world, hope for a better life, a different way, and a promise that if you work for your dreams, you can become whatever it is you desire to become. That's America. Some would criticize this rugged individualism and suggest in some sense it is greedy or self centered, but it is in this rugged individualism where the collective pursuit of happiness provides rays of hope, inspiration, and motivates the world over.

You see, the founders understood the proper place and role of the government was to ensure America remained the land of freedom and opportunity. When the Creator endowed the creation with this right, His desire was to prosper his children, to bring them hope and a future (Jeremiah

29:11).[138] In America, all have this right and we can choose to pursue it or not. We can choose in this great land to live above the level of mediocrity or to stay with the status quo. It isn't up to our friends, our family, or our government. This right is the promise made between Providence's call and a nation willing to follow. Our land broke down racial barriers, mass produced the automobile, and flew to the moon. When this gift is unleashed, there is no end in sight to the American dream. It has been the hope of each generation to leave this land more bountiful in opportunity. This is the American way! It is through this pursuit of happiness that the economic status and stature of America grew tall. Through the years, our influence around the globe grew, and so did the spread of liberty. This nation's pursuit of happiness has cured more diseases, saved more lives, and lifted more people out of poverty than any other land. It was in the master design of this country for the people to soar, and with them the world would follow. We brought capitalism and democracy to almost every part of the globe because we desired for others to share in destiny's bounty. It would serve us well to remember this gift was provided by the Creator, and we have Him to thank for it. With gratitude and praise, America, this right was given to us to be shared. The Creator knew that in order to find true contentment, we would need to reach the end of ourselves and attach ourselves to a greater cause. Wealth, fame, and success mean nothing when the goal is self-gratification. America, our purpose is clear and the path lies ahead. Let's take this right to help bring liberty to all!

Now America, be weary of the pursuit of happiness as an end to itself. It was never intended to work outside the bounds of the giver of this great gift, nor independent of the rights of life and liberty. In America, our dignity was not found through our bloodline, rather, it was defined by the individual's pursuit of happiness while bringing honor to the right of life and liberty. There are some in our culture of dependency who would lead us to believe that unless we receive help or a handout, we will never achieve our dreams. What these givers of other's belongings do not understand is the glory is in the pursuit, not in the result. Our founders knew the toils of pursuit well. For many years, they strived, suffered, and struggled, until one day this nation declared its independence and its readiness to place liberty on the map. We were never promised a life free from hardship,

---

138 Scripture taken from the Holy Bible, New International Version®. Copyright © 1973, 1978, 1984 by International Bible Society. Used by permission of Zondervan. All rights reserved.

where trials and tribulations would never show up. It is the trials of life that develop the character so desperately needed to contend with happiness.

What's wrong, America? Have we lost our independent spirit where joy was found in paving the way? The founders feared a government where people depended upon it for food, shelter, and clothing. In today's world, we know these things as Social Security, welfare, Medicare, and the 2010 universal healthcare reform legislation. The terms have changed, but nonetheless they result in people seeking their provisions not from the Creator or as a result of hard work, but from the arbitrary will of the government redistributing money it does not own. Our framers desired so much more for their people. They wanted us to be free from tyranny and independent from the state. To say government has no place in our land is untrue, but when government turns toward tyranny, it must be pushed back. America, seize this call! The time has come when we must reclaim our independence, or we will watch this right disappear.

THAT TO SECURE THESE RIGHTS

—————————— ⟬⟭ ——————————

*"**That to secure these rights,** Governments are instituted among Men, deriving their just powers from the consent of the governed, --That whenever any Form of Government becomes destructive of these ends, it is the Right of the People to alter or to abolish it, and to institute new Government, laying its foundation on such principles and organizing its powers in such form, as to them shall seem most likely to effect their Safety and Happiness. Prudence, indeed, will dictate that Governments long established should not be changed for light and transient causes; and accordingly all experience hath shewn, that mankind are more disposed to suffer, while evils are sufferable, than to right themselves by abolishing the forms to which they are accustomed. But when a long train of abuses and usurpations, pursuing invariably the same Object evinces a design to reduce them under absolute Despotism, it is their right, it is their duty, to throw off such Government, and to provide new Guards for their future security.--Such has been the patient sufferance of these Colonies; and such is now the necessity which constrains them to alter their former Systems of Government. The history of the present King of Great Britain is a history of repeated injuries and usurpations, all having in direct object the establishment of an absolute Tyranny over these States."*

- The Declaration of Independence (July 4, 1776)

So far, as we have sojourned through the Declaration of Independence, we have made our way from severing our ties with Great Britain to the front row seat where our founders planted the roots of unity, truth, and equality for all men. As the roots began to grow, the document announced to the world the mysterious link between this young nation, its Creator, and the unalienable rights given to the created. With the recognition of the fragility of such rights from within and from beyond our borders, Thomas Jefferson decided to place a bookend here by instituting the responsibility for securing those rights onto the governed. It wasn't the right given to the government, the president, or a king. Instead, the most solemn of duties was subscribed to the consent of the people. Unlike the prowess of a dictator who finds insecurity in the will of the people, our nation finds strength from our consent. Oh, the irony of democracy! It uses the greatest threat to tyranny as its greatest source of strength. Our nation recognizes the wisdom in a multitude of counselors by drawing upon the collective reasoning of its people. There is something comforting in knowing that the decisions for this land do not rest in the hands of a few, but in the wisdom of many. By now it is clear that when power is isolated, it will most certainly corrupt. Our framers were far too studious of the lessons of history to believe for one moment that government would never become corrupt. Those rights we hold so dear, the right to life, liberty, and the pursuit of happiness, most certainly need to be secured from a government that desires their destruction. This, my friends, is perhaps the most sacred of all duties for a citizen of our nation. Like a nation declaring war, this right of the people must be exercised with prudence and caution. In this area, we are to be slow to anger and slow to speak. God forbid this day arrive, but governments should beware, for when the white knight of liberty is pushed too far, he will grab his horse and begin a war. To allow these rights to drift off into history would open a door to a darkness the world has never seen. Take note, America. Lay hold to your duty, and stand at the gate and watch. Warn your comrades who find themselves in the elect of our government, for they only hold the power we give them, and as quick as it was given, it can be taken back.

To a person in the year 2010, these statements may seem overly bold. We may even label them as extremist or hate speech. This isn't a concept we created. Our source of wisdom tells us there is nothing new under the sun. When our elect push our rights aside to place more emphasis on themselves than we have given them consent to, when they use deceit to trick the land, when they show signs of conceit, and when they worm their way into homes to gain control over the weak-willed, then we will know our government has shifted away from goodness and truth and has moved toward evil. No man can say when this point is reached, but I believe the collective will of the people eventually reaches a boiling point, and they set a course for abolishing its leaders and beginning anew the process of instituting a government to once again receive the guardianship of the right to life, liberty, and the pursuit of happiness.

It is hard to say with great certainty where America sits on this map, but when our government seeks its will over the will of its people, one thing is guaranteed. We have come one step closer to a revolution. We live in an era of big government, big budgets, even larger deficits, and tremendous government overreach into the affairs of the individual and the affairs of free enterprise. Even one decade ago, it would have been hard to imagine an America in which a financially bankrupt government did not cut back or downsize, but instead spent at an astounding rate. Now, unlike anytime in history, our government has begun to exert influence onto the banks, the automobile industry, and the healthcare industry, and has recently begun dictating compensation to the private sector. We are witnessing state budgets being propped up from the federal government, and Washington dictates being shoved down the throats of state capitols. Are there ills that need to be corrected? You bet, but government is not the only solution. When government is the sole tool to solve all of society's ailments, we will find ourselves upon the slippery slope of tyranny. Two years ago, I was having a conversation with an Iraqi man who recently immigrated to the United States. I asked him what he thought about living in the land of liberty. Without hesitation he said, "America is not free. Everywhere you look there are rules, government, and taxes. I appreciate what America has done for me, but sometimes I feel like I had more freedom in Iraq." America, look around. Review your receipts. Look at your mortgages. There is nothing that isn't taxed. We buy a home only to pay taxes in perpetuity, so where is the ownership and who holds the rights? Are those rights with the people, or are they with the state?

Politicians, congressmen, senators, judges, governors, mayors, and yes, even the president of this great land, be weary of exercising your position beyond the will of the people, for your time is but a moment! Americans may take long to arise, but as Japan's Naval Marshal General Isoroku Yamamoto stated after Pearl Harbor, "I fear all we have done is to awaken a sleeping giant and fill him with terrible resolve."[139] The fury of the American will did not subside until the war ended and the world was safe. As Americans, we desire to believe in good, to trust, and to hope for the best, but when push comes to shove, we will stand up!

---

139 Source: http://www.pacaf.af.mil/news/story.asp?id=123034638

To Prove This, Let Facts Be Submitted To a Candid World

❦

"To prove this, let Facts be submitted to a candid world.

He has refused his Assent to Laws, the most wholesome and necessary for the public good.

He has forbidden his Governors to pass Laws of immediate and pressing importance, unless suspended in their operation till his Assent should be obtained; and when so suspended, he has utterly neglected to attend to them.

He has refused to pass other Laws for the accommodation of large districts of people, unless those people would relinquish the right of Representation in the Legislature, a right inestimable to them and formidable to tyrants only.

He has called together legislative bodies at places unusual, uncomfortable, and distant from the depository of their Public Records, for the sole purpose of fatiguing them into compliance with his measures.

He has dissolved Representative Houses repeatedly, for opposing with manly firmness his invasions on the rights of the people.

He has refused for a long time, after such dissolutions, to cause others to be elected, whereby the Legislative Powers, incapable of Annihilation, have returned to the People at large for their exercise; the State remaining in the mean time exposed to all the dangers of invasion from without, and convulsions within.

He has endeavoured to prevent the population of these States; for that purpose obstructing the Laws for Naturalization of Foreigners;

refusing to pass others to encourage their migrations hither, and raising the conditions of new Appropriations of Lands.

He has obstructed the Administration of Justice by refusing his Assent to Laws for establishing Judiciary Powers.

He has made Judges dependent on his Will alone for the tenure of their offices, and the amount and payment of their salaries.

He has erected a multitude of New Offices, and sent hither swarms of Officers to harass our people and eat out their substance.

He has kept among us, in times of peace, Standing Armies without the Consent of our legislatures.

He has affected to render the Military independent of and superior to the Civil Power."

(Note: For the remainder of the text see the complete Declaration of Independence found in Appendix A)

- The Declaration of Independence (July 4, 1776)

The light of liberty was brought to bear when the men who signed this document placed their grievances on display. Our land was initiated on unity, truth, and equality. As if those virtues weren't noble enough, our founders were compelled to add another to their rank. Its name was transparency. Our nation began by expelling the cloak of the king's darkness and placing the lamp of liberty high up for the world to see. They were not looking for the consent of others. Rather, they reestablished the standard for which governments would be judged. This moment, when the light of truth breaks out, is difficult to bear for all who know what happens at night. To be fair, we all know what happens when the sins we do in darkness are brought into the light. It exposes the evil, the corruption, and the abuse. For most people, shame would flood their minds. This was not so for the king, whose eyes were blinded with pride. All he could see was from his own eyes. As the list of grievances read, time after time the king usurped the will of the people for his own selfish gain. The selfish desire for power and control were always the motivators of a tyrant. Look at Jesus Christ when he was arrested and questioned before the high priest about his teachings. For we are instructed from Christ himself on the power of transparency and the barometer of a man's character. Jesus responds to the high priest by saying: "I have spoken openly to the world...I always taught in synagogues or at the temple, where all the Jews come together. I said nothing in secret (John 18:20)."[140] In response to the transparency of Christ the officials struck Him and ultimately Christ was led to His death. There were consequences for confronting the tyrant during the time of Christ, there were consequences during the time period when America declared independence, and there will be consequences today as America utilizes transparency to confront the forces of tyranny across our land. Through patience and long suffering, the colonists persevered. They petitioned for redress to no avail. America was left with but one choice: to declare war. They knew in their hearts liberty could not survive where its voice was not heard. With transparency on their side, they said, *"A Prince, whose character is thus marked by every act which may define a Tyrant, is unfit to be the ruler of a free people."*[141]

Perhaps there is a place in the heart of a man where the lust for power and selfish gain, pushes him beyond the point of no return into the character of a tyrant. Jesus came face-to-face with the religious and political tyrants of His day. He paid the ultimate sacrifice by giving His life so others could be free. As America defied its tyrant it too paid the ultimate sacrifice, by declaring war. In the end America's adherence to truth and willingness to confront the forces of evil led to the greatest nation on earth. Not to mention, liberty was birthed.

The United States of America eventually found its footing. Our national character began with unity, truth, equality, and transparency. The roots these great men established brought forth yet another fruit called trust, the sacred bond between a government and the people. When people have trust in their government, a nation can accomplish mighty things and move beyond its wildest expectations. This trust gave faith to the people and brought confidence to their stride, as this young nation endeavored into war. Our nation's treasury was poor and our military weak, giving us no rational reason to think we could win, but a nation full of unity, truth, equality, transparency, and trust can move beyond the borders of reason.

---

140 Scripture taken from the Holy Bible, New International Version®. Copyright © 1973, 1978, 1984 by International Bible Society. Used by permission of Zondervan. All rights reserved.

141 See Appendix A – The Declaration of Independence. The quote is found in the last sentence of the first paragraph following the list of grievances. The complete paragraph reads as follows: *"In every state of these Oppressions We have Petitioned for Redress in the most humble terms: Our repeated Petitions have been answered only by repeated injury. A Prince whose character is thus marked by every act which may define a Tyrant, is unfit to be the ruler of a free people."*

Our confidence wasn't in our wealth or might. It found its strength in our character and in our Creator. We held strong to the simple belief that when those ingredients exist, liberty is sure to follow!

When a nation loses her way, the future holds none of the answers to finding it again. Rather, it would be wise to heed the voices of our forefathers. If George Washington or Thomas Jefferson were here today, I believe they would speak with great passion and certain conviction. So, let go of today, and let's consider what Thomas Jefferson or George Washington might say:

> O, the land we love so dear, hear our voices from above. Turn from your path and return to your roots. You grew with such might and accomplished so much. With liberty as your goal and the vigor of youth, you turned the world upside down. Then, those years of adolescence appeared where you questioned your identity and destiny's call. Hear us clear, the land we love. Return to your roots where the voice of liberty was clear!

Here we have it. These men heard liberty's call. They faced war for the ideals of life, liberty, and the pursuit of happiness, and if they were wrong, it would take their deaths to prove it.

Nor Have We Been
Wanting in Attentions

--- ❦ ---

"Nor have We been wanting in attentions to our British brethren.
We have warned them from time to time of attempts by their legislature to
extend an unwarrantable jurisdiction over us. We have reminded them of
the circumstances of our emigration and settlement here. We have appealed
to their native justice and magnanimity, and we have conjured them by
the ties of our common kindred to disavow these usurpations, which would
inevitably interrupt our connections and correspondence. They too have been
deaf to the voice of justice and of consanguinity. We must, therefore, acquiesce
in the necessity, which denounces our Separation, **and hold them, as we**
hold the rest of mankind, Enemies in War, in Peace Friends."

- The Declaration of Independence (July 4, 1776)

The thirteen colonies had exhausted all their options and pursued every opportunity for their grievances to be heard, and Great Britain had but one answer: absolute submission to the crown, even to the point of breaking faith with their conscience. Recall the climate of Britain at this time. This was a land who had broken off relations with Rome and established the Church of England. The Church of England was the only state-sanctioned church, and was absolutely controlled by the monarch. Therefore, if the king allowed even the slightest bit of disobedience, word would get back to England and to Britain's other colonies around the globe. Simply put, no matter the merits of their grievances, nothing was going to change. Tyrants are threatened when they lose control, and the king of England was no exception to this truth.

To add insult to injury, this wasn't just another conquest of Great Britain. Most of these people considered England their home. They most certainly had family and friends who remained in England, but the relationship between the colonies and the British became so toxic they had to choose to hold onto the ties of old or break free from the bondage of a tyrant. With the benefit of history, we know the thirteen colonies severed their ties and declared war!

Imagine the courage it took to declare war on the British Empire. Imagine the shock the world must have felt, and the fear of uncertainty which ravaged the colonies as the reality of a war set in. Think about the boldness it took for this clan of colonies to take the leadership role in the negotiation and put Britain on notice they were now enemies of war! Imagine the rage this moment must have stirred in the king, for a group of lowly colonies to attempt to bring disgrace to the empire. Imagine the world hoping for America's victory, but feeling doubtful at best about the likelihood of this outcome. This entire situation, this moment, took the world by surprise. From this point forward, the world began to transform. Both parties had but one choice, and it was war. Amazingly, even in the face of a declaration of war, two more characteristics were added to our repertoire: long suffering and the willingness to place principles above self. So, when asked about the nature of American identity, we can respond with unity, truth, equality, transparency, trust, long suffering, and value of principles. The colonists were principled to the point they were willing to die for their cause. Talk about true Americans!

The statement from the Declaration of Independence which says "*... and hold them, as we hold the rest of mankind, enemies in war, in peace friends...*" provides remarkable insight into our national character. Have you ever heard of a nation declaring war on another nation, but also paving the way for forgiveness and reconciliation at the conclusion of the matter? It's remarkable if you ask me, and true to our ideals. America grew not because of the size of our land, the wealth of our resources, or the might of our military. We grew to fill the shoes of the stature of our character. Add two more virtues to the American identity: forgiveness and reconciliation. No wonder the world looked toward this land for answers and hope. We are, at our core, a land rich in ideals. Think about the wars we have had throughout our two-hundred year history. When Hitler was defeated, we helped to rebuild a better, peaceful, and more prosperous Germany. Yes, we maintained a military presence across Europe, but America forgave Germany and reconciled our nation by establishing a more healthy relationship. Look at Japan after Pearl Harbor. America delivered the deadly blows by dropping the atomic bomb on Hiroshima and Nagasaki. We didn't cut ties with Japan when the war was over. We forgave Japan, reconciled, and then helped them rebuild. Look at Afghanistan and Iraq. We could have just brought destruction and death to their land, but we have fought to rebuild and are still helping to do so. You see, our desire has never been and never will be to conquer another's land and occupy it for our own gain. We can't, for to do so goes against our unalienable rights of life, liberty, and the pursuit of happiness. We have been taught to love others as we desire to be loved, so to utilize tyranny to advance our cause would mean we have left the ideals of liberty behind.

Young America had declared war and paved the way for peace-time affairs, but there was one last thing that must be done. America had to declare themselves free by faith!

WE, THEREFORE, THE
REPRESENTATIVES

───────────── ✿ ─────────────

"We, therefore, the Representatives of the united States of America,
*in General Congress, Assembled, appealing to **the Supreme Judge of the***
***world** for the rectitude of our intentions, do, in the Name, and by Authority*
of the good People of these Colonies, solemnly publish and declare, That
these united Colonies are, and of Right ought to be Free and Independent
States, that they are Absolved from all Allegiance to the British Crown, and
that all political connection between them and the State of Great Britain,
is and ought to be totally dissolved; and that as Free and Independent
States, they have full Power to levy War, conclude Peace, contract Alliances,
establish Commerce, and to do all other Acts and Things which Independent
*States may of right do. -- And for the support of this Declaration, **with a***
***firm reliance on the protection of Divine Providence,** we mutually*
pledge to each other our Lives, our Fortunes, and our sacred Honor."
- *The Declaration of Independence (July 4, 1776)*

We declared a war that we neither asked for nor desired, but the winds of history placed this young land into a corner to fight for freedom or allow it to die. To conclude the document, our fathers of old had but one task left to accomplish—to declare to all America was now free. From this point forward, America would decide her destiny from a position of liberty, not behind the bondage of tyranny. Oh, the elation of freedom that must have rushed into the souls of all those brave men. America may have declared freedom from her British captives, but by being free, they chose faith in "... firm reliance on the protection of Divine Providence." America began this great quest by first acknowledging nature's God, and then, with grateful hearts, accepted the Creator's gifts, called unalienable rights. From here they appealed so fervently to the Supreme Judge of the world, for they were cognizant of eternal consequences, and from there they knew they would not overcome any great struggles without a firm reliance on the protection of Divine Providence.

The sentence which comes on the heels of the reference to Divine Providence states:

> ...*we mutually pledge to each other our Lives, our Fortunes, and our Sacred Honor.*

This statement reveals to America the depth of conviction, the extent of sacrifice, the firmness of commitment, and the permanent bond of love which ran among our forefathers. They were willing to sacrifice everything. In the book of Acts, we are told that the believers had devoted themselves to the purposes of the early church and were willing to sell their possessions and goods to anyone who was in need. This is a reflection of selflessness, a character trait of people living for a transcendent purpose (Acts 2:42–47).[142] As we know from history, the early church grew, but it too came at a cost, as most of the disciples died a martyr's death. Our founding fathers reached this point of selflessness too. As the call of liberty drew the hearts of our forefathers, the grasp of the vanities of life on earth was shattered. They rose to their moment in history and planted seeds of selflessness at the heart of America.

America, you decide. Did our founders have a faith? Did God exist in private, or was He woven into the fabric of our birth? As for me, I can only take away the belief that these authors recognized God, who created the wonder of nature and the laws that govern her. They understood the relationship between the Creator and the created. They possessed humility and were not ashamed that they were the receivers of life, not the givers. Perhaps that isn't evidence enough, but those fine men appealed to the Supreme Judge, before whom, when the brevity of life disappeared, they would lay bare to receive their rewards or just punishments. In the end, they did declare their faith in Divine Providence and not in men. We began this journey and discovered the character of this land, which includes unity, truth, equality, transparency, trust, long suffering, value of principles,

---

142 Scripture taken from the Holy Bible, New International Version®. Copyright © 1973, 1978, 1984 by International Bible Society. Used by permission of Zondervan. All rights reserved.

forgiveness, and reconciliation. All of these things began with God and were ended with His hand of providence. Was it by chance Nature's God began our story, in the text of the Declaration of Independence? Was it random to mention our Creator, who made the created, man, with the imprints of life, liberty, and the pursuit of happiness? Would our forefathers appeal to the Supreme Judge of this world (a phrase denoting awareness of eternal consequences) for mercy and direction if they did not believe in God Himself? As if this isn't evidence enough, placing eternity aside, look at where they placed their faith. Not in man, wealth, or might. They knew exactly where to go—their God known as Divine Providence.

As a nation that has arrived at the most secular time in our history, where saying the Pledge of Allegiance or citing a prayer is considered offensive, we must ask ourselves America: What are we afraid of? It was through God's mighty hand we were brought into this land and have what we have, so why is it so hard to see the reality of a God so near? We can twist and turn history on its head, but this young nation knew what was right and where all good things came from. It wasn't from man, but from God above. Our character concludes with unity, truth, equality, transparency, trust, long suffering, value of principles, forgiveness, reconciliation, generosity, and the climax of the matter is the solidity of our faith.

America, we must return to God Himself. What are we afraid of? He said it Himself, those who forgive will be forgiven. So suck up our pride. Acknowledge our mistakes, and go back to Him!

FOREFATHERS FOREVER

---⚬⚭⚬---

New Hampshire: Josiah Bartlett, William Whipple, Matthew Thornton
Massachusetts: John Hancock, Samuel Adams, John
Adams, Robert Treat Paine, Elbridge Gerry
Rhode Island: Stephen Hopkins, William Ellery
Connecticut: Roger Sherman, Samuel Huntington,
William Williams, Oliver Wolcott
New York: William Floyd, Philip Livingston, Francis Lewis, Lewis Morris
New Jersey: Richard Stockton, John Witherspoon, Francis
Hopkinson, John Hart, Abraham Clark
Pennsylvania: Robert Morris, Benjamin Rush, Benjamin
Franklin, John Morton, George Clymer, James Smith,
George Taylor, James Wilson, George Ross
Delaware: Caesar Rodney, George Read, Thomas McKean
Maryland: Samuel Chase, William Paca, Thomas
Stone, Charles Carroll of Carrollton
Virginia: George Wythe, Richard Henry Lee, Thomas Jefferson, Benjamin
Harrison, Thomas Nelson, Jr., Francis Lightfoot Lee, Carter Braxton
North Carolina: William Hooper, Joseph Hewes, John Penn
South Carolina: Edward Rutledge, Thomas Heyward,
Jr., Thomas Lynch, Jr., Arthur Middleton
Georgia: Button Gwinnett, Lyman Hall, George Walton

- The Declaration of Independence (July 4, 1776)

On our journey through the Declaration of Independence, we have made our way from severing our ties with Great Britain to the front row seat where our founders planted the roots of unity, truth, and equality for all men. The final step in completing the Declaration of Independence is the addition of the signatures of our forefathers. These aren't just any signatures. These are the names of the men who chose to submit to liberty's call despite the most uncertain odds. Often times we overlook the signatures or make light of them in our everyday speech. (Ex: "Give me your John Hancock.") Truth be told, there was something more profound with the formality of the moment. Before the ink had dried upon the page, these men had committed high treason against the English crown, a crime punishable by death. They undeniably recognized the magnitude of their role in the events surrounding the Revolutionary War and America's pursuit of independence, an act, once committed, they could never take back.

These men had to be men of courage, men of conviction, and men of faith. The odds were not in their favor. The reality of their military might was far from impressive, and the certain loss of life which was about to occur was heavy. I'm confident each of these men took turns struggling, straining, praying, and enduring those restless nights when the gravity of destiny, the anxiety of war, and the consequences of failure were more than any man could bear alone. This was their Gethsemane!

They forged ahead. They faced their fears head on. They placed trust in their convictions and saw, with eternal eyes of faith, beyond the clouds of the immediate. They knew that despite their agony and the agony ahead, there was but one path— to trust in liberty's call, to endure the suffering they were about to begin, and trust Divine Providence that their nation would be resurrected from death to life. As the events unfolded, the mocking of the British soldiers, the massacres, and the shortages of supplies and personnel they could have regretted grabbing hold of that feathered pen. As the curtain of the temple was torn, the tide began to turn. George Washington and his men strained to see victory. Through the ashes of the destruction, the stench of death, and the desperate condition of our military, liberty was born and the captives were released. The charge was clear and the path surely lit as America began her call to bring freedom to all nations and teach them why Providence granted humans those unalienable rights. Our forefathers created America upon the bedrock of bravery, the cornerstone of courage, and the foundation of faith. They are forefathers forever, and forever free!

Did the founding fathers really intend for America to be a completely independent nation, reliant upon self and man? Was it the intent of the

Declaration of Independence to fight for freedom so they could live a life free of dependence? Look around in modern America and you will see a culture hostile towards a God-centered worldview in favor of a man-centered worldview. This was never the intent of the founding fathers to declare independence from God. Their intent was to declare independence from a man, the king of England, otherwise known as a tyrant. The battle of independence was not a battle to be completely independent; it was a battle to decide where man would place his dependency. Think for a moment. When the Declaration of Independence was written, the writers chose to define liberty within the context of God. They never defined liberty absent from the existence of God.

As we've seen through the brief analysis of the Declaration of Independence the founding fathers placed four references to God. The references in the text are indicative of a nation who ran from the grip of man, the tyrant of a king, into the arms of God. They etched into the foundation of America, through the text of the Declaration of Independence, four distinct names of God: *Nature's God, the Creator, the Supreme Judge of this world, and Divine Providence.*[143] They sought the protection of Almighty God. Sadly, the modern American culture has attempted to marginalize, but cannot erase the unapologetic words of the Declaration of Independence which declare dependency upon the Almighty. The document could be titled *The Declaration of Dependence on God!* America, the Revolutionary War at its core was a war of control between man and God. It says in the book of Joshua, "But if serving the Lord seems undesirable to you, then choose for yourselves this day whom you will serve".[144] The last few versus in the *Star Spangled Banner* illustrate America's dependence upon God during that time when freedom was born. Read the last stanza of our beloved national anthem:

> *O, thus be it ever when freemen shall stand,*
> *Between their loved home and the war's desolation!*
> *Blest with victory and peace, may the heav'n-rescued land*
> *Praise the Power that hath made and preserved us a nation!*
> *Then conquer we must, when our cause. It is just,*
> *And this be our motto: "In God is our trust"*
> *And the star-spangled banner in triumph shall wave*
> *O'er the land of the free and the home of the brave!*[145]

143 See Appendix A - The Declaration of Independence.
144 Scripture taken from the Holy Bible, New International Version®. Copyright © 1973, 1978, 1984 by International Bible Society. Used by permission of Zondervan. All rights reserved.
145 Source: http://kids.niehs.nih.gov/lyrics/spangle.htm

Our national motto, *"In God We Trust,"* inspired by the Star Spangled Banner, signed into law on July 30, 1956 by President Dwight Eisenhower, and recognized by a Proclamation by the President of the United States of America, President George W. Bush, on the 50th anniversary in the year 2006, proclaims our dependence upon God.[146] The last sentence to the verse from the book of Joshua continues with "...but as for me and my household, we will serve the Lord (Joshua 24:15)".[147] Our forefathers made their choice in the Declaration of Independence in 1776, our national anthem proclaimed *"In God is our trust"* in 1814, and our law decreed *"In God We Trust"* as our national motto in 1956. Now, it is time for America in the twenty-first-century to choose.

Prayer

This prayer for taken from Congressional Record for the 108th Congress where Chaplain Dr. Lloyd John Ogilvie recognized February 24 as the day of George Washington's Farewell Address and felt it appropriate to recite the "Prayer for the United States of America" as it is preserved in the chapel at Valley Forge.[148]

Almighty God:

We make our earnest prayer that Thou wilt keep the United States in Thy Holy protection; that thou wilt incline the hearts of the Citizens to cultivate a spirit of subordination and obedience to Government, and entertain a brotherly affection and love for one another and for their fellow Citizens of the United States at large. And finally that Thou wilt most graciously be pleased to dispose us all to do justice, to love mercy, and to demean ourselves with that Love, humility and pacific temper of mind, which were the characteristics of the Divine Author of our blessed Religion, and without a humble imitation of whose example in these things we can never hope to be a happy nation. Grant our supplication, we beseech Thee, through Jesus Christ our Lord, Amen.

---

146 http://georgewbush-whitehouse.archives.gov/news/releases/2006/07/20060727-12.html

147 Scripture taken from the Holy Bible, New International Version®. Copyright © 1973, 1978, 1984 by International Bible Society. Used by permission of Zondervan. All rights reserved..

148 United States of America, Congressional Record, Proceedings and Debates of the 108th Congress First Session Volume 149-Part 3, Senate-Monday, February 24, 2003, Prayer by Chaplain Dr. Lloyd John Ogilvie who recognizes the day as George Washington's Farewell Address and says it is appropriate to recite the "Prayer for the United States of America as it is preserved in the chapel at Valley Forge," page 4198.

Section VI—The Final Branch

THE FINAL BRANCH

"In the beginning of the contest with Britain, when we were sensible of danger, we had daily prayers, in this room, for the divine protection. Our prayers, sir, were heard; and they were graciously answered. All of us, who were engaged in the straggle, must have observed frequent instances of a superintending Providence in our favor. To that kind Providence we owe this happy opportunity of consulting in peace on the means of establishing our future national felicity. And have we now forgotten that powerful Friend? or do we imagine we no longer need his assistance? I have lived, sir, a long time; and the longer I live, the more convincing proofs I see of this truth, that God governs in the affairs of men! And if a sparrow cannot fall to the ground without his notice, is it probable that an empire can rise without his aid? We have been assured, sir, in the sacred writings, that except the Lord build the house, they labor in vain who build it' I firmly believe this; and I also believe that without his concurring aid, we shall succeed in this political building no better than the builders of Babel: we shall be divided by our little partial, local interests, our projects will be confounded, and we ourselves shall become a reproach and a by-word to future ages. And what is worse, mankind may hereafter, from this unfortunate instance, despair of establishing government by human wisdom, and leave it to chance, war, and conquest."

Benjamin Franklin[149]

"The foundation of our national policy will be laid in the pure and immutable principles of private morality. The propitious smiles of

---

149 Everett, Edward, *Orations and speeches on various occasions, Volume 2,* C.C. Little and J. Brown, 1850.

*Heaven can never be expected on a nation that disregards the eternal
rules of order and right which Heaven itself has ordained ...."*

George Washington, First Inaugural, April 30, 1789[150]

*"I am the Alpha and the Omega," says the Lord God, "who
is, and who was, and who is to come, the Almighty."*

Revelation 1:8[151]

W hat is America to do when we have been failed repeatedly by
our executive branch, legislative branch, and judiciary branch
of government? Where are we to look when the magnitude of
our spending is on course to produce an economic implosion the likes of
which no American has seen? Where will the world turn when the hope
for liberty grows dim? Where will parents find peace when they attempt to
raise healthy children instilled with virtues when our communities are filled
with violence, hatred, immorality, and drugs? Where do followers of the
faithful find shelter when even the leaders of our churches fall prey to the
sexually perverse culture? Where do we go, America, when our finances, our
governmental institutions, our families, our churches, our traditions, and
our communities are crumbling before our eyes? We find ourselves at a crisis,
and the pressures are mounting on all sides. We have attempted everything
we know to do, but the enormity of our problems is beyond the capability
of our reach. Our culture is ill, sickened, and we need help. What are we
to do, America? Is it true, Armageddon is upon us? Is the end really near?
Unfortunately, we do not have the luxury of time to sit around and read the
signs or interpret the age. What we have been told to do is:

*"Stand at the crossroads and look; ask for the ancient paths, ask
where the good way is, and walk in it, and you will find rest for
your souls" (Jeremiah 6:16 NIV).*[152]

---

150 Source: http://www.archives.gov/legislative/features/gw-inauguration/
151 Scripture taken from the Holy Bible, New International Version®. Copyright © 1973,
1978, 1984 by International Bible Society. Used by permission of Zondervan. All rights
reserved.
152 Scripture taken from the Holy Bible, New International Version®. Copyright © 1973,
1978, 1984 by International Bible Society. Used by permission of Zondervan. All rights
reserved.

Unfortunately, the "whom" we are instructed to ask has been so marginalized in America. His names are nature's God, the Creator, the Supreme Judge of this world, and Divine Providence. He is so woven into the melody of the Declaration of Independence, yet if His name is spoken openly in the year 2010, it creates such hostility. I cannot tell you the number of times when I would tell family or friends I was writing a book about America and God, and people would say, "Be careful. Your writing is great, but you might want to remove that religious stuff." The infection grows deep.

There is and must be a role for God in America if America desires to remain relevant and vibrant in the world. Our forefathers acknowledged God in the founding documents, our state capitols throughout our land contain references to God, our currency refers to the Almighty, our Pledge of Allegiance[153] acknowledges our role under God, our courts swear on the Bible, our Congress begin each session with prayer, and our land has some of the richest and most diverse religious communities known to the world. America is not a secular country. It is not atheist or agnostic by design. America was never intended to exist in the zone of neutrality. Ironically, during the Civil War, both the North and the South made references to fighting for God. The President of the United States of America concludes each major speech by saying, "God Bless America." To conclude, America as a nation without faith is un-American.

There is great power in the invisible hand of Providence, herein known as *The Final Branch*. The Final Branch provides comfort during national tragedies, strength during times of national testing, endurance during times of great sacrifice, and hope that America can be better tomorrow than she is today. The Final Branch is a source of strength, not a weakness to be mitigated to the fringes of society. It is the magnificent centerpiece that makes us uniquely American. It is as important a branch of government as the executive, legislative, and judicial branches. Why has virtually every president consulted spiritual leaders throughout their terms? Why did Dr. Billy Graham meet with every president at one point or another to discuss personal and national matters of faith? Why, then, did George W. Bush meet with Christian leaders after the tragedy of September 11, 2001 to ask for their help in writing spiritual songs to comfort a hurting America? Why

---

153 Public Law 77-623. – 56 Stat. 377, Chap. 435, H.J.Res. 303, enacted June 22, 1942. Amended by Public Law 77-829. – 56 Stat. 1074, Chap. 806, H.J.Res. 359, enacted December 22, 1942. Public Law 83-396. – 68 Stat. 249, Chap. 297, H.J.Res. 243, enacted June 14, 1954. Public Law 94-344. – 90 Stat. 810, S.J.Res. 49, enacted July 7, 1976.

does the president say, "God Bless America," after each major address? It is part of our heritage. It is part of our upbringings, and it is the bookends to the life of our nation. Look at the Declaration of Independence. It begins with God being referred to as *nature's God and the Creator*, meaning they acknowledged God had created nature and all of which is contained in her, and then referred to God as *the Creator*, and man as *the created*. Our world and our lives began with God. Several paragraphs down, the authors place the other bookend into place, the Sovereign Judge of this world! Wow! God began life, and at the end of this life, He will be the judge of it! To conclude the matter, the authors of the text informed us on how to live through times of trial. We are to live through firm reliance on the protection of Divine Providence! Talk about having faith!

As we venture into *The Final Branch*, Americans will be provided irrefutable proof to resolve the conflict between theism and naturalism. Theism is the belief that there is a transcendent God who created the universe, a personal God of moral absolutes who possesses a unique relationship with man.[154] On the other hand, naturalism is the belief that natural causes alone are sufficient to explain everything that exists.[155] Naturalism is the idea that nature is all that exists, that life arose from a chance collision of atoms, evolving eventually into human life as we know it today.[156] By contrast, Christianity teaches that there is a transcendent God who existed before the world existed and who is the ultimate origin of everything else. The universe is dependent at every moment on His providential governance and care.[157] *The Final Branch* will demonstrate, through the four references to God found in The Declaration of Independence, why America and theism are interwoven at the core of this nation and why naturalism is incompatible with the founding fabric of America. This book will not make the claim that Christianity is the only religion that can exist in America. However, the book will demonstrate how Christianity was the dominant worldview which birthed America, defined liberty, and permanently imprinted theism into our national character. To modify this perspective is to create something less than the ideal of America.

It is time, America. As we stand at this crossroad and ask where the ancient path is, we begin unpacking the core of the American soul. It is long overdue to reach back through generations of history and go to the

154 Colson, Charles, and Nancy Pearcey. *How Now Shall We Live?* Tyndale House Publishing, Inc., 1999.
155 Ibid.
156 Ibid.
157 Ibid.

source of what spoke us into existence. Let's take this journey together as we begin to dig deeper and see what it means when we unearth and re-institute the four cornerstones to our land. What does it mean and what will it look like? Only He knows, but for the moments of these pages, let's start bridging the gap between America in 2010 and the ancient American path.

NATURE'S GOD

⁓☙⟐❧⁓

"In the beginning God created the heavens and the earth."
Genesis 1:1 (NIV)[158]

*"I form the light and create darkness, I bring prosperity and
create disaster; I, the Lord, do all these things."*
Isaiah 45:7 (NIV)[159]

*"Behold, I will create new heavens and a new earth. The former
things will not be remembered, nor will they come to mind."*
Isaiah 65:17 (NIV)[160]

I n America, in the year 2010, there is a fierce battle occurring within
our midst over who or what created the earth. Many would argue
it was random chance, that life was birthed out of an explosion (a
big bang). Others subscribe to a combination of evolution, the big bang
theory, and the existence of God. Still others believe life occurred solely
in the way it has been accounted for in God's Holy Word—the Bible.
There are really only two choices. Either life was created randomly, or
nature's God does exist and had specific plans and intelligent designs. For

---

158 Scripture taken from the Holy Bible, New International Version®. Copyright © 1973,
1978, 1984 by International Bible Society. Used by permission of Zondervan. All rights
reserved.
159 Ibid
160 Ibid.

centuries, even before the birth of America, it was accepted that nature's God was responsible for what we have come to know as the heavens and the earth. There was no radioactive dating, mathematical models, or computer simulations. People simply believed in something more vast, more superior, and more wise than the limitations of the human mind. This isn't to say history didn't have its doubts, but the clear foundation and fabric built into the Declaration of Independence subscribes to the account that there is an all-knowing, ever present God who chose to put this earth, the animals, the plants, the universe, and man himself into existence. There is such comfort and such security when humans place their confidence into the existence of a God who, with order and purpose, made life. To place our confidence into randomness, chance, or evolution of any sort leads us quickly down a road of chaos, confusion, and anxiety. Furthermore, the first reference to God in the Declaration of Independence concerning the laws of nature and Nature's God could possibly co-exist with the naturalist perspective on man, morality, and creation (recall that naturalism is the idea that nature is all that exists, that life arose from a chance collision of atoms, evolving eventually into human life).[161] Unfortunately for the naturalist, the authors of the Declaration of Independence made three additional references to God—Creator, Supreme Judge of the World, and Divine Providence. Taken as a whole, the claims of the naturalist cannot coexist within the framework of the Declaration of Independence. Either the naturalist is correct and America was built upon a flawed worldview, or the naturalists are wrong and are out of step with the core of our American belief system.

War is a perfect example to make our point. When the United States military goes into a war, the amount of planning, communication, preparation, and training that goes into a single battle is astounding. Think about the simple task of just getting fuel and food to all those vehicles and men and women stretched across a continent. There is a clear chain of command, and there are contingency plans for unplanned events (which actually means they are planning for them). War is complex to say the least, and to go into battle without a strategy, without adequate planning and ample preparation, is suicide. Truth be told, it is because of this rigid structure the US military has been largely successful over its history. There is security for the soldier and the sailor in knowing that when they go into battle, there has been planning conducted. For the most

---

161 Colson, Charles, and Nancy Pearcey. *How Now Shall We Live?* Tyndale House Publishing, Inc., 1999.

part, they have been training for years before the actual engagement. Now contrast this with the Iraqi military right after the second gulf war. They were poorly organized, poorly trained, not accustomed to planning and preparation for conflicts, and soon enough chaos and insecurity erupted amongst the troops and the countryside. The point of the matter isn't to analyze military preparation. Rather the idea is to establish the fact that when we begin to believe the earth was created out of randomness, then we have opened the doors to chaos, anxiety, disunity, and insecurity. We inadvertently cut the umbilical cord to the peace, security, and tranquility of our land. Essentially, we are trying to grow and mature without the nutrients required for a stable, secure, vibrant society. Instead, chaos and insecurity ensue and we are left to begin searching for something solid, something permanent, and something that will not change. Therein lies the reason some have fashioned their security in the government, their wealth, their intellect, their community, or their church. The truth is, America is deeply insecure and desperately in need of something stable to plant our feet upon.

Stability is defined as "not likely to change or fail; firmly established."[162] We live in the age of change, and it seems like nothing is consistent. I mean everything, even the meaning of Christmas, is changing. When those young revolutionaries were preparing for war, the air was filled with uncertainty. As the young, rag tag group of colonists were about to face the most powerful military on earth, instead of turning inward or placing their confidence in fleeting objects or people, the great men of that day returned to basics. First, they acknowledged the fact that nature's God did exist, and it was because of nature's God that they were at this moment in history. This provided comfort and security to a young nation that had the confidence in something wiser than all of them, and could guide them through the ensuing days. Second, they recognized their role as the created, not the Creator. They based their confidence in the imprint of this creator on all of mankind by acknowledging each person's unalienable rights of life, liberty, and the pursuit of happiness. Third, as they announced their intentions before the world, they asked for the Supreme Judge of this world to guide, direct, and ensure their intentions were on the right side of history. There is strength and security that comes when we share burdens with someone else, and this someone happened to be God. Finally, they acknowledged the path toward liberty was cloudy and confusing. Therefore, they placed

---

162 *The New Oxford American Dictionary, Second Edition*, Erin McKean (editor), 2051 pages, May 2005, Oxford University Press, ISBN 0-19-517077-6.

firm reliance on Divine Providence. This reliance, known as faith, gave them somewhere to go when they were unsure of themselves. When the death toll mounted, when the family homes burned to the ground, when their national treasury emptied, they knew exactly where to go.

Unfortunately, America, we are about to face the same forces of tyranny and desperation, but we are starting from an even more elementary perspective. To restore America, we need to renew the hearts and minds across this land. We cannot afford to remove a cornerstone of the stability and security of America. Our founders recognized the strength found in God so many years before. They realized its importance enough to place it in the first sentence in the Declaration of Independence. There are many resources available to learn about creation and God's role in creating the universe. So seek those sources out. For parents, you need to instill this into your children so they can grow up with security, comfort, and humility even during moments of great uncertainty. Government leaders and politicians, you need to put aside the rhetoric and start engaging in straight talk with your constituents about re-instituting the Christian heritage and Christian version of creation in our schools, history books, and public life overall. Educators, you are some of our best defenses on this. It is up to you to teach the truth across America and dispel the lies being taught across this land. Church leaders, pastors, and priests across America, you need to teach, preach, and speak with fervency, and help your flock understand the critical concept of who is responsible for creation.

Our journey begins here, America, as we re-affirm and re-institute the wisdom of our forefathers. Focus, you great patriots, on the task at hand. Look past the crumbling culture around us. See above the uncertainty and the insecurity. As we re-establish our historical heritage within our culture, the tide will turn. After all, God is faithful and true, and has assured us with His words.

> *Be strong and courageous. Do not be afraid or terrified because of them, for the Lord your God goes with you; he will never leave you nor forsake you.*
>
> *Deuteronomy 31:6 (NIV)[163]*

---

163 Scripture taken from the Holy Bible, New International Version®. Copyright © 1973, 1978, 1984 by International Bible Society. Used by permission of Zondervan. All rights reserved.

Do you not know? Have you not heard? The Lord is the everlasting God, the Creator of the ends of the earth. He will not grow tired or weary, and his understanding no one can fathom. He gives strength to the weary and increases the power of the weak. Even the youths grow tired and weary, and young men stumble and fall; but those who hope in the Lord will renew their strength. They will soar on wings like eagles; they will run and not grow weary, they will walk and not be faint.

Isaiah 40:28–31 (NIV)[164]

He is the source of life. He created the heavens and the earth, and He created you and me. As we become weary, America, as our land bleeds, let's go back to nature's God. He's promised us that the eagle will soar! Try it, America, as the role of man decreases and the role of nature's God increases. Watch the landscape of our nation transform from chaos to calm!

---

164 Ibid.

THE CREATOR

∽◌◉◌∼

*"So God created man in his own image, in the image of God
he created him; male and female he created them."*

Genesis 1:27 (NIV)[165]

*"The Lord God formed the man from the dust of the ground and breathed
into his nostrils the breath of life, and the man became a living being."*

Genesis 2:7 (NIV)[166]

Amazingly, the Declaration of Independence opens by referencing nature's God, then continues with the second reference to the Creator, and defines the unique relationship that exists between the Creator and the created. Just to refresh our memories a bit, here is what the text of the Declaration of Independence says:

> *We hold these truths to be self-evident, that **all men are created equal**, that they are endowed by their **Creator** with certain unalienable Rights, that among these are Life, Liberty and the pursuit of Happiness.*

The Signers of the Declaration of Independence could have chosen any other words, but instead decided to highlight the unique relationship

---

165 Scripture taken from the Holy Bible, New International Version®. Copyright © 1973, 1978, 1984 by International Bible Society. Used by permission of Zondervan. All rights reserved.

166 Ibid.

between the Creator and the created. Unlike the first sentence, which refers to nature's God, this shows a sense of pride, a sense of uniqueness, a sense of an artist proud of His masterpiece. Our forefathers clearly believed the Creator held man as the crown jewel of His creation. It is interesting the authors referred to those attributes given by the Creator to all men, those unalienable rights. As we've discussed before, *unalienable* denotes something which cannot be given or taken away from the possessor. Therefore, it is fair to say our Creator, through the wisdom of His design, made all men to possess dignity. We are told in the book of Genesis that God created man in his own image (Genesis 1:27),[167] and He breathed life into man's nostrils (Genesis 2:7).[168] We are, have been, and will always be the highlight of His creation. This captivation by God is startling. It is humbling to think of the depth and breadth of His affection toward mankind. He tells us repeatedly we are the apple of His eye (Zechariah 2:8),[169] which affords us a sense of protection and security. The protection and security are natural. Who doesn't want to protect their most prized possessions? Where do you keep your diamond rings, ladies? Moreover, this unique status man possesses with his Creator implies man has a distinctly different relationship with God than any other plant, animal, or creature roaming the earth or the sea. God desires a close relationship with the created! The *deist*, who believes in a God which is distant, foreign, or alien, would agree God created man and the universe, but left it to run on its own.[170] The deist's view would have been compatible with the Declaration of Independence had the founding fathers left the final two references to God (Supreme Judge of the World, and with reliance upon the protection of Divine Providence) out of the Declaration of Independence—especially the reference to Divine Providence. If you recall from an earlier section, the national seal of the United States of America, as seen on the back of the one dollar bill, contains an unfinished pyramid with an eye on the top. The unfinished pyramid is known as the Eye of Providence which symbolizes God's involvement and favor upon America. Either the deist is correct or the text of the Declaration of Independence is flawed.

---

167 Scripture taken from the Holy Bible, New International Version®. Copyright © 1973, 1978, 1984 by International Bible Society. Used by permission of Zondervan. All rights reserved.

168 Ibid.

169 Ibid.

170 Sire, James W., *The Universe Next Door, A Basic Worldview Catalog Fourth Edition.* InterVarsity Press USA, 2004.

America, when we decided to move down the path of disavowing ourselves to this unique place in creation, we ventured outside Divine Providence's security and protection. Our forefathers went in the exact opposite direction during their season of uncertainty. As we walk further and further away from His shelter, the insecurity across our land ensues. Think about it. A child who is raised with a loving, supportive, disciplining, and involved father will, on average, turn out to be much more secure with him or herself than children raised in broken homes, shelters, and orphanages outside the protection a loving dad affords. As a nation, it stands to reason that if we encouraged a worldview that acknowledged God as the Creator, security would begin to take grip again. I fear we have reached a tipping point in America (or we're closing in on it) where we have replaced God as the center of creation with other, more transient means (e.g., government, randomness, the environment) and something less wise (e.g., man himself). We have been attempting to redefine this universal truth for the last fifty years, and now, one decade into the twenty-first century, we find ourselves broken, immoral, and more fearful for the future than ever. Perhaps those men of old invoked great wisdom into this land, and as wise students of history, it is now our turn to trust the choice of their words by believing in the Creator even more.

The second facet of the Creator that our forefathers told us about is the Creator's desire for a close relationship with His created. How can you arrive at this conclusion from one sentence in the document? Simply put, the authors of this great document decided to place the microscope on the Creator-created relationship over any other relationship or organism throughout all of creation. It was this relationship which found itself expressed in the Declaration of Independence. Furthermore, our forefathers communicated a sense of order and authority by capitalizing the Creator and leaving "...all men created..." in lowercase. Coincidence? I doubt it. This manuscript was read and edited by many hands before it was signed.

America, there is a gap right now, a gap between where our culture sits, how it relates to the Creator, and the role both of them play in our society. For decades we have taken step upon step away from recognition of how life should be ordered. We are exchanging this for a godless society, which will lead to the inevitable collapse of our nation. If you are one who counts themselves as one of the faithful, then press on for the prize. For those of you who are lukewarm and have been sitting around playing both sides of the fence, it is time to make a choice. For those of you who have wholesale rejected any notion of the Creator and do not desire to come into harmony with nature's laws, my heart hurts for you.

To take back our land and reclaim what was entrusted to us over two hundred years ago, we must reestablish the preeminence of God as Creator all across our society. We are out of sync, America, for we have been going about this liberty thing all wrong. As my grandpa used to say, "We have the cart before the horse." I get it. Our culture continues to desire to move God to the fringes because our society says it is unfashionable to be a person of faith. The rooster will crow sooner or later, and one day we will all awaken before the Supreme Judge of the world to account for this life.

THE SUPREME JUDGE OF THE WORLD

―――――――――― ⟡ ――――――――――

"Then I saw a great white throne and him who was seated on it. Earth and sky fled from his presence, and there was no place for them. And I saw the dead, great and small, standing before the throne, and books were opened. Another book was opened, which is the book of life. The dead were judged according to what they had done as recorded in the books ... if anyone's name was not found written in the book of life, he was thrown into the lake of fire."

Revelation 20:11–15 (NIV)[171]

"Come near, you nations, and listen; pay attention, you peoples! Let the earth hear, and all that is in it, the world, and all that comes out of it! The Lord is angry with all nations; his wrath upon all their armies. He will totally destroy them, he will give them over to slaughter. Their slain will be thrown out, their dead bodies will send up a stench; the mountains will be soaked with blood."

Isaiah 34:1–3[172]

Those words—Supreme Judge of the world—what majesty, what power, and what fear those words instill. Think about this for a moment. Our forefathers were about to enter the war of all wars. Lives were going to be lost, families would be torn apart, and cities would be burned to the ground. As they were about to conclude their declaration of war, they made an appeal to who? To the Supreme Judge of the World. The word *supreme* is defined as

―――――――――――――――

171 Scripture taken from the Holy Bible, New International Version®. Copyright © 1973, 1978, 1984 by International Bible Society. Used by permission of Zondervan. All rights reserved.
172 Ibid.

"superior to all others, strongest, most important, or most powerful."[173] The word *judge* denotes "someone who decides authoritatively after deliberation."[174] This isn't just the Supreme Court judge or your local city court judge. This is the Judge of all judges. To build upon this, the most powerful person with the force of authority is going to cast judgment upon the intentions and actions of men here on earth. There are several things that are most notable. First, there is a supreme judge, and the actions of men will come before this Supreme Judge of the world. The implication is that the Supreme Judge of this world has the ultimate and final authority to deliberate over what happens in this world. By utilizing the word *world,* it denotes this person or figure stands over top of or above what he is judging, meaning this super-sized judge must be in a position to know all sides of the actions he will be judging. Just like in a court of law, the prosecutor will bring the evidence and reasons why someone should be convicted of the crime, and the defense attorney will present the evidence why the person should not be convicted of a crime. It is the judge who sits above both the plaintiff and the defendant, and knows all sides of the case to cast judgment. That's one intelligent being! Therefore, the Supreme Judge of the world must know the law and all sides of the actions He will be casting a judgment upon. Now, for a judge to do this in one legal proceeding for a single crime with skilled attorneys arguing opposing sides is difficult enough, but to do this for all men everywhere, for every action, and to cast just judgments is entirely different. This judge must possess intelligence far superior than any man. If these men, who signed the Declaration of Independence, came from across Europe, then Christianity would have influenced their view of the world. After all, the epicenters of the Roman Catholic Church, the Protestant Movement, and the Church of England were located in Europe placing Christianity at the forefront of most of the cultural rifts and national conflicts in the centuries preceding the birth of America. Therefore, if you or your ancestors were from Europe during the eighteenth century and you find yourself writing, reviewing, and signing the Declaration of Independence, then your worldview would have been strongly influenced by Christianity. As a result, you would be concerned about the Supreme Judge of this world and eternal consequences, and how this judge can know all the facts for every action of every person and have perfect knowledge of the judicial code to cast just judgment. This refers to a term known as *omniscience* in Christianity. Omniscience can be defined as:

> *The state of being all-knowing which theology ascribes to God. Though Scripture affirms God's immeasurable understanding, God's omniscience is not a matter of abstract speculation. Rather, God's knowing is a matter*

---

173 *The New Oxford American Dictionary, Second Edition,* Erin McKean (editor), 2051 pages, May 2005, Oxford University Press, ISBN 0-19-517077-6.
174 Ibid.

of personal experience. God knows us personally. Such knowledge is cause for alarm for the unrighteous, but for confidence for God's saints.[175]

Therefore, we have a Supreme Judge of the world who is all-knowing (omniscient) who was referenced in the Declaration of Independence, who our forefathers were appealing to with the belief that this super-sized judge knew everything.

From the text of the Declaration of Independence there is no doubt men are accountable for their actions on this earth. If men are accountable for their actions on earth, then someone must be aware of the actions of all men and make a record of those actions, good or bad. Just like when a defendant goes into the courtroom, there must be evidence and knowledge presented to the judge that a crime was committed. How can anyone be in all places at all times to record the actions, the words, the thoughts, and inner motivations of all men? If these men, who signed the Declaration of Independence, came from across Europe, then Christianity would have influenced their view of the world. After all, the epicenters of the Roman Catholic Church, the Protestant Movement, and the Church of England were located in Europe placing Christianity at the forefront of many of the cultural rifts and national conflicts in the centuries preceding the birth of America. Therefore, if you or your ancestors were from Europe during the eighteenth century and you find yourself writing, reviewing, and signing the Declaration of Independence, then your worldview would have been strongly influenced by Christianity. As a result, you would be concerned about the Supreme Judge of this world and eternal consequences, and how this judge can be everywhere at all times. This refers to a term known as *omnipresent in Christianity.* Omnipresence is:

Derived from Latin, to speak of God's presence everywhere in all the world's spaces. The Bible speaks of God's presence in two major ways: in space and in terms of relationships.[176]

We have a Supreme Judge of the world who is all-knowing (omniscient), all-present (omnipresent), who was referenced in the Declaration of Independence, and to whom our forefathers were appealing to with an obvious belief that all of their actions have ultimate accountability. Like any legal proceeding, a just punishment must fit the deed.

---

175 *Holman Bible Dictionary,* Trent C. Butler (editor), 1458 pages, © Copyright 1991 Holman Bible Publishers, ISBN: 1-55819-053-8.

176 *Holman Bible Dictionary,* Trent C. Butler (editor), 1458 pages, © Copyright 1991 Holman Bible Publishers, ISBN: 1-55819-053-8.

Judgment denotes there will either be a reward or some sort of punishment after judgment has passed. This indicates the conviction of some sort of heaven or hell, where this super judge has the sole power to give rewards or inflict punishment. If this is the correct definition, then this judge would be the *most powerful* judge the world has known. In a Christian worldview, this characteristic is known as *omnipotence*. Omnipotence can be defined as:

> *The state of being all powerful which theology subscribes to God. Scripture often affirms that all power belongs to God (Psalm 147:5),[177] that all things are possible for God (Luke 1:37; 19:26),[178] and that God's power exceeds what humans can ask or think (Ephesians 3:20).[179] For Scripture, God's omnipotence is not a matter of abstract speculation but a force to be reckoned with.[180]*

America, right in the Declaration of Independence our founders are telling us they are concerned with the punishments or rewards which an omnipotent—all-powerful—God may inflict upon them and their nation. If we take the last sentence of the definition above seriously, "a force to be reckoned with," then there must have been a deep-seated fear and respect for this God. To conclude otherwise would be contextually inaccurate.

If there is judgment that will result in rewards or punishment, the next obvious question is where do we find the criteria for how we will be judged? For example, in the United States' code for criminal statues, there are elements defining a crime which must be met. When the elements are met, then a punishment commensurate with the crime is assigned. This naturally begs the question: What is the Supreme Judge of this world's code or criteria used for judging the actions of men on earth? Truthfully, when you are about to send your nation to war, you are aware of an ultimate judgment. It is only logical the writers would have searched far and wide to ensure they knew the elements of the Supreme Judge's statute. Stay with me, America. If these men who signed the Declaration of Independence, came from across Europe, then Christianity would have influenced their view of the world. After all, the epicenters of the Roman Catholic Church, the Protestant Movement, and the Church of England were located in Europe placing Christianity at the forefront of many cultural rifts and national conflicts in the centuries preceding the birth of

---

177 Scripture taken from the Holy Bible, New International Version®. Copyright © 1973, 1978, 1984 by International Bible Society. Used by permission of Zondervan. All rights reserved.
178 Ibid.
179 Ibid.
180 *Holman Bible Dictionary*, Trent C. Butler (editor), 1458 pages, © Copyright 1991 Holman Bible Publishers, ISBN: 1-55819-053-8.

America. Therefore, if you or your ancestors were from Europe during the eighteenth century and you find yourself writing, reviewing, and signing the Declaration of Independence, then your worldview would have been shaped by Christianity. As a result, you would be concerned about the Supreme Judge of this world's judicial code. There is only one source in which this code could be found—the inspired Word of God, the Bible. This is pretty deep, America. Now we have ourselves some meat to chew on!

There is a multicultural movement, sometimes known as postmodernism, within America where all cultures are treated as morally equivalent and reduced all ideas to social constructions shaped by class, gender, and ethnicity.[181] Chuck Colson and Nancy Pearce, in their book, *How Now Shall We Live?*, state:

> *The philosophy of existentialism, a precursor of postmodernism, proclaims that life is absurd, meaningless, and that the individual self must create his own meaning by his own choices. Choice was elevated to the ultimate value, the only justification for any action. Contemporary trends like postmodernism and multiculturalism are rooted in naturalism, for if there is no transcendent source of truth or morality, then we find our identity only in our race gender, or ethnic group.[182]*

It would seem, even to the novice, that the reference in the Declaration of Independence to a Supreme Judge directly contradicts the philosophy of existentialism, where choice and self are held up as opposed to a transcendent judge of this universe. More specifically, the letter and the spirit of the Declaration of Independence where the Supreme Judge of this world is referenced are consistent with a Christian worldview. A Christian worldview never equates truth with the limited perspective of any group.[183] Colson and Pearcey also state that truth is God's perspective, as revealed in Scripture. Hence, while Christians appreciate the cultural diversity, Christians insist on the propriety of judging particular cultural practices as morally right or wrong. Therefore, a postmodern worldview is not compatible with the text of the Declaration of Independence, whereas a Christian worldview is highly compatible. Our founding fathers did not appeal to the choice of the individual regarding morality, or define morality in terms of race, gender, or ethnic group. Could you imagine having a different set of laws for each race, gender, ethnic group, and perhaps even each individual? To do so would undermine the Declaration of Independence and make the lofty aspirations within the Constitution, to establish justice and ensure domestic tranquility, a virtual

181 Colson, Charles, and Nancy Pearcey. *How Now Shall We Live?* Tyndale House Publishing, Inc., 1999.
182 Ibid.
183 Ibid.

impossibility. Besides, our beloved Declaration of Independence says all men were created equal. If we buy into equality, then all of us should be judged equally. Just look at Lady Justice, a statue found in courts across this land, where she sits blindfolded and administering justice without regard to class, gender, or ethnicity. Perhaps we should heed the words of the Reverend Martin Luther King, Jr.'s "I have a dream" speech:

> *Let freedom ring. And when this happens—when we allow freedom to ring from every village and every hamlet, from every state and every city, we will be able to speed up that day when all of God's children—black men and white men, Jews and Gentiles, Protestants and Catholics—will be able to join hands ...*[184]

In summary, our forefathers appealed to the Supreme God of this world, and in order to be the ultimate judge of this world, the Supreme God must be all-knowing (omniscient) to know all the facts of every action of all men, be everywhere at all times to make a record of each man's actions (omnipresent), and possess the power to either punish or reward men for their actions (omnipotent). To be held accountable, man must know the judicial code being used to judge him, and given the fact that the framers came primarily from Europe, the epicenter of Christianity, by definition their source of God's judicial code would have been the Bible. To conclude, listen to the words of Benjamin Franklin delivered on June 28, 1787 when he so eloquently refers to *the sacred writings* as he implored Congress to draw upon prayer.

> *I have lived, Sir, a long time, and the longer I live, the more convincing proofs I see of this truth; that God Governs in the affairs of men. And if a sparrow cannot fall to the ground without his notice, is it probable that an empire can rise without his aid? We have been assured, Sir, in the **sacred writings**, that 'except the Lord build the House they labour in vain that build it.' I firmly believe this; and I also believe that without his concurring aid we shall succeed in this political building no better, than the Builders of Babel...I therefore beg leave to move—that henceforth prayers imploring the assistance of Heaven, and its blessings on our deliberations, be held in this Assembly every morning before we proceed to business, and that one or more of the Clergy of this City be requested to officiate in that Service.*[185]

---

184 Bennett, William J., and John T.E. Cribb. *The American Patriot's Almanac.* Thomas Nelson, Inc., 2008.
185 Source: http://chaplain.house.gov

DIVINE PROVIDENCE

⁕

"And now these three remain: faith, hope, and
love. But the greatest of these is love."
1 Corinthians 13:13[186]

"Reliance on Divine Providence" is the fourth reference to God in the Declaration of Independence. The document begins by acknowledging nature's God, who created the heavens and the earth. Our forefathers let us know where life began, who designed it, and when they utilized the third reference to God, the Supreme Judge of this world, they let us know where life ends. This brings new meaning to the Scripture:

> *I am the Alpha and the Omega," says the Lord God, "who is, and who was, and who is to come, the Almighty.*
>
> *Revelation 1:8 (NIV)[187]*

If I could paraphrase for a moment, our founders were informing us that this nation began with God, and this nation will end with God. The second reference to God as the Creator allows us to get a close up view of God's masterpiece—man. I believe our forefathers were communicating the depth of affection God has for us, and his desire to know and be involved in the affairs

---

186 Scripture taken from the Holy Bible, New International Version®. Copyright © 1973, 1978, 1984 by International Bible Society. Used by permission of Zondervan. All rights reserved.

187 Ibid.

of men. Then we come to the third reference of God, the Supreme Judge of this world, meaning all of us, men and women alike, are going to have to face this judge for our actions here on earth. To accomplish His role as the Supreme Judge of this world, God must be all-knowing (omniscient), present everywhere at all times (omnipresent), and all-powerful (omnipotent) to have the ability to reward and punish all people of every nation throughout the world. This brings us to the fourth reference to God in our reliance on the protection of Divine Providence, where we are provided the means to ensure we are measuring up to what is expected from the Supreme Judge of this world. Did you catch that? God created the heavens and the earth, then created man. He holds us accountable and judges us for our actions, and the icing on the cake is we have the answer to how we will receive a favorable judgment—*reliance on the protection of Divine Providence.* Let's unpack this concept further.

Reliance is defined as dependence or trust in someone or something.[188] The definition for *faith* is complete trust or confidence in someone or something.[189] Incredibly, the definitions are almost identical. Therefore, it is fair to use the term *faith* in place of the word *reliance.* The term *protection* is defined as a person or thing that prevents someone or something from suffering harm or injury.[190] Now, the term *divine*[191] is defined as of, from, or like God. The term *providence*[192] is defined as the protective care of God. So the phrase "*firm reliance on the protection of Divine Providence,*" in modern day terms, means placing our faith in God for protective care. If we place this in the context of our forefathers, they placed their faith in God for protection during the war that was about to begin, and from the judgment of the Supreme Judge of this world. Actively seeking the protection of Divine Providence conjures up an image of a God who has the capacity and desire to intervene into the affairs of the American colonies—a personally involved God. For example, have you ever noticed how close in proximity the United States Secret Service Agents are to the President of the United States. The Secret Service Agents are ready to rescue the President from danger in seconds. It would be impossible for the Secret Service Agents to protect the President if they were far away from the President. Typically, the smaller the distance between the security personnel and the person they are protecting the greater the probability of ensuring a safe outcome. Think about providing protection for America through the

---

188 *The New Oxford American Dictionary, Second Edition,* Erin McKean (editor), 2051 pages, May 2005, Oxford University Press, ISBN 0-19-517077-6.
189 Ibid.
190 Ibid.
191 Ibid.
192 Ibid.

Revolutionary War. Our forefathers, by placing faith in God's protection, logically did not perceive God as distant or uninvolved in 1776 nor would they perceive God as distant in modern day America. If He was a distant God then our forefathers would have chosen different words to express their sentiments.

America's reckoning with liberty was radically different than anything the world had seen. They were fleeing a governmental system that was not based in faith in a Creator, God. It was based upon one man—the king. Our forefathers knew all too well that when a nation placed its faith in a man, it led to tyranny. You see, when a man finds himself in the position of king, czar, or dictator where his power is unchecked, it is a sure bet corruption will soon follow. This was one of the primary theological issues between the Protestant Reformation and the Catholic Church during the sixteenth century. Historically, the Catholic Church placed a sense of infallibility upon its central authoritative figure, which we all know as the Pope. In time, the Pope became an extremely powerful figure, and it was difficult to challenge, change, or correct his judgment. The only option was to wait upon the next Pope. Dissention was not tolerated, and power was centralized within the Catholic Church. Men like Martin Luther, John Knox, and John Calvin were used to revolutionize how man would relate to God and to the church. No longer did any one man have the right to stand between another man and truth.[193] The rights of the individual and his relationship with the Almighty were declared. Man could read and learn for himself (*sola scriptura*) God's Holy Word. Man was also free to be justified to God not on the basis of works, wealth, or any action of the church, but through faith alone (*sola fide*). With these two transformational freedoms came direct accountability between the individual and God Himself. The reverberations across Europe must have been profound and shaped the worldview of our founding fathers. Two centuries later, our forefathers left the shores of Europe for America where they were about to radically transform how man would relate to his government. The founders of our land were part of Europe, the very countries who witnessed the breaking off of the Church of England, the Protestant Reformation, and ultimately, life under the king of England. You could say the winds of history, both from a spiritual dimension and from the civil governmental perspective, taught these keen students of history and experience that unchecked centralized power would always lead to power and corruption.

Wow! A quick rundown of two hundred years of history brings us to the crux of this last reference to God. Therefore, the men who were inspired to

---

193 Hough Lynn Harold, *The Significance of the Protestant Reformation*. The Abdingdon Press, 1918.

write the document believed in placing their faith not in man, but in God. History had taught them that placing their faith in a man was fleeting and usually resulted in great tragedy. It is with this backdrop that America must discover what it means to place its faith in God. Our forefathers understood it, they referenced it, they wrote about it, and they relied upon it to get them through the toughest of times. Could it be they placed this reference for the whole world to see, for all generations? Could it be they knew there would come a time when the foundation of America would be shaken? Could it be they wanted to leave this nation a heritage by providing the blueprint of how a nation and her people are to relate to God? America, this cannot be a mere coincidence. The historical context just doesn't support it. Besides, the words are written in black and white and witnessed by many by their signatures at the bottom of the text. It is historically accurate. The time has come for each man, in his own way, to learn to place his confidence in Divine Providence. America, for too long the focus has been on man, on our intelligence, on our insight, on our accomplishments, and very much on ourselves. By placing our faith in man, America finds herself on the verge of an economic implosion (not to mention what is occurring in Europe). Faith in a man will always fail. Our gracious God didn't leave us directionless. He left us His Word as a lamp unto our feet and light unto our path (Psalm 119:105).[194]

The great faith chapter, known as Hebrews 11, provides a run down of virtually every major biblical figure used by God. Hebrews says that faith *"... is being sure of what we hope for and certain of what we do not see. This is what the ancients were commended for" (Hebrews 11:1–2).*[195] Did you see this, America? It says *"... this is what the ancients were commended for ...?"* The ancients, the ancients, hang onto those words for just a moment. We began this journey by referencing the following Scripture in Section I of this book:

> *This is what the Lord says:*
> *Stand at the crossroads and look; ask for the **ancient** paths,*
> *Ask where the good way is, and walk in it, and you will find*
> *Rest for your souls. But you said, "We will not walk in it."*
> *Jeremiah 6:16 (NIV)*[196]

---

194 Scripture taken from the Holy Bible, New International Version®. Copyright © 1973, 1978, 1984 by International Bible Society. Used by permission of Zondervan. All rights reserved.
195 Ibid.
196 Ibid.

Here we are, our land of liberty. We have come full circle. We were instructed in the book of Jeremiah to "... *stand at the crossroads and look; ask for the **ancient paths,** ask where the good way is ...*" Then our founders told us when they concluded the text to place faith in God. We went to Scripture to find out how God defines faith. It says, essentially, the **ancients** were commended for having faith in God. America, like the book of Jeremiah, we are standing at a crossroads of epic proportions. Our God, in His wisdom, knew we would approach this point, and so did the forefathers of America because they were at that point themselves. They were at a crossroads between declaring liberty or facing certain death through tyranny. Our forefathers placed their choice in permanent ink by faith in God (firm reliance upon divine providence), and they soon discovered the ancient path, the good way, and rest for their souls. Will Americans of the twenty-first century, who are sitting at the crossroads of destiny, ask for the ancient path and follow God's prescription and our founders' testament to place our faith into Christ Himself? Come, America. Come now, and look down this path of faith. The record of history stands at your side, "... *for you did not receive a spirit that makes you slave again to fear, but you received the spirit of sonship. And by him we cry out Abba Father" (Romans 8:15).*"[197]

---

197 Scripture taken from the Holy Bible, New International Version®. Copyright © 1973, 1978, 1984 by International Bible Society. Used by permission of Zondervan. All rights reserved.

FREEDOM'S PLAN

❦

The sacred rights of mankind are not to be rummaged for, among old parchments, or musty records. They are written, as with a sun beam in the whole volume of human nature, by the hand of the divinity itself; and can never be erased or obscured by mortal power.

Alexander Hamilton, 1775 (Source: National Archives)[198]

America, our forefathers provided us a prescription through the text of the Declaration of Independence, a place where we are to go when we are faced with the crossroads of existence. They called it divine providence. We, in modern America, would call it faith in Jesus Christ. It is through faith in Jesus Christ that America will discover the ancient path and be commended by God for doing so. The challenge for many Americans is to take the first step and choose to believe the promises of Scripture and the prescription of our founders. It is frightening when the hope we placed in the things of this earth—the government, our finances, our family, our jobs, and our communities—fail us. Fear not, America. You are not without direction in this unfamiliar territory, but you are left with a personal choice. It is quite simple. Our nation can continue down the path of trusting in man and trusting in the failed institutions around us, or choose a different path known as the ancient path. Therefore, sons and daughters of liberty, you can place your faith in Divine Providence and begin your own personal journey to return to your roots, or we can

---

198 Source: http://www.archives.gov/exhibits/charters/charters_of_freedom_7.html#

continue to flounder in despair, hopelessness, and fretting throughout the night.

There are some who will pick up this book and chalk it up to another religious zealot's attempt to push his form of religion down America's throat. Other people may read this and tacitly agree with the major tenets, but dismiss the sense of urgency and call to action. An even smaller proportion of people will identify with this book with great passion and steadfast conviction. No matter your current religious standing or position on this book, there is an undeniable battle being waged for control of the American heart. This battle has found its expression in many forms, but the most lethal is in Islamic extremism—commonly known as terrorism. The war on terrorism is an ideological war where the ideology of America is under attack from the ideology of radical Islam. The ultimate objective of radical Islam is not simply to have equal rights in America or to destroy a few cities. Although traumatic, these events are mere tactics of the enemy's larger strategy. The jihadists desire to dominate America through implantation of *sharia* law into our civilization. *Sharia law* is defined as Islamic canonical law based on the teachings of the Koran and traditions of the Prophet (Hadith and Sunna), prescribing both religious and secular duties and sometimes retributive penalties for lawbreaking.[199] Ultimately, the radical Islamists desire to conform our civilization into that of an Islamic nation—radically transforming western civilization. At the core of any civilization lies the wellspring, the dominant religious worldview where it draws its morality, develops its legal system, and provides the characteristics from which a national identity is formed. For more than two hundred years, our nation's morality, legal system, and identity found roots in our Christian heritage. For the past fifty years, we have seen a continued denial and rewriting of history to remove any remnants of our Christian identity. If the radical Islamists are successful, this trend will continue and either America's personality will be supplanted by *sharia* law or we will become an impotent influence around the world. There are stark differences between *sharia* law and a nation built upon Christian principles. If you've asked yourself throughout this book why we chose to invoke God, the name of Jesus Christ, and so many references to the Holy Bible, the response is simple. America's heritage, history, faith, founding documents, and Christianity are so interwoven. To tug at one is to tug at

199 *The New Oxford American Dictionary, Second Edition*, Erin McKean (editor), 2051 pages, May 2005, Oxford University Press, ISBN 0-19-517077-6.

all of them. Together they comprise the national identity of the United States of America—the very heart and soul of this land. By unraveling the tapestry of America's character, the Islamic extremist will remake the essence of the American soul. This struggle is not new to America. We've faced similar threats throughout our history. The difference doesn't lie in the world's latest brand of tyranny; it lies with America's disconnect with her heritage, history, faith, founding documents, and Christianity. Believe me, the jihadists are determined to continue to drive a wedge between American roots and the present-day culture.

Choose, America. Choose wisely, for your choice is part of this great experiment in America, where all men were created equal and endowed with certain unalienable rights. The first right afforded to you under the Bill of Rights is freedom of religion, and may you, America, exercise that right by placing your faith in, "... *Son of Man who did not come to be served, but to serve, and to give his life as a ransom for many" (Matthew 20:28)."*[200] You see, the founders of this land were willing to give their lives for the ransom of generations to follow. Listen to the words of George Mason as he answers the call of liberty with fervor and passion of conviction.

> *When the last dutiful & humble petition from Congress received no other Answer than declaring us Rebels, and out of the King's protection, I from that Moment look'd forward to a Revolution & Independence, as the only means of Salvation; and will risque the last Penny of my Fortune, & the last Drop of my Blood upon the Issue.*
>
> *George Mason, October 2, 1778 (Source: National Archives)*[201]

These men were just ordinary men selected to be a part of an extraordinary set of events. They were willing to risk their fortunes and the last drops of their blood for liberty. Will you, America, be so bold to heed the voice of destiny and be willing to "... *sell everything you have and give to the poor and you will have treasure in heaven" (Mark 10:21)?*[202]

---

200 Scripture taken from the Holy Bible, New International Version®. Copyright © 1973, 1978, 1984 by International Bible Society. Used by permission of Zondervan. All rights reserved.

201 Source: http://www.archives.gov/exhibits/charters/charters_of_freedom_1.html

202 Scripture taken from the Holy Bible, New International Version®. Copyright © 1973, 1978, 1984 by International Bible Society. Used by permission of Zondervan. All rights reserved.

America, as the skies of our future look bleak, we can grab hold of hope, because we are promised, "... *with man this is impossible, but not with God; all things are possible with God"(Mark 10:27).*[203]

Prayer

The following prayer was the First Prayer of the Continental Congress, 1774. The prayer was given by Reverend Jacob Duché, Rector of Christ Church of Philadelphia, Pennsylvania given on September 7, 1774, at 9 o'clock in the morning.[204]

O Lord our Heavenly Father, high and mighty King of kings, and Lord of lords, who dost from thy throne behold all the dwellers on earth and reignest with power supreme and uncontrolled over all the Kingdoms, Empires and Governments; look down in mercy, we beseech Thee, on these our American States, who have fled to Thee from the rod of the oppressor and thrown themselves on Thy gracious protection, desiring to be henceforth dependent only on Thee. To Thee have they appealed for the righteousness of their cause; to Thee do they now look up for that countenance and support, which Thou alone canst give. Take them, therefore, Heavenly Father, under Thy nurturing care; give them wisdom in Council and valor in the field; defeat the malicious designs of our cruel adversaries; convince them of the unrighteousness of their Cause and if they persist in their sanguinary purposes, of own unerring justice, sounding in their hearts, constrain them to drop the weapons of war from their unnerved hands in the day of battle!

Be Thou present, O God of Wisdom, and direct the councils of this honorable assembly; enable them to settle things on the best and surest foundation. That the scene of blood may be speedily closed; that order, harmony and peace may be effectually restored, and truth and justice, religion and piety, prevail and flourish amongst the people. Preserve the health of their bodies and vigor of their minds; shower down on them and the millions they here represent, such temporal blessings as Thou seest expedient for

---

203 Ibid.

204 Source: http://chaplain.house.gov/archive/continental.html

them in this world and crown them with everlasting glory in the world to come. All this we ask in the name and through the merits of Jesus Christ, Thy Son and our Savior.

Amen.

Section VII—Joy Cometh in the Morning

THE BATTLE CRY

―――――――――――― ⋘⚬⋙ ――――――――――――

"And I have also heard the groaning of the children of Israel, whom the Egyptians keep in bondage: and I have remembered my covenant. Wherefore say unto the children of Israel, I am the Lord, and I will bring you out from under the burdens of the Egyptians, and I will rid you out of their bondage, and I will redeem you with a stretched out arm and with great judgments: And I will take you to me for a people, and I will be to you a God; and ye shall know that I am the Lord your God, which bringeth you out from under the burdens of Egyptians."

Exodus 6:5–7 (NIV)[205]

This was the cry of an enslaved people who found themselves face to face with the wicked cycle of history, where the love affair with liberty becomes ensnared to the bondages of tyranny. Liberty, the gift provided from Providence's hand to the United States of America, finds herself under siege from virtually every direction. The land of the free and the home of the brave, those sworn to protect this vital right, have themselves become entangled in the grip of this world's king, known as the tyrant. The forces of tyranny are subtle, crafty, and sly. He prowls around looking to make free men fall, and fall we have (1 Peter 4:8).[206] We have fallen so far we do not know what it is like to be free any longer. Our minds

---

205 Scripture taken from the Holy Bible, New International Version®. Copyright © 1973, 1978, 1984 by International Bible Society. Used by permission of Zondervan. All rights reserved.

206 Scripture taken from the Holy Bible, New International Version®. Copyright © 1973, 1978, 1984 by International Bible Society. Used by permission of Zondervan. All rights reserved.

are tainted, our souls in turmoil, and our hearts grieving as the shadows of this dark force push us deeper into its evil lair. Yet, there is another aspect to this epic struggle. When the hearts of the faithful find no strength within themselves, they reach for strength from their Maker.

The Maker of this place we call earth is not a distant and uninvolved God. He is personal and deeply interested in the affairs of His most prized possession, the crown jewel of His creation—mankind. He knows the slant of our hearts, the conditions of our brokenness. Our current state of affairs is no surprise to our heavenly Father. He hears our cries, our desire to be free. This is His story, the one He unfolded from the Old Testament to the New, where the ruler of this world intends our present ailments for evil, but God uses our ailments for good. We find ourselves in bondage again as slaves to Pharaoh. It would seem that the harder we attempt to find freedom and to break free, the more arduous our work becomes. We slave on, we hope, we pray, but in those moments when we see some light, there is yet again another failing, another fault, and another destruction of an ancient stone. We are commanded by Scripture to remain in hope. We are told there will be hardship for sure, but as we see our families, churches, communities, and institutions moving forward with disappointment, we find it hard to hang onto hope.

The elderly of our land cannot believe their eyes. Things they thought were rare and only done in secret are now done openly and with great frequency across this land. The middle-aged struggle as they near retirement, for the promises of financial security, prosperity, and good healthcare now appear to be a lie. Their life plans are in a shambles as they attempt to find economic security in a culture that values youth over experience. Those who find themselves raising children with the desire to instill strong values find their homes are under siege from the television, Internet, billboards, their schools, and a culture which has become violently opposed to anyone who attempts to maintain the traditions of their faith. The young are confused. They are attempting to launch themselves into a world which grows smaller, less loyal, and ever more distant from the red, white, and blue where faith, family, and country were once the norm. There isn't much cause for hope, and a person could find themselves at the depths of despair, and in the grips of depression.

There is a roadmap to find our way home. God provided it to us in His Holy Word. He provided us countless examples of what happens when His people, a people born to be free, choose the path of bondage and begin the slow path toward taking His abounding grace for granted. The Israelites were no strangers to the dictates of bondage. They slaved and slaved until God heard their cries. With confidence, they put their faith in God to liberate their people through Moses' leading. Moses heeded his call after meeting the great I Am at that burning bush. It was at this moment when Moses, a man in exile, was used to answer the cries of the faithful while the grip of tyranny pressed in. Moses confronted the tyrant with a brother named Aaron. Pharaoh did not respond immediately, but then, in protest, he clamped down on God's children by enforcing longer work hours and higher work quotas. They were sentenced to more hard labor, and in this moment they began to doubt Moses and God's answer to their plea.

Despite the wavering of their faith, Moses did not give up or leave God's children to the plight of that tyrant. Moses pressed on. He continued to confront great Pharaoh with plague after plague, until Pharaoh's fist was unclenched from the necks of the Israelites. This wasn't an easy task for Pharaoh to do. After each concession, he rescinded his offer until God brought such force and such weight as to kill every first born in the Egyptian nation including Pharaoh's son. Pharaoh released this nation into the hands of Moses. Even after the tragedy of the first born, Pharaoh rescinded his decision and decided to pursue Moses, for a tyrant without slaves is nothing at all. Did God allow Pharaoh to pursue Moses for some greater purpose, or was it Pharaoh's pride that led him to desperation, to the moment where his entire army was drowned in the sea? We may never know, but one thing is for sure. God heard their cries.

God heard the prayers of His people, and he brought them to freedom. They found themselves free again, and ready to rebuild their nation. America, God shed His grace on thee over the centuries and desires to shed it again. He has blessed America and prospered our land. His promises in Scripture tell us that if we obey, we will be blessed for generations to come. He has been faithful to our land. Our history is short, but our successes are great. However, America, we are in a struggle for our souls to be free. We have fought for others, we have died to allow them to be free, but now we find ourselves in the stranglehold of Pharaoh. This was not God's desire, nor was this part of His plan. He has remained steady and prepared to heal our land. As we unite in our prayers over the condition of our land, as we express to the heavens the depths of our grief, as we struggle, strain, and suffer, God will hear us again.

There is no indication in Scripture why God chose that moment in Israel's history to reunite them with freedom. Was it because enough Israelites were humbled? Was it God's mercy as He witnessed the persecution of His people? Perhaps it was just God's grace, because He himself was saddened. From the beginning, God designed His people to be free. The rewards of freedom are unparalleled when they choose to obey, but the risk of freedom is that they may fall from God's design. Who knows the exact root cause. One thing we can have confidence in is God does bring freedom to those He calls His own.

When God liberates His people, the process of liberation takes time. There will be struggle, strain, and suffering. Without pain and sacrifice, freedom will not last. Look at a child who gets whatever he asks for. That child rarely appreciates the more virtuous things of life. How could he? God loves us, America, and has heard the cry of our hearts. He longs to restore freedom. It will come through the years of struggle to break the back of the tyrant. From the roadmap of old we know the Israelites were sent to the desert to prepare themselves for this great gift. There was much change and purification that occurred in those dry days. As the days in the scorching heat ended, our friends received their gift of grace—The Promised Land. It is time, America, to begin our journey to break the forces of tyranny which reign in our nation. From there we can head to the desert, where we will find His hand leading us through a great famine. When all is said and done, America will be better, more pure, and prepared to fully reclaim one nation, under God!

THE YEARS OF FAMINE

⸙⸙⸙

"Then Joseph said to Pharaoh, "The dreams of Pharaoh are one and the same. God has revealed to Pharaoh what he is about to do. The seven good cows are seven years, and the seven good heads of grain are seven years; it is one and the same dream. The seven lean, ugly cows that came up afterward are seven years, and so are the seven worthless heads of grain scorched by the east wind; They are seven years of famine."

Genesis 41:25–27 (NIV)[207]

"If my people, who are called by my name, will humble themselves and pray and seek my face and turn from their wicked ways, then will I hear from heaven and will forgive their sin and will heal their land. Now my eyes will be open and my ears attentive to the prayers offered in this place."

2 Chronicles 7:14, 15 (NIV)[208]

As America emerges from the hand of Pharaoh, we will find ourselves in the midst of a famine. We are a land that has lost our way. We have become so soiled, musty, and cold. The strength of our prosperity has gone astray as America loses its trust in her societal institutions. These things were supposed to be pure, strong, and faithful. How could they fail? Many Americans see it coming, and others would rather not. The beauty of this famine is it will bring all things into the

---

207 Scripture taken from the Holy Bible, New International Version®. Copyright © 1973, 1978, 1984 by International Bible Society. Used by permission of Zondervan. All rights reserved.
208 Ibid.

light. God did not leave us without a guiding light. His name is Joseph, a man rejected by his family and sold into slavery. Through a divine set of events, he rose to run a nation through its most severe time.

As those things around us are pruned and trimmed, God will provide a Joseph to guide us through the night. Joseph was provided as a gift from above to interpret dreams and to see the will of the Almighty. Joseph foretold the years of prosperity for his nation, but he also predicted through Pharaoh's dream that there would be seven years of famine in which the land of plentiful would be no more. Joseph knew if he prepared the land correctly, they could endure. It started simply by Joseph being placed in charge and establishing the storehouse to prepare for the coming calamity. He didn't act in anxious energy or fret through the night.

As the famine began and people ran out of resources, they came to Joseph to ask for help. It started with those that had the least, and then it continued with those who had even more. Even the wealthy of the land ultimately begged Joseph for help. Can you imagine the societal angst as food, water, and sustenance evaporated? Can you imagine the adjustments, the rationing, and the changes to the social fabric that must have occurred during those years of famine? The stress and strain must have been immense. There must have been uprisings as desperation grew. When people move from luxury to necessity, it has an affect on our human psyche. Their society must have been like a grape in a wine press, pressured on all sides, never knowing when it would end and if they would survive. There must have been much crying, praying, and tears as a land known for wealth kept to the bare minimum. This is what occurs when any nation goes through such a dramatic transformation.

America, does this sound familiar? A land that possesses such resources, such wealth, and such influences, finds itself brought low. We can see it upon the horizon as the bankruptcy reaches our shores, the bankruptcy of a nation that has spent much more than she has earned, that has marginalized the traditions of her faith, and with grave concern, witnessed the destruction of the sacred trust between a nation, a people born free, and those institutions where we could anchor our lives. America would be wise to begin the process of preparing for the impending famine that is coming to our land. We would be wise to build our storehouse, strengthen our positions, and seek the hand of prudence. There are major adjustments coming to our land. As the famine emerges, we too will move from luxury to necessity. This a most uncomfortable position, just as it was in the 1930s when America knew this level of desperation. Some may criticize the presentation of the reality of our national issues and the presentation of the ensuing consequences as stirring up needless hysteria. We need look no further than the debt clock, however, which ticks ahead at such a pace that there is rarely an American who can comprehend its affect. The changes to the fabric of America must be both deep and widespread to have any lasting affect. These changes must shake the very foundation of our land in order to break the back of this tyrant's hold. No one can predict for certain, but the vast changes that are needed shall begin with the spiritual heart of America.

God's greatest concern is not with our comfort, convenience, or pleasure, for He is a jealous God who desires the heart of this land and the heart of each American. He isn't looking for commercialized Christianity or the appearance of reverence. Rather, God is about the purity of this nation's faith and its willingness to humble our land at the foot of Almighty God. This change will begin first in the steeples of the churches across our land that are effective at entertaining people of our culture, but struggle at cultivating rooted people of faith. God will demand from the pulpit a generation of faithful leaders who are His hands, His voice, and His feet. They will enable God to produce a deep repentance, cleansing, and ultimately, a deeper faith in the lives of His people. Recall the apostles in the book of Acts, who lived a life of fervency and conviction even to the point of willingly facing the same fate as Christ—a martyr for God. They were commanded to be God's witnesses in Jerusalem, in all of Judea and Samaria, and to the ends of the earth (Acts 1:8).[209] God provided a roadmap for the emergence of the church as a force to be reckoned with. These disciples began in earnest in the city of Jerusalem, and then moved on from behind the comfortable walls of their home field advantage. As the strength of the early church grew, the church began moving into Judea, Samaria, and ultimately, into the rest of the world, or the hub of the world, known as Rome. In America, our land has become comfortable. Pleasure and entertainment have supplemented boldness, fervency, and conviction unto death. Like the land of Israel and the time of the Roman Empire, there always remained a remnant of those devout faithful whose clothing remained white and unblemished from the culture. This will not be easy or slight of change, for many churches will see their memberships tumble and their programs shrink as they reorient themselves to God's

---

209 Scripture taken from the Holy Bible, New International Version®. Copyright © 1973, 1978, 1984 by International Bible Society. Used by permission of Zondervan. All rights reserved.

true Word. When the two-edged sword is preached, it will most certainly create reactions, upset partnerships, and make many angry. In America, our churches have become infected to the point that it is hard to determine where the culture ends and the church begins. You see, God designed the church to be unique, to be set apart from the world. Not removed from the world, but distinct. It doesn't operate the way a business runs. It is different. It is God's great hand. So, as our churches adjust, there will be great angst and frustration, but in the end the faithful will see the Rock of all ages emerge better, stronger, and brighter. This is where the change must begin. This is the front line, where tyranny has had its reign. With the armor of our great God, we must take back our churches from deception and implant into their hearts the unadulterated truth of God (Ephesians 6:10-20).[210]

As the churches regain their footing and the battle line moves, the famine will continue, for the war has not concluded. It has just begun. The culture has infected our businesses, our schools, our communities, and our government. The disease has grown so slowly, it is becoming difficult to recognize its progression. As for the governments of this land, they have become our god, our spouses, our families, and ourselves. For many, this phenomenon has occurred for generations. It is an addiction which receives its fix from state capitols across this land and Washington itself. Millions upon millions line up for checks and food stamps as if there was no other way to subsist. For those who find themselves in this position, addictions are difficult to see, to accept, and even harder to break free from. The truth of the matter is your dealer is about to run out of your drug. The government finds itself facing an unimaginable fiscal crisis—the likes of which this nation has never seen. For the wise of heart, it would be advisable to break from this addiction, for in the end it will be up to you and your rugged individualism to restore vitality again. For those who cannot bring themselves to heal this disease, there is the force of a system that can no longer stand, which will push you to an even more vulnerable place. Prepare, America. Prepare, like Joseph of old, for government was never intended to be so large and overpowering. When the adjustment comes, don't lose hope or fall into despair. These will be hard times, but the goal of the matter is to remove government as your god. When this tyrant is removed, you can begin finding your faith and confidence again in something more eternal than the fleeting handouts of governments.

---

210 Scripture taken from the Holy Bible, New International Version®. Copyright © 1973, 1978, 1984 by International Bible Society. Used by permission of Zondervan. All rights reserved.

For those of you who have paid your dues and expect the financial rewards of a life well spent: at our current trajectory, our land will be broke and our government will not be able to support you. This is a sad and an unfortunate affair, when a nation who made so many promises and gladly took money from our hands cannot honor its commitments. At these various points, the temptation will be to give in to anger, resentment, and most certainly for some, revolt. Look at the streets of Greece in the year 2010. They are faced with a government gone bankrupt. There have been riots, protests, and uprising as the anger erupts toward the government. The people are angry, for they were given a whole lot of promises that the government of Greece was unable to keep. Some anticipate the same fate for other nations across the European Union who, like Greece, are in an unsustainable financial position. The United Kingdom is also struggling with record debt levels, which may affect their bond ratings. The world is in a very jittery state right now. It's as if we do not know where the next fire will erupt. We are scared, uncertain, and desperately looking to grasp onto something secure. Some even predict China will be faced with major financial adjustments as worldwide demand decreases at and many of their internal social and economic issues come to a boiling point. People will be hungry, and people will be looking for somewhere to place their faith.

As for the Christian, we must see past the pain of the moment and look toward our Creator, who will provide. For families young and old across this land, the lives you once took for granted will dramatically change. For the old, you will work for more years, so prepare your bodies, your minds, and hearts that retirement may not be exactly as you planned. For the young, get ready. Don't plan to depend upon old Uncle Sam. You must turn to God and the individual gifts He provided you. You must undertake the work ethic of old and the desire to see greater hope. At this juncture, you will have to bear the brunt of financial responsibility for supporting your elders. The easy years of retirement will no longer exist as it becomes obvious both the government and those guaranteed pension plans are at risk or lost altogether. This seismic shift in responsibility will strain and change your family for sure. This will be a time when relying on faith in our God and family will be the pillars to getting ourselves through. Prepare, America. Prepare, for the world we know is changing.

As government continues to falter upon its promises, responsibility will fall to churches, charities, and communities to step into the gap and fulfill these needs. This could be looked upon as an impossible challenge, one which you feel ill-equipped to meet. As people struggle to support themselves and to survive, God's servants will have an opportunity to meet needs with the water that promises everlasting life. It is imperative for our churches to begin this change now. Like the hands of the Great Shepherd in heaven, they must be ready to receive His sheep. The sheep will come first for food, then for shelter, and then they will ripen for something more eternal. Prepare, oh faithful servants, the remnant of God. Ready yourselves with urgency, and cover yourselves in love. For the Christian who is sitting, debating his calling, get out of the boat, Peter, for you know not who it is that is walking on the water beside the boat. There are many faithful who have delayed and made excuses not to leave their riches and follow the King of all Kings. Now is the time to reckon with God, to seek His purpose for you and your placement in the great working of the body. We need you, faithful. We need you, servants, for we cannot meet the needs of the great famine with so few hands and feet. Move out of the pews, the comforts of life, and get ready as God readies you for the fight of all fights. It is in this moment when desperation meets reconciliation, when hunger meets eternal bread, and thirst meets living water.

As the pressure grows, governments falter, and resources are consumed, our economic world will change. It will begin slowly at first, as luxury items like vacations, ski boats, fine wine, jewelry, and four wheelers become less in demand. It will drift toward stores where generic brand sales will soar, and the average family goes from two, three, four, or even more automobiles down to one. This will be a painful period as we move from luxury to necessity. It can never be easy. Rest assured, America, our pleasures and comforts, where wants are mistaken for needs, will be pulled away. We will be better, stronger, and a more virtuous nation in the end. This will reverberate across the globe as America consumes less and conserves more. This shift in mentality will not be easy, nor should it be taken lightly. A child who has grown accustomed to so many toys does not give them up without a fight. There will be tremendous adjustments to our nation, our people, and our land as the priorities of the last several decades are rearranged to those of our Maker!

You see, as a government begins to go defunct, its stream of income dries up. There must be economic consequences when either payments to its citizens decrease, taxes go up, or even worse, both. There are some who argue we could just cut tax rates, and the revenue to the federal treasury will go through the roof. There is some merit to this argument, but there is a point when even soaring revenue will not be enough to pay the bills. It is then that government must shrink. Where are all the people, who have known nothing else, supposed to go? The market will flood with laborers at a time when consumption is on the decline and businesses are contracting. The need to provide for food, shelter, and clothing will increase, with less government handouts and a business community in reduction. This is what happens when a nation endures a famine. It gets tough. It gets ugly, and without good leadership, it can become a mess. People who find themselves at a loss will turn toward a few great options: God, family, friends, and their community. The chasms of the past will be removed as the needs of the moment begin to take precedence. The men and women who are called the faithful should look toward the book of Acts, where the church became the source of support for the homeless, the widows, and the orphans. Perhaps many would have to sell their possessions and open their doors to a wayward neighbor in need of a warm home cooked meal. The adjustments will be great, and the potential for violence and riots may occur, but keep focused, God's children, for out of the famine will come a hunger for the great I Am the likes of which America has never seen.

The story of Joseph is not only one of famine or the angst of a society made to adjust. It is also a story of a man born free, sold into slavery, who regained his freedom. It was during the trials of his life that Joseph learned to keep his eyes up on high. He never compromised his integrity, not for one moment, and in the end God brought him great glory. Through the famine, Joseph found the purpose of his life. It would be easy to get caught up in the pain, the changes, and the suffering brought about by a famine, but God always uses what we perceive as evil for His good. As America begins her journey through this tough land, there will be changes and challenges that lie ahead. However, we can have faith, for the purposes of this famine are not intended to incite tyranny. Rather, they are intended to bring about the rebirth of liberty. Hold on, America, as the road gets bumpy and the path becomes unclear. We must not fear, for our confidence is not by the sight of the world, but in our faith in the great I Am. He has brought us this far, He has been faithful through the ages, and He has heard our cries. He longs for us to be free again so we can choose to praise His name.

THE TWENTY-FIRST-CENTURY
AMERICAN REFORMATION

&

*We, the people, are the rightful masters of both Congress
and the courts, not to overthrow the Constitution, but to
overthrow men who pervert the Constitution."*

Abraham Lincoln[211]

*"We have it in our power to begin the world over again. A
situation, similar to the present, hath not happened since the days
of Noah until now. The birthday of a new world is at hand."*

Thomas Paine, February 14, 1776[212]

*"... God forbid we should ever be twenty years without such a rebellion.
The people cannot be all, and always, well informed. The part which is
wrong will be discontented, in proportion to the importance of the facts
they misconceive. If they remain quiet under such misconceptions, it is
lethargy, the forerunner of death to the public liberty ... And what country
can preserve the spirit of resistance? Let them take arms. The remedy is to
set them right as to the facts, pardon and pacify them. What signify a few
lives lost in a century or two? The tree of liberty must be refreshed from time
to time, with the blood of patriots and tyrants. It is its natural manure."*

Thomas Jefferson Papers, 334 (C.J. Boyd, Ed., 1950)[213]

---

211 Linus Pierpont Brockett, *The life and times of Abraham Lincoln, sixteenth president of
the United States: including his speeches, messages, inaugurals, proclamations, etc., etc,* 3rd
Edition, Bradley & Co., 1865.

212 *http://www.archives.gov/exhibits/charters/charters_of_freedom_4.html*

213 *http://www.loc.gov/exhibits/jefferson/jefffed.html*

In 1814 Francis Scott Key recorded our beloved "Star Spangled Banner," which heralds the call of freedom and touches the soul of each American. Imagine being a part of the first years of this young nation called the United States of America, who bravely declared independence and broke free from the tyrannical chains of England. After the dust settled, the smoke cleared, and the sounds of warfare disappeared, our great flag, the red, the white, and the blue, was still gleaming. Imagine the excitement from the sense of freedom that came across the thirteen colonies, the sense of possibilities and the dreams of this young nation, who dared to be different and risked it all for the possibility of freedom. Think about the parents who gave to their children the gift of liberty, and broke the chains of a class-based society. In this new land, in this America, you could be anything you desired to be, and nothing, I mean nothing, stood in your way except the extent of your imagination and the faith of your convictions. What a moment, what a call, and what a mysterious turn of history when liberty was unveiled as a free gift provided by our Creator. Imagine a land where every man and every woman could begin the great pursuit of liberty for all. Imagine all those Americans who could now answer the deep cry of their souls, which yearned for freedom and hungered for liberty. Once destiny and the gasp of the human heart were united, America was delivered from the mighty grip of tyranny and birthed into the nurturing arms of freedom. Despite the death, despite the destruction, and despite the bloodshed, something uniquely different had come to the shores of America. No doubt the hand of the Creator brought forth the gift of freedom and charged America to be its guardian. The birth of liberty wasn't the end of young America's call. It was the beginning. I recall scenes from the movie *Braveheart*.[214] The main character, William Wallace, played by Mel Gibson, was thrust into the clash between a free Scotland and the tyranny of England. Wallace and his comrades turned the tide on English rule. Wallace inspired thousands of Scottish peasants and nobles alike to fight and die for freedom, or else live in tyranny, which was worse than death itself. You see, Wallace understood that in every man was this desire to be free, and to live any other way meant you stopped living. It wasn't Wallace who placed this yearning into the human soul. Rather, he just recognized the undeniable truth that it existed. It is this truth, the truth of the human condition that aches for freedom, that motivated young America to take a stance. In the words of Patrick Henry, "Give me liberty or give me death." Wow! Give me liberty or

---

214 *Braveheart*. CD. Directed by Mel Gibson. United States: Distributed by Paramount Pictures.

give me death. Let that soak into your soul for a bit, simmer in your mind, and ignite your heart.

It ignited the hearts of those young revolutionaries who fought with passion, conviction, and great courage for their freedom. Amazingly, with each passing political cycle we are offered a new vision for America, a new direction, and a new hope for the future. One thing is for sure, with each passing politician a vision comes and a vision goes, but America need only to reconnect with the passion and conviction which brought us into existence. From the onset, we have existed for one reason. At times we have lost our way, but America, as it says in The Star Spangled Banner *"... And the rocket's red glare, the bombs bursting in air, Gave proof through the night that our flag was still there. Oh, say, does that star-spangled banner yet wave, O'er the land of the free and the home of the brave?"* You heard it, America. Old Glory is still here, it is still waving over the land of the free and the home of the brave. You see, those men and women of old didn't have the modern comforts of the twenty-first century, but they did have the simplicity of knowing the yearning for freedom. In those moments when they became conscious of living in liberty, they recognized death was a small price to pay, because to live with the void of not knowing freedom wasn't living, it was merely existing to exist. We Americans, we have purpose. We have a direction, and we have a cause—liberty for all! It was our cause from the beginning, and it will be until the end.

Now, back to William Wallace. The movie ends with Wallace being caught by the English authorities. Wallace is placed on trial, convicted, and sentenced to death unless he would renounce his allegiance to freedom and submit to the king. Wallace resists to the end, and is ultimately put to death for his high treason. With each passing moment of the film, it becomes obvious Wallace is going to die. In William Wallace's mind, however, he wasn't about to die. He was finally going to live! As he takes his last breaths and the death squad closes in, William Wallace exclaims, "Freedom! Freedom!" You see, Wallace wasn't broken by the grip of tyranny. Wallace submitted to the cause of freedom and placed his faith in the hands of his Creator God to usher freedom to his soul, and ultimately bring freedom across Scotland. America, each of us loses our way when we live for something less epic than our calling of liberty, when we exist for such shallow values as the comforts and securities of this earth over the honor of serving liberty. The call from heaven above is clear: to usher this gift across America and the globe. Our lives are lacking the real reason we call America home, for we birthed liberty across this land, and now, in the year 2010, we must go back to those inspiring moments and bring back the hope of liberty!

The Great Awakening of the Twenty-First Century

My fellow countrymen (and countrywomen), our reckoning with destiny is upon us. Liberty is calling us back, and back we must go. We must reconnect with the vision of our past and begin building a bridge from our modern society to the highly flammable passion of liberty that birthed America. We must shake off the chains of political correctness, put behind us the culture of death, resurrect The Final Branch of American governance, restore a sense of responsibility, and rebuild our moral integrity. We must take back our nation from the hands of tyranny and the forces of evil that would like to see America fall to ashes and the cause of liberty become a distant thought of the past.

The epic struggle to stoke the flames of freedom isn't a call to arms. Rather, it is a call to touch the hearts and minds of every person who considers America home. It is a call to help Americans reconnect with the yearning for freedom, and to cultivate the courage and conviction to face the forces of tyranny head on. No longer will we stand for removing God from the public square. No longer will we allow our churches to be watered down and pushed to the fringes of society. No longer will we stand on the sidelines and watch political correctness dismantle our nation, and no longer will we allow the culture of corruption and moral demise to expand. It is time, America, to place our ailments on notice. It is time to put a stake in the ground and declare a revolutionary moment; a moment not unlike that of our forefathers when they stood up to the king of England and said, "No more. We will not be kicked, we will not be pushed, and we will not be bullied any longer." In the words of my feisty wife, "It is time to knock them right across the temple, hard and fast." You know, America. You know in your sphere of influence when it is time to take that stance. You know, America, when it is time to say "no more" in your communities, and you know, America, when enough is enough. Let your soul shout, "Give me liberty, or give me death!" Let your voice be heard. Let it be counted. It is time to stand. It is time to fight. Watch out, tyranny and the oppressive forces of evil! We began with a revolution when few thought we had a chance, so while the tide is not in our favor and the naysayers sit on the sidelines, we will begin our advancement toward reclaiming our reckoning with liberty.

Radical Revolutionaries

This manuscript calls for *radical revolutionaries* from every corner of the United States of America. We need radical revolutionaries to establish themselves in every inch and sect of American society. We need revolutionaries to infect our community of faith and demand the purity, the holiness, and the unobstructed dedication to the teaching and preaching of the unabridged Word of God. We need our faith communities to touch the hearts and minds of Americans and restore a sense of civility and morality to our culture. We need radicals to defend the traditional family in America to the death. We need family fanatics to advance the cause of strong families. We need radicals to take charge of the defenseless and find a loving, strong home for every orphaned child across America, and put to an end the needless loss of life through abortion. We need a set of radical revolutionaries, engaged in political positions at every level of government, to take America back to the cause of liberty and the traditions of our heritage. We need radical revolutionaries to flank the untrustworthy media and develop freedom-loving, liberty-focused, truth seeking media outlets that do not compromise integrity for sensationalism. We need radical revolutionaries to penetrate the academic sectors of America and put a stop to the theft of the American minds and value systems. We need radical educators who are devoted to teaching the truth and shepherding our young minds responsibly, and with deference to the "In God We Trust" national motto we have come to know and love. We need radical revolutionaries who are willing to speak truth to the politically correct culture which values comfort and feelings over reality and truth. We must begin to restore Superman-like ideals: truth, justice, and the American Way. We need radical revolutionaries who are willing to stand up to the destruction of our cities from the plague of entitlements, who are willing to face their peer groups head on, confront their racial sects, and turn the tide on the dependency culture. We need radical youth who demonstrate passion, conviction, and a sense of duty and responsibility toward their families, friends, communities, and nation. We need radical cultural revolutionaries prepared to combat the onslaught upon liberty wherever and whenever it is under siege. Liberty is beckoning America back to herself, so it is time to stand for liberty, or accept a life devoid of purpose. It's your call, it's our time, and it is all of our purposes!

Your Call, Your time, Our Purpose

The title of this book, *The Final Branch* is intended to be a call to each and every American. We can no longer afford benchwarmers and citizens who shallowly seek self interests. We must stop catering to those forces which attack the unalienable rights guaranteed by the Declaration of Independence. Time is of the essence, and our reckoning with liberty is calling Americans, Christians, and patriots alike. This isn't a call for a violent or forceful revolution. It is a call for a participatory revolution, where the God-fearing citizenry stand up and are counted. All of us who have straddled the fence of service must seize the moment, take our God-given gifts and talents, and dedicate them to the sole purpose of the restoration of America, the land of the free, the home of the brave.

For those who have played the game of faith, it is time to get right with God. For those who have fallen away from the faith or just denied the need for God, the time has come to make the decision and be counted as one of God's children. God has plans for you and for your life. God desires to use your gifts, talents, and abilities to do your part in helping America achieve her destiny with liberty. As Scripture says, *"The body is a unit, though it is made up of many parts; and though all its parts are many, they form one body" (1 Corinthians 12:12).*[215] You are important. God considers you important, and America considers you important. If you consider America your nation, then you are absolutely a part of God's purpose for America, to be the beacon of liberty and bring light into darkness. You see, our choice isn't about whether or not God has a purpose for America. The choice is really whether we decide to accept God's purpose for us as part of the collective body known as America. It is commitment time, America. It is the fourth quarter with two minutes left to go, and we are down by ten points. It is now or never to forget what is behind and strain toward what lies ahead (Philippians 3:13-14).[216] Americans, press on toward liberty to win the prize for which God has called this nation. It is our call. It is our duty. It is our joy. Now, make that commitment to God to get into the game and bring liberty to all!

Stand up, America. Stand now, and let the cowboy ride again!

---

215 Scripture taken from the Holy Bible, New International Version®. Copyright © 1973, 1978, 1984 by International Bible Society. Used by permission of Zondervan. All rights reserved.

216 Scripture taken from the Holy Bible, New International Version®. Copyright © 1973, 1978, 1984 by International Bible Society. Used by permission of Zondervan. All rights reserved.

Prayer

The Gettysburg Address, given by Abraham Lincoln on November 19, 1863. Lincoln encouraged the nation to continue the fight and live up to its founding principles. The last sentence of the Gettysburg Address is the inspiration for the prayer below.[217]

Almighty God:

May the purpose granted to America and those patriots who have sacrificed much for the ideals known as America be not in vain— that this nation, under God, shall have a new birth of freedom— and that government of the people, by the people, for the people, shall not perish from the earth. Amen.

217 Bennett, William J., and John T.E. Cribb. *The American Patriot's Almanac.* Thomas Nelson, Inc., 2008.

EPILOGUE

⁂

We began our journey to discover the heart of America in the twenty-first century and quickly jumped to the eighteenth century when the Constitution, the Bill of Rights, and the Declaration of Independence were written. At the onset of this journey, my purpose was to discover the heart and soul of this nation, with the goal of sharing a message of hope with my fellow countrymen (and women). As the writing and research for this book unfolded, my heart was even more captivated by the majesty of America than when I began. The foresight of our forefathers and the intervention of Divine Providence into the affairs of America should make Americans feel honored, proud, and most of all, humble. The further I dug, the more I recognized how God had interwoven the American version of faith, liberty, and history into the strands of my own heart. They weren't always apparent, but when they were touched I certainly knew it. To tug at one of those strands is to tug at all of them. Our culture has been tugging for far too long. Either we are going to return to the roots of this land or the ideal known as America will cease to exist. This is the struggle of our time.

The goal of this book was to unravel the mystery of our nation without the benefit of historians or legal scholars, for at the core of this manuscript is the fundamental belief that each man and woman can discover for themselves liberty's plan and purpose for America by simply reading the actual documents. By removing the barriers between each American and the words of our forefathers, perhaps America would reunite with the spirit of the Revolutionary War, and the same passion would awaken which transformed how man related to his government. For it is here, America, when we follow the trail of liberty through the travails of our nation's history, where the Twenty-First Century American Reformation will be born, and from there, where twenty-first century Americans will regain their footing to once again receive destiny's call—Liberty for All!

This is the end of our journey together. My prayer is that your heart has been touched and your purpose as an American made clear. I would like to part on a high note, for as the tide rises and tribulations mount, we will find hope not in man, but in God's providential care. For in His heart He saw fit to walk by our side.

Jeffrey J. DiQuattro

Appendices

APPENDIX A—THE DECLARATION OF INDEPENDENCE

―――――― cⱷⱺⱷ ――――――

The decision to place the texts of our founding documents into an appendix came with the hope each American will read, analyze, and think about the spirit and the letter of each document. We each possess the capability to comprehend the essential tenets of each document without being a scholar of history. Their greatness is in their simplicity. The authors understood the twists and turns of history, but no greater theme did they etch into these pieces of paper than the reliance on the wisdom of the people. We, the people, should heed the lessons of history and the wisdom of simplicity, and spend time simmering with the texts as a reminder of our national identity, a guide to our past, and a compass for our future.

The Declaration of Independence: A Transcription[218]

IN CONGRESS, July 4, 1776.

The unanimous Declaration of the thirteen united States of America,

When in the Course of human events, it becomes necessary for one people to dissolve the political bands which have connected them with another, and to assume among the powers of the earth, the separate and equal station to which the Laws of Nature and of Nature's God entitle them, a decent respect to the opinions of mankind requires that they should declare the causes which impel them to the separation.

---

218 U.S. National Archives & Records Administration, 8601 Adelphi Road, College Park, MD, 20740-6001,• 1-86-NARA-NARA• 1-866-272-6272; taken from http://www.archives.gov/exhibits/charters/declaration_transcript.html.

We hold these truths to be self-evident, that all men are created equal, that they are endowed by their Creator with certain unalienable Rights, that among these are Life, Liberty and the pursuit of Happiness.--That to secure these rights, Governments are instituted among Men, deriving their just powers from the consent of the governed, --That whenever any Form of Government becomes destructive of these ends, it is the Right of the People to alter or to abolish it, and to institute new Government, laying its foundation on such principles and organizing its powers in such form, as to them shall seem most likely to effect their Safety and Happiness. Prudence, indeed, will dictate that Governments long established should not be changed for light and transient causes; and accordingly all experience hath shewn, that mankind are more disposed to suffer, while evils are sufferable, than to right themselves by abolishing the forms to which they are accustomed. But when a long train of abuses and usurpations, pursuing invariably the same Object evinces a design to reduce them under absolute Despotism, it is their right, it is their duty, to throw off such Government, and to provide new Guards for their future security.--Such has been the patient sufferance of these Colonies; and such is now the necessity which constrains them to alter their former Systems of Government. The history of the present King of Great Britain is a history of repeated injuries and usurpations, all having in direct object the establishment of an absolute Tyranny over these States. To prove this, let Facts be submitted to a candid world.

He has refused his Assent to Laws, the most wholesome and necessary for the public good.

He has forbidden his Governors to pass Laws of immediate and pressing importance, unless suspended in their operation till his Assent should be obtained; and when so suspended, he has utterly neglected to attend to them.

He has refused to pass other Laws for the accommodation of large districts of people, unless those people would relinquish the right of Representation in the Legislature, a right inestimable to them and formidable to tyrants only.

He has called together legislative bodies at places unusual, uncomfortable, and distant from the depository of their public Records, for the sole purpose of fatiguing them into compliance with his measures.

He has dissolved Representative Houses repeatedly, for opposing with manly firmness his invasions on the rights of the people.

He has refused for a long time, after such dissolutions, to cause others to be elected; whereby the Legislative powers, incapable of Annihilation, have returned to the People at large for their exercise; the State remaining in the mean time exposed to all the dangers of invasion from without, and convulsions within.

He has endeavoured to prevent the population of these States; for that purpose obstructing the Laws for Naturalization of Foreigners; refusing to pass others to encourage their migrations hither, and raising the conditions of new Appropriations of Lands.

He has obstructed the Administration of Justice, by refusing his Assent to Laws for establishing Judiciary powers.

He has made Judges dependent on his Will alone, for the tenure of their offices, and the amount and payment of their salaries.

He has erected a multitude of New Offices, and sent hither swarms of Officers to harrass our people, and eat out their substance.

He has kept among us, in times of peace, Standing Armies without the Consent of our legislatures.

He has affected to render the Military independent of and superior to the Civil power.

He has combined with others to subject us to a jurisdiction foreign to our constitution, and unacknowledged by our laws; giving his Assent to their Acts of pretended Legislation:

For Quartering large bodies of armed troops among us:

For protecting them, by a mock Trial, from punishment for any Murders which they should commit on the Inhabitants of these States:

For cutting off our Trade with all parts of the world:

For imposing Taxes on us without our Consent:

For depriving us in many cases, of the benefits of Trial by Jury:

For transporting us beyond Seas to be tried for pretended offences

For abolishing the free System of English Laws in a neighbouring Province, establishing therein an Arbitrary government, and enlarging its Boundaries so as to render it at once an example and fit instrument for introducing the same absolute rule into these Colonies:

For taking away our Charters, abolishing our most valuable Laws, and altering fundamentally the Forms of our Governments:

For suspending our own Legislatures, and declaring themselves invested with power to legislate for us in all cases whatsoever.

He has abdicated Government here, by declaring us out of his Protection and waging War against us.

He has plundered our seas, ravaged our Coasts, burnt our towns, and destroyed the lives of our people.

He is at this time transporting large Armies of foreign Mercenaries to compleat the works of death, desolation and tyranny, already begun with circumstances of Cruelty & perfidy scarcely paralleled in the most barbarous ages, and totally unworthy the Head of a civilized nation.

He has constrained our fellow Citizens taken Captive on the high Seas to bear Arms against their Country, to become the executioners of their friends and Brethren, or to fall themselves by their Hands.

He has excited domestic insurrections amongst us, and has endeavoured to bring on the inhabitants of our frontiers, the merciless Indian Savages, whose known rule of warfare, is an undistinguished destruction of all ages, sexes and conditions.

In every stage of these Oppressions We have Petitioned for Redress in the most humble terms: Our repeated Petitions have been answered only by repeated injury. A Prince whose character is thus marked by every act which may define a Tyrant, is unfit to be the ruler of a free people.

Nor have We been wanting in attentions to our British brethren. We have warned them from time to time of attempts by their legislature to extend an unwarrantable jurisdiction over us. We have reminded them of the circumstances of our emigration and settlement here. We have appealed to their native justice and magnanimity, and we have conjured them by the ties of our common kindred to disavow these usurpations, which, would inevitably interrupt our connections and correspondence. They too have been deaf to the voice of justice and of consanguinity. We must, therefore, acquiesce in the necessity, which denounces our Separation, and hold them, as we hold the rest of mankind, Enemies in War, in Peace Friends.

We, therefore, the Representatives of the united States of America, in General Congress, Assembled, appealing to the Supreme Judge of the world for the rectitude of our intentions, do, in the Name, and by Authority of the good People of these Colonies, solemnly publish and declare, That these United Colonies are, and of Right ought to be Free and Independent States; that they are Absolved from all Allegiance to the British Crown, and that all political connection between them and the State of Great Britain, is and ought to be totally dissolved; and that as Free and Independent States, they have full Power to levy War, conclude Peace, contract Alliances, establish Commerce, and to do all other Acts and Things which Independent States may of right do. And for the support of this Declaration, with a firm reliance on the protection of divine Providence, we mutually pledge to each other our Lives, our Fortunes and our sacred Honor.

The 56 signatures on the Declaration appear in the positions indicated:

Column 1
>**Georgia:**
>Button Gwinnett
>Lyman Hall
>George Walton

Column 2
>**North Carolina:**
>William Hooper
>Joseph Hewes
>John Penn
>
>**South Carolina:**
>Edward Rutledge
>Thomas Heyward, Jr.
>Thomas Lynch, Jr.
>Arthur Middleton

Column 3

Massachusetts:
John Hancock

Maryland:
Samuel Chase
William Paca
Thomas Stone
Charles Carroll of Carrollton

Virginia:
George Wythe
Richard Henry Lee
Thomas Jefferson
Benjamin Harrison
Thomas Nelson, Jr.
Francis Lightfoot Lee
Carter Braxton

Column 4

Pennsylvania:
Robert Morris
Benjamin Rush
Benjamin Franklin
John Morton
George Clymer
James Smith
George Taylor
James Wilson
George Ross

Delaware:
Caesar Rodney
George Read
Thomas McKean

Column 5

New York:
William Floyd
Philip Livingston
Francis Lewis
Lewis Morris

New Jersey:
Richard Stockton
John Witherspoon
Francis Hopkinson
John Hart
Abraham Clark

Column 6

New Hampshire:
Josiah Bartlett
William Whipple

Massachusetts:
Samuel Adams
John Adams
Robert Treat Paine
Elbridge Gerry

Rhode Island:
Stephen Hopkins
William Ellery

Connecticut:
Roger Sherman
Samuel Huntington
William Williams
Oliver Wolcott

New Hampshire:
Matthew Thornton

Appendix B—The Constitution of the United States

―――――――――― ⌘ ――――――――――

The Constitution of the United States: A Transcription[219]

Note: *The following text is a transcription of the Constitution in its **original** form. Items that are hyperlinked have since been amended or superseded.*

We the People of the United States, in Order to form a more perfect Union, establish Justice, insure domestic Tranquility, provide for the common defence, promote the general Welfare, and secure the Blessings of Liberty to ourselves and our Posterity, do ordain and establish this Constitution for the United States of America.

Article. I.

Section. 1.

All legislative Powers herein granted shall be vested in a Congress of the United States, which shall consist of a Senate and House of Representatives.

Section. 2.

The House of Representatives shall be composed of Members chosen every second Year by the People of the several States, and the Electors in each State shall have the Qualifications requisite for Electors of the most numerous Branch of the State Legislature.

---

219 U.S. National Archives & Records Administration, 8601 Adelphi Road, College Park, MD, 20740-6001,• 1-86-NARA-NARA• 1-866-272-6272; taken from http://www.archives.gov/exhibits/charters/constitution_transcript.html.

No Person shall be a Representative who shall not have attained to the Age of twenty five Years, and been seven Years a Citizen of the United States, and who shall not, when elected, be an Inhabitant of that State in which he shall be chosen.

Representatives and direct Taxes shall be apportioned among the several States which may be included within this Union, according to their respective Numbers, which shall be determined by adding to the whole Number of free Persons, including those bound to Service for a Term of Years, and excluding Indians not taxed, three fifths of all other Persons. The actual Enumeration shall be made within three Years after the first Meeting of the Congress of the United States, and within every subsequent Term of ten Years, in such Manner as they shall by Law direct. The Number of Representatives shall not exceed one for every thirty Thousand, but each State shall have at Least one Representative; and until such enumeration shall be made, the State of New Hampshire shall be entitled to chuse three, Massachusetts eight, Rhode Island and Providence Plantations one, Connecticut five, New York six, New Jersey four, Pennsylvania eight, Delaware one, Maryland six, Virginia ten, North Carolina five, South Carolina five, and Georgia three.

When vacancies happen in the Representation from any State, the Executive Authority thereof shall issue Writs of Election to fill such Vacancies.

The House of Representatives shall chuse their Speaker and other Officers; and shall have the sole Power of Impeachment.

Section. 3.

The Senate of the United States shall be composed of two Senators from each State, chosen by the Legislature thereof for six Years; and each Senator shall have one Vote.

Immediately after they shall be assembled in Consequence of the first Election, they shall be divided as equally as may be into three Classes. The Seats of the Senators of the first Class shall be vacated at the Expiration of the second Year, of the second Class at the Expiration of the fourth Year, and of the third Class at the Expiration of the sixth Year, so that one third may be chosen every second Year; <u>and if Vacancies happen by Resignation, or otherwise, during the Recess of the Legislature of any State, the Executive thereof may make temporary Appointments until the next Meeting of the Legislature, which shall then fill such Vacancies.</u>

No Person shall be a Senator who shall not have attained to the Age of thirty Years, and been nine Years a Citizen of the United States, and who shall not, when elected, be an Inhabitant of that State for which he shall be chosen.

The Vice President of the United States shall be President of the Senate, but shall have no Vote, unless they be equally divided.

The Senate shall chuse their other Officers, and also a President pro tempore, in the Absence of the Vice President, or when he shall exercise the Office of President of the United States.

The Senate shall have the sole Power to try all Impeachments. When sitting for that Purpose, they shall be on Oath or Affirmation. When the President of the United States is tried, the Chief Justice shall preside: And no Person shall be convicted without the Concurrence of two thirds of the Members present.

Judgment in Cases of Impeachment shall not extend further than to removal from Office, and disqualification to hold and enjoy any Office of honor, Trust or Profit under the United States: but the Party convicted shall nevertheless be liable and subject to Indictment, Trial, Judgment and Punishment, according to Law.

Section. 4.

The Times, Places and Manner of holding Elections for Senators and Representatives, shall be prescribed in each State by the Legislature thereof; but the Congress may at any time by Law make or alter such Regulations, except as to the Places of chusing Senators.

The Congress shall assemble at least once in every Year, and such Meeting shall <u>be on the first Monday in December</u>, unless they shall by Law appoint a different Day.

Section. 5.

Each House shall be the Judge of the Elections, Returns and Qualifications of its own Members, and a Majority of each shall constitute a Quorum to do Business; but a smaller Number may adjourn from day to day, and may be authorized to compel the Attendance of absent Members, in such Manner, and under such Penalties as each House may provide.

Each House may determine the Rules of its Proceedings, punish its Members for disorderly Behaviour, and, with the Concurrence of two thirds, expel a Member.

Each House shall keep a Journal of its Proceedings, and from time to time publish the same, excepting such Parts as may in their Judgment require Secrecy; and the Yeas and Nays of the Members of either House on any question shall, at the Desire of one fifth of those Present, be entered on the Journal.

Neither House, during the Session of Congress, shall, without the Consent of the other, adjourn for more than three days, nor to any other Place than that in which the two Houses shall be sitting.

Section. 6.

The Senators and Representatives shall receive a Compensation for their Services, to be ascertained by Law, and paid out of the Treasury of the United States. They shall in all Cases, except Treason, Felony and Breach of the Peace, be privileged from Arrest during their Attendance at the Session of their respective Houses, and in going to and returning from the same; and for any Speech or Debate in either House, they shall not be questioned in any other Place.

No Senator or Representative shall, during the Time for which he was elected, be appointed to any civil Office under the Authority of the United States, which shall have been created, or the Emoluments whereof shall have been increased during such time; and no Person holding any Office under the United States, shall be a Member of either House during his Continuance in Office.

Section. 7.

All Bills for raising Revenue shall originate in the House of Representatives; but the Senate may propose or concur with Amendments as on other Bills.

Every Bill which shall have passed the House of Representatives and the Senate, shall, before it become a Law, be presented to the President of the United States: If he approve he shall sign it, but if not he shall return it, with his Objections to that House in which it shall have originated, who shall enter the Objections at large on their Journal, and proceed to reconsider it. If after such Reconsideration two thirds of that House shall agree to pass the Bill, it shall be sent, together with the Objections, to the other House, by which it shall likewise be reconsidered, and if approved by two thirds of that House, it shall become a Law. But in all such Cases the Votes of both Houses shall be determined by yeas and Nays, and the Names of the Persons voting for and against the Bill shall be entered on the Journal of each House respectively. If any Bill shall not be returned by the President within ten Days (Sundays excepted) after it shall have been presented to him, the Same shall be a Law, in like Manner as if he had signed it, unless the Congress by their Adjournment prevent its Return, in which Case it shall not be a Law.

Every Order, Resolution, or Vote to which the Concurrence of the Senate and House of Representatives may be necessary (except on a question of Adjournment) shall be presented to the President of the United States; and before the Same shall take Effect, shall be approved by him, or being disapproved by him, shall be repassed by two thirds of the Senate and House of Representatives, according to the Rules and Limitations prescribed in the Case of a Bill.

Section. 8.

The Congress shall have Power To lay and collect Taxes, Duties, Imposts and Excises, to pay the Debts and provide for the common Defence and general Welfare of the United States; but all Duties, Imposts and Excises shall be uniform throughout the United States;

To borrow Money on the credit of the United States;

To regulate Commerce with foreign Nations, and among the several States, and with the Indian Tribes;

To establish an uniform Rule of Naturalization, and uniform Laws on the subject of Bankruptcies throughout the United States;

To coin Money, regulate the Value thereof, and of foreign Coin, and fix the Standard of Weights and Measures;

To provide for the Punishment of counterfeiting the Securities and current Coin of the United States;

To establish Post Offices and post Roads;

To promote the Progress of Science and useful Arts, by securing for limited Times to Authors and Inventors the exclusive Right to their respective Writings and Discoveries;

To constitute Tribunals inferior to the supreme Court;

To define and punish Piracies and Felonies committed on the high Seas, and Offences against the Law of Nations;

To declare War, grant Letters of Marque and Reprisal, and make Rules concerning Captures on Land and Water;

To raise and support Armies, but no Appropriation of Money to that Use shall be for a longer Term than two Years;

To provide and maintain a Navy;

To make Rules for the Government and Regulation of the land and naval Forces;

To provide for calling forth the Militia to execute the Laws of the Union, suppress Insurrections and repel Invasions;

To provide for organizing, arming, and disciplining, the Militia, and for governing such Part of them as may be employed in the Service of the United States, reserving to the States respectively, the Appointment of the Officers, and the Authority of training the Militia according to the discipline prescribed by Congress;

To exercise exclusive Legislation in all Cases whatsoever, over such District (not exceeding ten Miles square) as may, by Cession of particular States, and the Acceptance of Congress, become the Seat of the Government of the United States, and to exercise like Authority over all Places purchased by the Consent of the Legislature of the State in which the Same shall be, for the Erection of Forts, Magazines, Arsenals, dock-Yards, and other needful Buildings;--And

To make all Laws which shall be necessary and proper for carrying into Execution the foregoing Powers, and all other Powers vested by this Constitution in the Government of the United States, or in any Department or Officer thereof.

Section. 9.

The Migration or Importation of such Persons as any of the States now existing shall think proper to admit, shall not be prohibited by the Congress prior to the Year one thousand eight hundred and eight, but a Tax or duty may be imposed on such Importation, not exceeding ten dollars for each Person.

The Privilege of the Writ of Habeas Corpus shall not be suspended, unless when in Cases of Rebellion or Invasion the public Safety may require it.

No Bill of Attainder or ex post facto Law shall be passed.

No Capitation, or other direct, Tax shall be laid, <u>unless in Proportion to the Census or enumeration herein before directed to be taken.</u>

No Tax or Duty shall be laid on Articles exported from any State.

No Preference shall be given by any Regulation of Commerce or Revenue to the Ports of one State over those of another; nor shall Vessels bound to, or from, one State, be obliged to enter, clear, or pay Duties in another.

No Money shall be drawn from the Treasury, but in Consequence of Appropriations made by Law; and a regular Statement and Account of the Receipts and Expenditures of all public Money shall be published from time to time.

No Title of Nobility shall be granted by the United States: And no Person holding any Office of Profit or Trust under them, shall, without the Consent of the Congress, accept of any present, Emolument, Office, or Title, of any kind whatever, from any King, Prince, or foreign State.

Section. 10.

No State shall enter into any Treaty, Alliance, or Confederation; grant Letters of Marque and Reprisal; coin Money; emit Bills of Credit; make any Thing but gold and silver Coin a Tender in Payment of Debts; pass any Bill of Attainder, ex post facto Law, or Law impairing the Obligation of Contracts, or grant any Title of Nobility.

No State shall, without the Consent of the Congress, lay any Imposts or Duties on Imports or Exports, except what may be absolutely necessary for executing it's inspection Laws: and the net Produce of all Duties and Imposts, laid by any State on Imports or Exports, shall be for the Use of the Treasury of the United States; and all such Laws shall be subject to the Revision and Controul of the Congress.

No State shall, without the Consent of Congress, lay any Duty of Tonnage, keep Troops, or Ships of War in time of Peace, enter into any Agreement or Compact with another State, or with a foreign Power, or engage in War, unless actually invaded, or in such imminent Danger as will not admit of delay.

Article. II.

Section. 1.

The executive Power shall be vested in a President of the United States of America. He shall hold his Office during the Term of four Years, and, together with the Vice President, chosen for the same Term, be elected, as follows:

Each State shall appoint, in such Manner as the Legislature thereof may direct, a Number of Electors, equal to the whole Number of Senators and Representatives to which the State may be entitled in the Congress: but no Senator or Representative, or Person holding an Office of Trust or Profit under the United States, shall be appointed an Elector.

The Electors shall meet in their respective States, and vote by Ballot for two Persons, of whom one at least shall not be an Inhabitant of the same State with themselves. And they shall make a List of all the Persons voted for, and of the Number of Votes for each; which List they shall sign and certify, and transmit sealed to the Seat of the Government of the United States, directed to the President of the Senate. The President of the Senate shall, in the Presence of the Senate and House of Representatives, open all the Certificates, and the Votes shall then be counted. The Person having the greatest Number of Votes shall be the President, if such Number be a Majority of the whole Number of Electors appointed; and if there be more than one who have such Majority, and have an equal Number of Votes, then the House of Representatives shall immediately chuse by Ballot one of them for President; and if no Person have a Majority, then from the five highest on the List the said House shall in like Manner chuse the President. But in chusing the President, the Votes shall be taken by States, the Representation from each State having one Vote; A quorum for this purpose shall consist of a Member or Members from two thirds of the States, and a Majority of all the States shall be necessary to a Choice. In every Case, after the Choice of the President, the Person having the greatest Number of Votes of the Electors shall be the Vice President. But if there should remain two or more who have equal Votes, the Senate shall chuse from them by Ballot the Vice President.

The Congress may determine the Time of chusing the Electors, and the Day on which they shall give their Votes; which Day shall be the same throughout the United States.

No Person except a natural born Citizen, or a Citizen of the United States, at the time of the Adoption of this Constitution, shall be eligible to the Office of President; neither shall any Person be eligible to that Office who shall not have attained to the Age of thirty five Years, and been fourteen Years a Resident within the United States.

In Case of the Removal of the President from Office, or of his Death, Resignation, or Inability to discharge the Powers and Duties of the said Office, the Same shall devolve on the Vice President, and the Congress may by Law provide for the

Case of Removal, Death, Resignation or Inability, both of the President and Vice President, declaring what Officer shall then act as President, and such Officer shall act accordingly, until the Disability be removed, or a President shall be elected.

The President shall, at stated Times, receive for his Services, a Compensation, which shall neither be increased nor diminished during the Period for which he shall have been elected, and he shall not receive within that Period any other Emolument from the United States, or any of them.

Before he enter on the Execution of his Office, he shall take the following Oath or Affirmation:--"I do solemnly swear (or affirm) that I will faithfully execute the Office of President of the United States, and will to the best of my Ability, preserve, protect and defend the Constitution of the United States."

Section. 2.

The President shall be Commander in Chief of the Army and Navy of the United States, and of the Militia of the several States, when called into the actual Service of the United States; he may require the Opinion, in writing, of the principal Officer in each of the executive Departments, upon any Subject relating to the Duties of their respective Offices, and he shall have Power to grant Reprieves and Pardons for Offences against the United States, except in Cases of Impeachment.

He shall have Power, by and with the Advice and Consent of the Senate, to make Treaties, provided two thirds of the Senators present concur; and he shall nominate, and by and with the Advice and Consent of the Senate, shall appoint Ambassadors, other public Ministers and Consuls, Judges of the supreme Court, and all other Officers of the United States, whose Appointments are not herein otherwise provided for, and which shall be established by Law: but the Congress may by Law vest the Appointment of such inferior Officers, as they think proper, in the President alone, in the Courts of Law, or in the Heads of Departments.

The President shall have Power to fill up all Vacancies that may happen during the Recess of the Senate, by granting Commissions which shall expire at the End of their next Session.

Section. 3.

He shall from time to time give to the Congress Information of the State of the Union, and recommend to their Consideration such Measures as he shall judge necessary and expedient; he may, on extraordinary Occasions, convene both Houses, or either of them, and in Case of Disagreement between them, with Respect to the Time of Adjournment, he may adjourn them to such Time as he shall think proper; he shall receive Ambassadors and other public Ministers; he shall take Care that the Laws be faithfully executed, and shall Commission all the Officers of the United States.

Section. 4.

The President, Vice President and all civil Officers of the United States, shall be removed from Office on Impeachment for, and Conviction of, Treason, Bribery, or other high Crimes and Misdemeanors.

Article III.

Section. 1.

The judicial Power of the United States shall be vested in one supreme Court, and in such inferior Courts as the Congress may from time to time ordain and establish. The Judges, both of the supreme and inferior Courts, shall hold their Offices during good Behaviour, and shall, at stated Times, receive for their Services a Compensation, which shall not be diminished during their Continuance in Office.

Section. 2.

The judicial Power shall extend to all Cases, in Law and Equity, arising under this Constitution, the Laws of the United States, and Treaties made, or which shall be made, under their Authority;--to all Cases affecting Ambassadors, other public

Ministers and Consuls;--to all Cases of admiralty and maritime Jurisdiction;--to Controversies to which the United States shall be a Party;--to Controversies between two or more States;--between a State and Citizens of another State,--between Citizens of different States,--between Citizens of the same State claiming Lands under Grants of different States, and between a State, or the Citizens thereof, and foreign States, Citizens or Subjects.

In all Cases affecting Ambassadors, other public Ministers and Consuls, and those in which a State shall be Party, the supreme Court shall have original Jurisdiction. In all the other Cases before mentioned, the supreme Court shall have appellate Jurisdiction, both as to Law and Fact, with such Exceptions, and under such Regulations as the Congress shall make.

The Trial of all Crimes, except in Cases of Impeachment, shall be by Jury; and such Trial shall be held in the State where the said Crimes shall have been committed; but when not committed within any State, the Trial shall be at such Place or Places as the Congress may by Law have directed.

Section. 3.

Treason against the United States, shall consist only in levying War against them, or in adhering to their Enemies, giving them Aid and Comfort. No Person shall be convicted of Treason unless on the Testimony of two Witnesses to the same overt Act, or on Confession in open Court.

The Congress shall have Power to declare the Punishment of Treason, but no Attainder of Treason shall work Corruption of Blood, or Forfeiture except during the Life of the Person attainted.

Article. IV.

Section. 1.

Full Faith and Credit shall be given in each State to the public Acts, Records, and judicial Proceedings of every other State. And the Congress may by general Laws prescribe the Manner in which such Acts, Records and Proceedings shall be proved, and the Effect thereof.

Section. 2.

The Citizens of each State shall be entitled to all Privileges and Immunities of Citizens in the several States.

A Person charged in any State with Treason, Felony, or other Crime, who shall flee from Justice, and be found in another State, shall on Demand of the executive Authority of the State from which he fled, be delivered up, to be removed to the State having Jurisdiction of the Crime.

No Person held to Service or Labour in one State, under the Laws thereof, escaping into another, shall, in Consequence of any Law or Regulation therein, be discharged from such Service or Labour, but shall be delivered up on Claim of the Party to whom such Service or Labour may be due.

Section. 3.

New States may be admitted by the Congress into this Union; but no new State shall be formed or erected within the Jurisdiction of any other State; nor any State be formed by the Junction of two or more States, or Parts of States, without the Consent of the Legislatures of the States concerned as well as of the Congress.

The Congress shall have Power to dispose of and make all needful Rules and Regulations respecting the Territory or other Property belonging to the United States; and nothing in this Constitution shall be so construed as to Prejudice any Claims of the United States, or of any particular State.

Section. 4.

The United States shall guarantee to every State in this Union a Republican Form of Government, and shall protect each of them against Invasion; and on Application of the Legislature, or of the Executive (when the Legislature cannot be convened), against domestic Violence.

Article. V.

The Congress, whenever two thirds of both Houses shall deem it necessary, shall propose Amendments to this Constitution, or, on the Application of the Legislatures of two thirds of the several

States, shall call a Convention for proposing Amendments, which, in either Case, shall be valid to all Intents and Purposes, as Part of this Constitution, when ratified by the Legislatures of three fourths of the several States, or by Conventions in three fourths thereof, as the one or the other Mode of Ratification may be proposed by the Congress; Provided that no Amendment which may be made prior to the Year One thousand eight hundred and eight shall in any Manner affect the first and fourth Clauses in the Ninth Section of the first Article; and that no State, without its Consent, shall be deprived of its equal Suffrage in the Senate.

Article. VI.

All Debts contracted and Engagements entered into, before the Adoption of this Constitution, shall be as valid against the United States under this Constitution, as under the Confederation.

This Constitution, and the Laws of the United States which shall be made in Pursuance thereof; and all Treaties made, or which shall be made, under the Authority of the United States, shall be the supreme Law of the Land; and the Judges in every State shall be bound thereby, any Thing in the Constitution or Laws of any State to the Contrary notwithstanding.

The Senators and Representatives before mentioned, and the Members of the several State Legislatures, and all executive and judicial Officers, both of the United States and of the several States, shall be bound by Oath or Affirmation, to support this Constitution; but no religious Test shall ever be required as a Qualification to any Office or public Trust under the United States.

Article. VII.

The Ratification of the Conventions of nine States, shall be sufficient for the Establishment of this Constitution between the States so ratifying the Same.

The Word, "the," being interlined between the seventh and eighth Lines of the first Page, the Word "Thirty" being partly written on an Erazure in the fifteenth Line of the first Page, The Words "is tried" being interlined between the thirty second and thirty third Lines of the first Page and the Word "the" being interlined between the forty third and forty fourth Lines of the second Page.

Attest William Jackson Secretary

Done in Convention by the Unanimous Consent of the States present the Seventeenth Day of September in the Year of our Lord one thousand seven hundred and Eighty seven and of the Independence of the United States of America the Twelfth In witness whereof We have hereunto subscribed our Names,

Go. Washington
President and deputy from Virginia

Delaware
Geo: Read
Gunning Bedford jun
John Dickinson
Richard Bassett
Jaco. Broom

Maryland
James McHenry
Dan of St Thos. Jenifer
Danl. Carroll

Virginia
John Blair
James Madison Jr.

North Carolina
Wm. Blount
Richd. Dobbs Spaight
Hu Williamson

South Carolina
J. Rutledge
Charles Cotesworth Pinckney
Charles Pinckney
Pierce Butler

Georgia
William Few
Abr Baldwin

New Hampshire
John Langdon
Nicholas Gilman

Massachusetts
Nathaniel Gorham
Rufus King

Connecticut
Wm. Saml. Johnson
Roger Sherman

New York
Alexander Hamilton

New Jersey
Wil Livingston
David Brearley
Wm. Paterson
Jona. Dayton

Pennsylvania
B Franklin
Thomas Mifflin
Robt. Morris
Geo. Clymer
Thos. FitzSimons
Jared Ingersoll
James Wilson
Gouv Morris

Appendix C—The Bill of Rights

⁓⊙⊙⊙⊙⌇

The Bill of Rights: A Transcription[220]

The Preamble to The Bill of Rights

Congress of the United States
begun and held at the City of New-York, on
Wednesday the fourth of March, one thousand
seven hundred and eighty nine.

THE Conventions of a number of the States, having at the time of
their adopting the Constitution, expressed a desire, in order to prevent
misconstruction or abuse of its powers, that further declaratory and
restrictive clauses should be added: And as extending the ground of public
confidence in the Government, will best ensure the beneficent ends of its
institution.

RESOLVED by the Senate and House of Representatives of the United
States of America, in Congress assembled, two thirds of both Houses
concurring, that the following Articles be proposed to the Legislatures
of the several States, as amendments to the Constitution of the United
States, all, or any of which Articles, when ratified by three fourths of the
said Legislatures, to be valid to all intents and purposes, as part of the said
Constitution; viz.

---

220 U.S. National Archives & Records Administration, 8601 Adelphi Road, College Park,
MD, 20740-6001,• 1-86-NARA-NARA• 1-866-272-6272; taken from http://www.
archives.gov/exhibits/charters/bill_of_rights_transcript.html.

ARTICLES in addition to, and Amendment of the Constitution of the United States of America, proposed by Congress, and ratified by the Legislatures of the several States, pursuant to the fifth Article of the original Constitution.

Note: The following text is a transcription of the first ten amendments to the Constitution in their original form. These amendments were ratified December 15, 1791, and form what is known as the "Bill of Rights."

Amendment I

Congress shall make no law respecting an establishment of religion, or prohibiting the free exercise thereof; or abridging the freedom of speech, or of the press; or the right of the people peaceably to assemble, and to petition the Government for a redress of grievances.

Amendment II

A well regulated Militia, being necessary to the security of a free State, the right of the people to keep and bear Arms, shall not be infringed.

Amendment III

No Soldier shall, in time of peace be quartered in any house, without the consent of the Owner, nor in time of war, but in a manner to be prescribed by law.

Amendment IV

The right of the people to be secure in their persons, houses, papers, and effects, against unreasonable searches and seizures, shall not be violated, and no Warrants shall issue, but upon probable cause, supported by Oath or affirmation, and particularly describing the place to be searched, and the persons or things to be seized.

Amendment V

No person shall be held to answer for a capital, or otherwise infamous crime, unless on a presentment or indictment of a Grand Jury, except in cases arising in the land or naval forces, or in the Militia, when in actual service in time of War or public danger; nor shall any person be subject for the same offence to be twice put in jeopardy of life or limb; nor shall be compelled in any criminal case to be a witness against himself, nor be deprived of life, liberty, or property, without due process of law; nor shall private property be taken for public use, without just compensation.

Amendment VI

In all criminal prosecutions, the accused shall enjoy the right to a speedy and public trial, by an impartial jury of the State and district wherein the crime shall have been committed, which district shall have been previously ascertained by law, and to be informed of the nature and cause of the accusation; to be confronted with the witnesses against him; to have compulsory process for obtaining witnesses in his favor, and to have the Assistance of Counsel for his defence.

Amendment VII

In Suits at common law, where the value in controversy shall exceed twenty dollars, the right of trial by jury shall be preserved, and no fact tried by a jury, shall be otherwise re-examined in any Court of the United States, than according to the rules of the common law.

Amendment VIII

Excessive bail shall not be required, nor excessive fines imposed, nor cruel and unusual punishments inflicted.

Amendment IX

The enumeration in the Constitution, of certain rights, shall not be construed to deny or disparage others retained by the people.

Amendment X

The powers not delegated to the United States by the Constitution, nor prohibited by it to the States, are reserved to the States respectively, or to the people.

Note: The capitalization and punctuation in this version is from the enrolled original of the Joint Resolution of Congress proposing the Bill of Rights, which is on permanent display in the Rotunda of the National Archives Building, Washington, D.C.

ACKNOWLEDGEMENTS

‿✿◎✿‿

I would like to acknowledge God Himself for His providential care, inspiration, and motivation to write this book. Throughout the process, my faith in God was strengthened and my conviction that America holds a unique place in the Creator's heart was solidified. Much gratitude is due to my wife, Kimberly, who picked up the extra load in my absence from home. To spend countless hours writing is no small undertaking. She too has a heart for America and a willingness to sacrifice for the cause of liberty. To my dear son, Benjamin (and, Lord willing, if we have another), you have been such an inspiration to take up the call of liberty. Amazing how children affect a father's heart. I would like to thank my father and mother, Frank and Marie DiQuattro; my brother Kevin DiQuattro; friends; and other family members who affirmed me throughout the writing process. Your encouragement nourished my motivation to birth *The Final Branch*. I would also like to thank Don Schenkel and Marie Evans from the Service Corps of Retired Executives (SCORE), Lubbock District Office, who provided assistance in bringing this endeavor to completion.

CPSIA information can be obtained at www.ICGtesting.com
Printed in the USA
LVOW062314031011

248974LV00002B/1/P

9 781615 075720